Published in the United States of America by
Michigan Publishing Services
Manufactured in the United States of America

ISBN 978-1-60785-362-6 (paper)

Photographs by Jared Ragland, The University of Alabama at Birmingham, Department of
Art and Art History, except: page 38 by Zach Gibson, VCUarts; page 63 by Devin Lunsford,
The University of Alabama at Birmingham, Department of Art and Art History; and pages
72, 112, and cover by Joseph Xu, University of Michigan, College of Engineering.

When electronically viewing this document as a PDF,
please refer to the pages numbers printed on the document.

SURVEYING
THE LANDSCAPE:
Arts Integration at Research Universities

A Review of Best Practices and Challenges
for Arts Integration in Higher Education

BRUCE M. MACKH, PhD
Director, Mellon Research Project

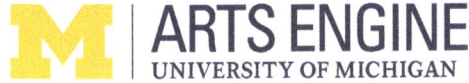

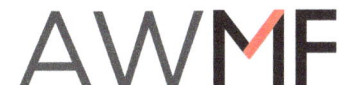

EXECUTIVE SUMMARY

Under the auspices of **ArtsEngine**[1,2] at the University of Michigan, the Mellon Research Project examines the increasingly prevalent integration of arts practice and study at research universities. ArtsEngine National's[3] initial mission to "transform the research university through the infusion of arts practice" in response to growing recognition of the value of arts integration practices across the landscape of higher education led to a $500,000 grant from **The Andrew W. Mellon Foundation**. This grant supported an initial investigation of present practices in arts integration at research universities, encompassing a national network of faculty and administrators who embrace innovative methods in teaching, research, and co-curricular programming linking the arts to other disciplinary domains.

This study presents "best practices in the integration of arts practice in U.S. research universities . . . , fulfill[ing] the need for a document that articulates models, obstacles, implementation strategies, costs, and impact on students and faculty as well as on research, practice, and teaching in other knowledge areas" (ArtsEngine). Rather than providing a detailed set of instructions, this document maps the landscape of arts integration at 30 partner institutions in the Alliance for the Arts in Research Universities (a2ru) and at 16 other institutions. It highlights aspirational models and presents an overall guide to current practices linking the arts to other learning areas.

---

1 Academic deans at the University of Michigan came to the realization that the arts were notably absent in discussions of interdisciplinarity in research universities. This grew into a partnership known as Arts on Earth in 2006, renamed ArtsEngine in 2010. This initiative was intended to enhance creativity among students, faculty, and staff by integrating research, theory, and coursework in the visual, performing, and literary arts with engineering, architecture, and other academic disciplines.
2 Hyperlinks were correct at the time of this study's publication.
3 ArtsEngine National was the precursor to a2ru (Alliance for the Arts in Research Universities), founded in 2012.

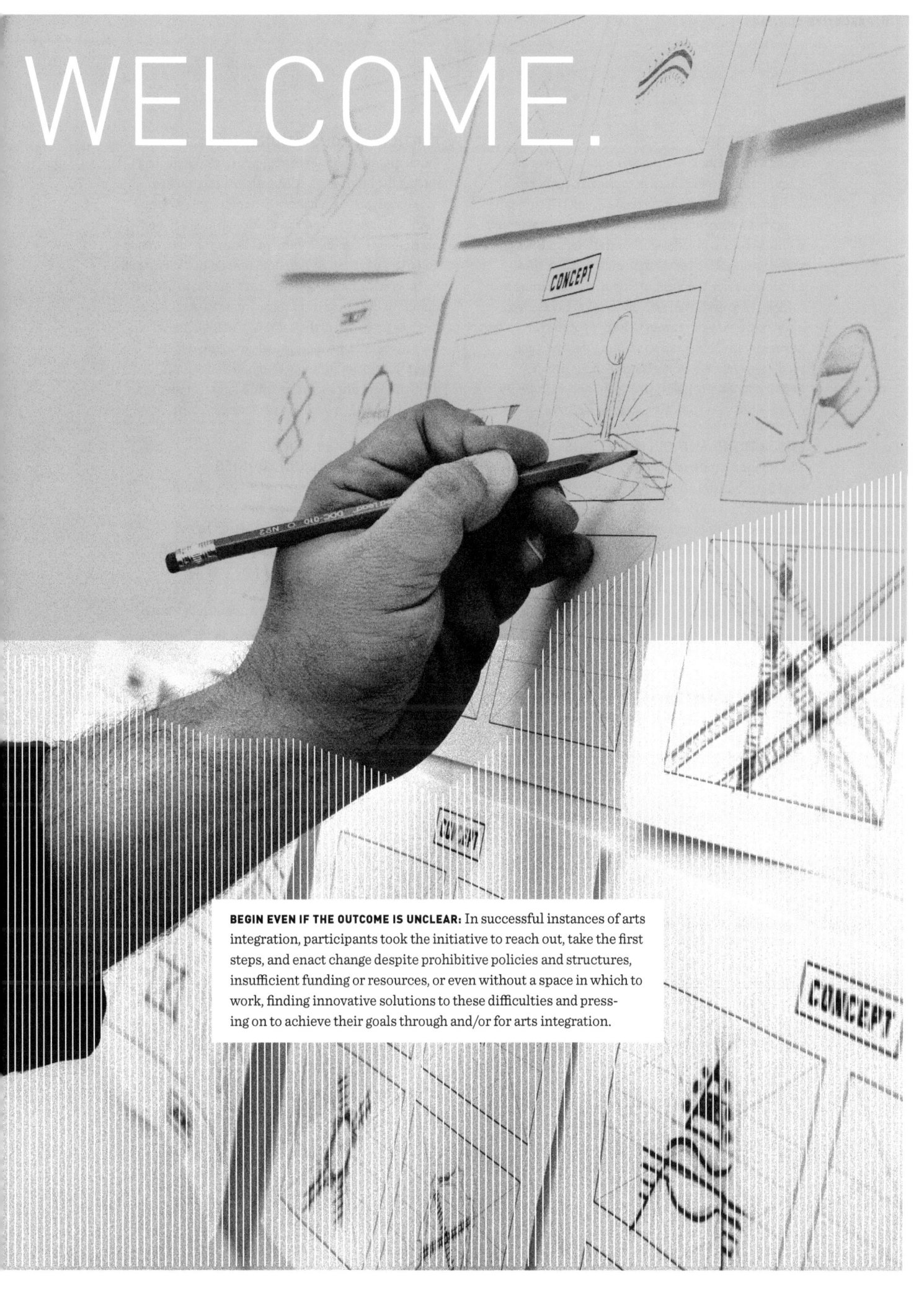

WELCOME.

BEGIN EVEN IF THE OUTCOME IS UNCLEAR: In successful instances of arts integration, participants took the initiative to reach out, take the first steps, and enact change despite prohibitive policies and structures, insufficient funding or resources, or even without a space in which to work, finding innovative solutions to these difficulties and pressing on to achieve their goals through and/or for arts integration.

METHODOLOGY

Using a mixed methodological approach favoring ethnography, researchers examined 46 higher educational institutions in the U.S. and UK through interviews with 965 individuals, including university administrators, faculty, staff, and students. By nature qualitative rather than quantitative, these narratives form the basis of this study, providing a subjective overview of arts integration in research universities as seen through the eyes of the interview participants. This project is among the first such studies specifically concerned with the arts in higher education, making it a groundbreaking work of potential value to future arts researchers.

LIMITATIONS AND DELIMITATIONS

The foundational assumption that arts integration is beneficial and desirable within research universities provides the philosophical basis of this investigation, attracting participants with a presumed bias toward arts integration. Likewise, sites visited included institutions affiliated with ArtsEngine's National Network or a2ru, as well as higher educational institutions known to engage in arts integration.

This study's scope encompasses sufficient breadth to have warranted three separate projects, examining research collaborations with the arts, curricular arts integration, and co-curricular arts programming as distinct topics. Interview scripts and grant proposal language delimited data collected. The study relies on participant interviews rather than extensive collection of evidentiary materials. Limited to those sources interviewees chose to provide, collected documents consisted mostly of course syllabi rather than budgets, grant proposals, research reports, or similar items that would have affected the scope of research.

Although grant language addressed costs and impacts of arts integration, participants largely chose not to share specifics regarding budgets or measurements of success, speaking mainly about their views on disciplinarity and arts integration, generally describing their projects or courses and addressing challenges they faced. Few interviewees provided specific or detailed information about how they assessed the impact of their courses, projects, or programs. The study resulted in a subjective, richly textured picture of present practices as portrayed by the participants, rather than an objective or empirical collection of data appropriate for comparisons or numerical analysis.

PARTICIPANT QUOTATIONS

Participants' statements appear exactly as spoken during the interviews. Although extemporaneous spoken language tends to be less polished or formal than scholarly writing, the flavor and character of participants' candid comments brings an uncommon voice to this study. Statements remain in their original form with minimal editorial intervention in order to maintain the integrity of these remarks. As the research process progressed, the value of participants' whole narratives became increasingly evident; relaying these full stories remains an opportunity for future development during the second Mellon-funded grant project recently awarded to ArtsEngine/a2ru.

ANALYSIS OF KEY TERMS AND CONCEPTUAL CATEGORIES

The language and ideas conveyed by participants' responses to interview questions regarding their experience with arts integration reveal issues related to such efforts at the sites visited. In a representative sample, research assistants searched 117 recorded interviews collected at 8 institutions, identifying key terms and conceptual categories conveying these issues, identifying 1,152 instances across 39 conceptual designations. This analysis provides a tool for understanding characteristic responses, utilizing frequency of terms in order to generate categorical comparisons.

FREQUENCY OF TERMS. Key terms occurring in 30 or more of the sampled interviews identify areas of concern, involvement, or interest. Of the top 5 terms, 59% of participants spoke about grants and external funding, and 59% mentioned impact and dissemination of research and creative production; 46% discussed promotion and tenure; 45% spoke about arts practice; and 44% cited disciplinary hierarchies.

TYPE OF CURRICULAR ARTS INTEGRATION. Within the Mellon Research Project, investigators utilized three categories of arts integration:

1) fusion refers to a course fully merging one or more academic disciplines with one or more areas of the arts; 2) infusion indicates collaborations in which the arts support teaching and learning in another discipline; and 3) diffusion refers to courses in which non-arts students engage in immersive study in the arts. Investigators categorized 62% of the 42 identified instances of these curricular collaborations as fusion, 37% as infusion, and only 1% (one instance) as diffusion.

INTERVIEW FOCUS. The focus of participants' remarks demonstrates distribution across the conceptual areas of the Mellon Research Project. As can be seen in figure 5 in chapter 1, curricular development provided a focus in 12% of the sample interviews, and 24% centered on arts practice. Participants discussed arts curricula in 22% and research in 21% of interviews. Co-curricular discussions appeared in 12% of interviews and STEAM (Science, Technology, Engineering, Arts, and Mathematics) considerations in 10%. With a data range of just 14%, these categories reflect the relatively even attention paid to these areas of interest throughout the research process.

INITIATION OF PARTNERSHIP. Examination of the initiation of research or curricular partnerships showed the arts originating partnerships more frequently in curricular settings (68%) while non-arts partners initiated more research collaborations (56%). Further, 101 participants spoke about initiating research partnerships while 56 interviewees mentioned curricular partnerships. Of these 157 partnerships, the arts initiated 83 collaborations while another discipline initiated 74, a difference of only 5%.

DISCIPLINARY IDENTITY. Views on disciplinarity indicate that 18 individuals held anti-disciplinary or post-disciplinary views, 29 interviewees identified as interdisciplinary or transdisciplinary, and 4 individuals adhered to strict disciplinarity. Views on disciplinarity may influence participants' willingness to engage in arts integration or the types of arts-integrative activities in which they choose to participate.

Because this analysis encompasses only 12% of all interviews and 17% of all institutions included in the full Mellon Research Project, caution should be employed when drawing conclusions based on a relatively small representative sample. However, characteristics identified among participants' responses and the relationships of key terms and conceptual categories serve to illuminate subsequent discussions in this study. Full transcription of all recorded interviews will help to reaggregate these terms and concepts into the participants' narratives, providing greater contextualization of issues encountered with arts integration.

FINDINGS

Arts integration occurs at each of the campuses visited, existing across a vast range of cases from small individual research projects and single courses to institution-wide emphases on the arts. The Mellon Research Project identified instances of arts integration in a wide variety of academic settings, presenting findings in the following chapters categorized by:

1) models of arts integration;
2) student needs and perceptions;
3) challenges and administrative concerns; and
4) best practices. Areas of study within this framework feature arts integration efforts in curricular, research, and co-curricular settings.

MODELS OF ARTS INTEGRATION

» *Curricular arts integration varies in the depth of partnership between the arts and affiliated disciplines, ranging from full integration and equal partnership to courses utilizing the arts in support of teaching or learning in another discipline, sometimes limited to a single class period.*

» *Research collaborations also vary in depth and focus. Artists expressed skepticism regarding instrumentalization of their creative practice when applied to research in other disciplines as data visualization, sonification, or embodiment. Participants perceived equal partnerships as more desirable than those in which one discipline supports research in another knowledge area.*

» *Centers and institutes incorporating the arts can foster collaborative research and teaching, often in conjunction with partners from other university units, community organizations, or corporate sponsors.*

» *Co-curricular programs provide opportunities for students to engage in the arts in addition to their curricular involvement. These programs allow them to experience the benefits of arts participation even though they may be enrolled in highly demanding degree programs that may preclude arts-based or arts-integrated electives.*

STUDENT NEEDS AND PERCEPTIONS

» Students described themselves as "native to interdisciplinarity," expressing a strong desire for a community of like-minded people seeking to engage in arts integration.

» Students also desire authentic engagement in impactful, meaningful learning experiences integrating the arts. They reported concerns about financial pressures, conflicting messages regarding career preparation and self-discovery, and other issues common to university students across learning areas.

CHALLENGES AND ADMINISTRATIVE CONCERNS

» Promotion and tenure remain primary concerns for faculty involved in research or teaching outside of their primary discipline; faculty reported difficulty in achieving acceptance of these activities by promotion and tenure committee members or conveyed reluctance to engage in arts-integrative collaborations prior to achieving tenure. Administrators expressed related concerns about policy in connection with arts-integrative teaching or research crossing disciplinary lines.

» Funding of arts-integrated projects or courses was identified as a challenge, especially when accompanied by perceived inequitable resource allocation and status differentials between the arts and STEM areas. Interviewees also cited problems finding space in which to conduct arts-integrative research or co-teaching, and have co-curricular organizations meet.

» Differences in departmental cultures, disciplinary vernaculars, and definitions of research can complicate arts-integrative collaborations. Similarly, university structures or policies such as contact hour and credit hour requirements, teaching loads, or policies for addressing instructor displacement when co-teaching provide obstacles to arts integration.

» Further challenges arose relative to perceived recognition of faculty efforts in arts integration. When participants feel their efforts are not recognized or when peers or administrators demonstrate little support, motivation may suffer.

BEST PRACTICES

» Co-teaching and cross-listing arts-integrated courses proved successful options for curricular collaborations involving the arts, especially when accompanied by administrative consideration of faculty teaching loads, instructor displacement, and support for course development.

» Liberal interpretation of existing policies for promotion and tenure can facilitate faculty participation in arts-integrative teaching and research. This strategy is

most effective when applied comprehensively on an institutional level rather than the more commonly identified practice of case-by-case evaluation.

» Centers and institutes establish shared spaces for arts-integrated research and teaching, fostering a professional community of scholars whose work transcends traditional disciplinary boundaries. Funding models relying on stable revenue streams, such as university-level support or tuition-based income, allow for greater sustainability than grant funding alone, although grants provide support for programs or projects not otherwise feasible under limited institutional budgets.

» Research including the arts as equal partners from the onset of a project enhances collaboration and avoids perceived instrumentalization of arts practice only for purposes of illustration or demonstration. Successful research partnerships may endure for years, producing long-term benefit for both partners.

» Best practice also encompasses partnerships between stand-alone art schools and research universities, community engagement, and efforts to support and improve arts practice.

Overall, those engaging in arts integration encounter opportunities and issues similar to faculty and administrators across higher education, who experience environments conducive to intellectual inquiry and creativity, as well as concerns of funding, space, promotion and tenure, and university support, at least to some extent. Arts-integrative curricular and research endeavors, however, exist outside of established disciplinary norms and structures, requiring flexibility and creativity in meeting their emerging needs. Recommendations for best practice in this study may help to ensure the integrity of interdisciplinary arts-integrative efforts by providing stability for programs or projects, fostering faculty support and recognition, and establishing the value of the arts across the campus.

RECOMMENDATIONS

BEGIN EVEN IF THE OUTCOME IS UNCLEAR: In successful instances of arts integration, participants took the initiative to reach out, take the first steps, and enact change despite prohibitive policies and structures, insufficient funding or resources, or even without a space in which to work, finding innovative solutions to these difficulties and pressing on to achieve their goals through and/or for arts integration.

INSTITUTIONALIZATION: Although arts integration may begin through the efforts of one person and in the absence of tangible support, long-term sustainability arises through institutionalization of such efforts, made possible by policy reform, by establishment of programmatic structures supporting arts integration, and in the most exemplary instances, by institution-wide efforts to weave the arts into the fabric of academic life.

GENUINE PARTNERSHIPS: Collaborations recognizing the arts as an equal partner help to establish genuine partnerships that generate benefits for both the arts and the other disciplines involved. Persistent inequities should be identified and addressed, ensuring that all participants perceive the collaboration as an equitable value proposition.

ENDURING VALUE: Integrating the arts within the classroom, the laboratory, and in students' academic lives remains the focus of the Mellon Research Project. We seek to brand, market, and communicate this integration so that the intrinsic importance of the arts as valuable contributors to the university is illuminated and understood. Moreover, even as the focus on the positive impact of arts integration in other academic areas grows in prominence, we should also recognize that such engagement holds value for the arts, leading to improved creative practice, enhanced professional standing, and enriched student learning within the arts themselves.

OPPORTUNITIES FOR ADDITIONAL STUDY

ArtsEngine and a2ru have received a second grant from The Andrew W. Mellon Foundation; this grant will help to create additional resources based on this rich database of participant information, allowing:

» Complete transcription of interviews, to be archived and made available.

» Mining of the full transcriptions of participant narratives for additional quantitative data.

» Gathering of additional documentation from partner institutions in order to update existing data and generate an archive and repository of supporting materials (see "Development of resources" bullet, below).

» Creation of Partner Profiles of each of the a2ru participating institutions to contain synthesized information gathered via interviews, peer comparisons, and recommendations.

» Development of Shared Practice Modules, produced by a2ru partners and illuminating areas such as arts and health, arts and humanities, and arts and STEM, creative placemaking, and other areas within emerging and evolving arts-integrative fields.

» Production of a "Keystone Guide" for facilitating arts-integrated teaching, learning, and research.

» Regional training workshops for arts-integrated interdisciplinary approaches to teaching, learning, practice, and research.

» Development of resources tailored to the informational needs of different groups featured in this report, specifically:

*- **Administrators:*** Create an archive of promotion and tenure policies supportive of arts-integrative efforts for use by administrators seeking to revise or reinterpret their existing policies.

*- **Artists:*** Compile a database of funding opportunities available to artists in order to build greater capacity to contribute to arts-integrative projects.

*- **Students:*** Formulate a resource for students seeking to develop co-curricular groups, clubs, or organizations involving the arts, providing coaching on fund-raising and group management.

*- **All Participants:*** Generate guidelines for communicating between, across, and among disciplines, anticipating common obstacles and supporting skill development in conducting fluent discourse spanning diverse academic fields.

» Deeper examination of the complex relationship between institutional context or structure and the success of arts integration at a given institution. For example, researchers will consider the organization of different colleges, schools, or departments in terms of governance structures, fund-raising, affiliated learning areas, and the impact of these aspects on administrative and faculty actions when seeking to pursue arts integration. The overall strength of the arts at any given institution is the key to effective local arts integration.

Arts integration can demonstrate potential benefit for all participants, whether from the arts or other academic areas. The growing prevalence of arts-integrated scholarly activity and increasing institutional recognition of the arts can be viewed as valuable to the overall mission of the university, thus providing impetus for faculty and administrators to pursue arts integration. Such a move will create lasting programs and systems that allow innovative collaborations to continue to grow and thrive within research universities.

This project was made possible through the generous support of **The Andrew W. Mellon Foundation**, not only through its substantial monetary gift but also through the leadership of Vice President Mariët Westermann, for whose guidance we offer our deepest gratitude. Second, we would like to express our appreciation to the North Campus deans at the **University of Michigan**, to each of the founding members of the **Michigan Meetings, ArtsEngine, and a2ru**, and to the countless faculty members and administrators who served on committees, task forces, and work groups leading to the creation of this project. Next, our thanks go to the 965 individuals who participated in the project's interviews for the stories they shared and for allowing their personal experience to become part of this groundbreaking research.

Sincere thanks and admiration go to research assistant David Hiemstra and graduate research assistant Malcolm MacLachlan, who dedicated hundreds of hours over the past year to viewing and analyzing the entire body of collected video recordings, editing and providing materials for all chapters, building the data set for chapter 1, and helping to write chapter 3. This document is tangibly stronger directly because of their efforts. David and Malcolm continue to provide tireless support, intelligent contributions, and keen understanding of the importance of this project.

Also at the University of Michigan's ArtsEngine, thanks to Communications Specialist Michelle Krell Kydd, who helped write a source document for chapter 3, and Education Specialist Lauren Fretz Thompson, who helped write a source document for chapter 2. Both of them also served as proofreaders and editors for this study. Michelle and Lauren were endlessly patient, encouraging, and supportive. Thanks to ArtsEngine's administrative assistant, Elizabeth Rohr, for her contributions to the project, and to Anthony Kolenic for his participation, especially in coauthoring the source documents for chapters 2 and 3. Deepest appreciation goes to John Marshall for his moral support and many productive conversations, as well as for envisioning the Fusion-Infusion-Diffusion model.

We would also like to recognize ArtsEngine Executive Director Laurie Baefsky and Jean Wineman of the A. Alfred Taubman College of Architecture and Urban Planning for support during the project's times of transition. Additional thanks are offered to the design/editing team: Doug Barrett, design; Jared Ragland, photo editor; Linda Tate, copy editor; and Danielle LaVaque-Manty, proofreader.

Our sincere appreciation goes to those who served as readers for this study, who accomplished their task in a remarkably short time frame, providing sound advice and needed encouragement: Laurence Kaptain, Dean of the **College of Arts and Media, University of Colorado Denver**; Lauren Lake, Chair of **Art and Art History at the University of Alabama at Birmingham**; Golan Levin, Director of the **Frank-Ratchye STUDIO for Creative Inquiry at Carnegie Mellon University**; Robert Palazzo, Dean of the **College of Arts and Sciences at the University of Alabama at Birmingham**; Robin Romans, Associate Provost at the **University of Southern California**; and Tamara Underiner, Associate Dean for Research at the **Herberger Institute for Design and the Arts at Arizona State University**.

We would also like to acknowledge Theresa Reid, the original Executive Director of ArtsEngine and a2ru and first Principal Investigator of the Mellon Research Project, for the vision and foresight in bringing this project to life and shepherding it through its early stages.

Finally, we would like to recognize the reader of this document: by investigating these pages, you participate in the movement toward a more whole university through the integration of the arts.

For all of this and more, our most sincere thanks and humble gratitude.

Bruce M. Mackh, PhD
Mellon Research Project Director
on behalf of ArtsEngine

LIST OF TABLES AND FIGURES

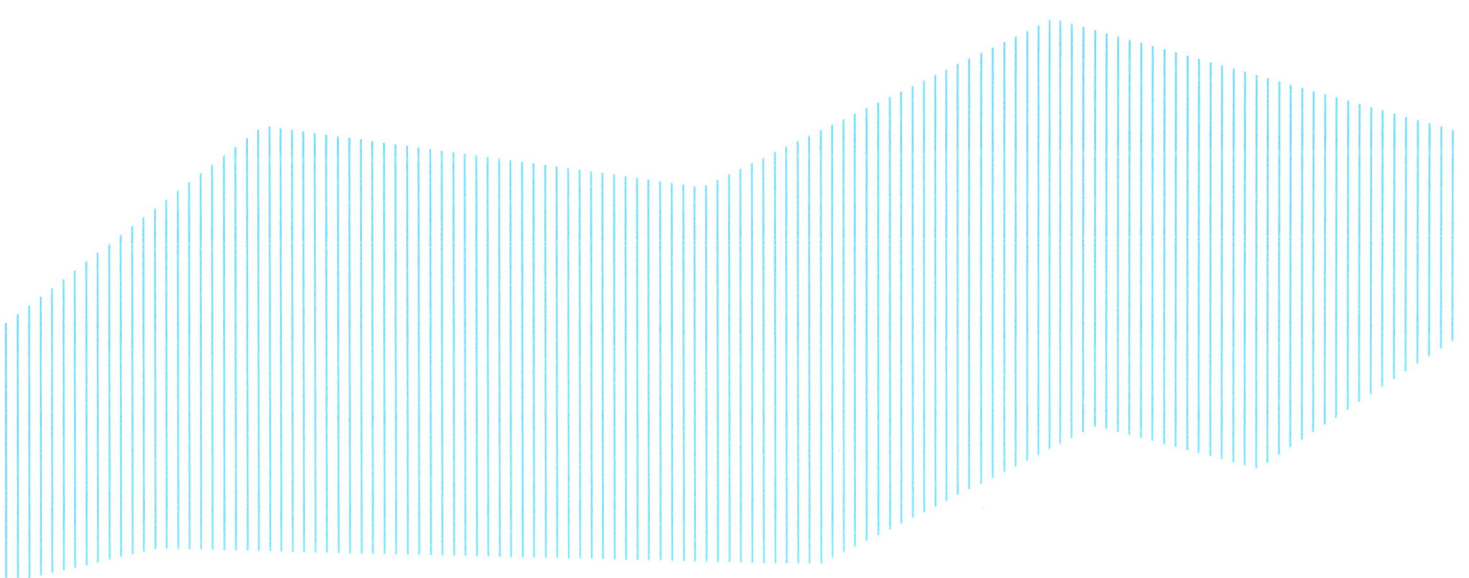

TABLE OF CONTENTS

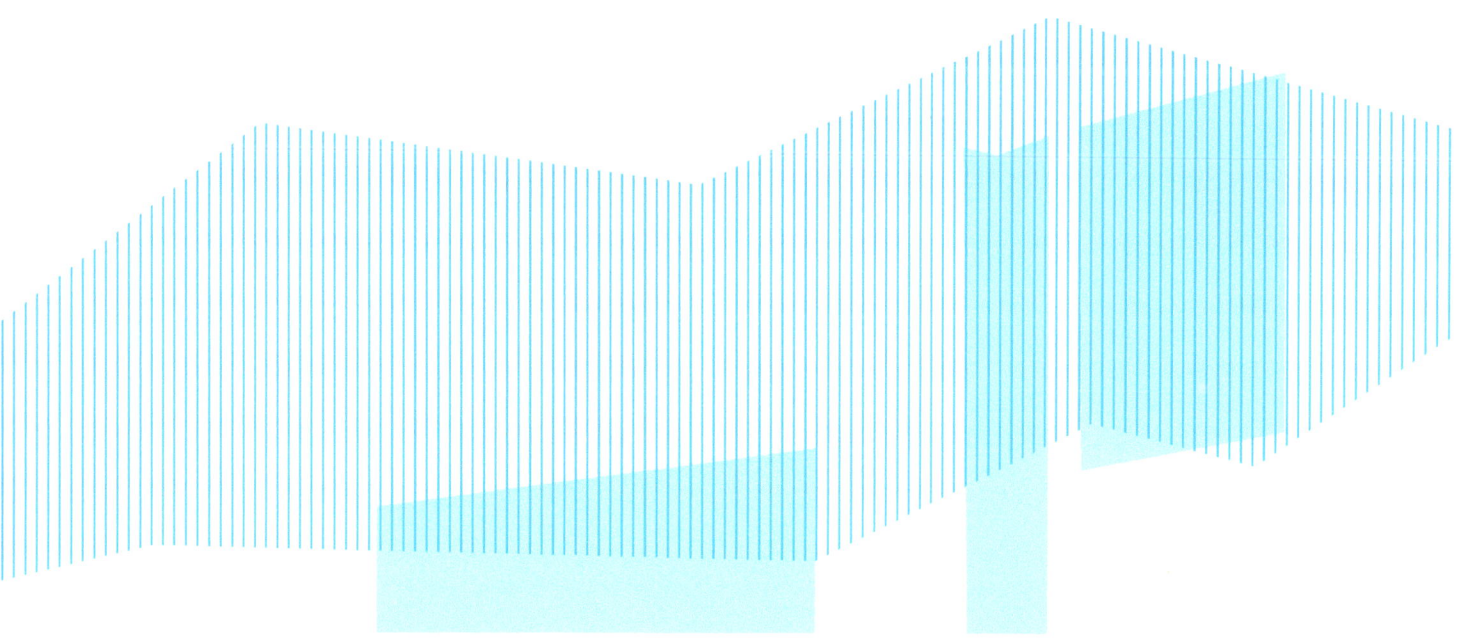

CHAPTER ONE

THE MELLON RESEARCH PROJECT

The purpose of the Mellon Research Project was to gather and publish evidence of the impact of arts integration on research, practice, and teaching in other knowledge areas and to develop schemas for diversifying and scaling opportunities for arts-infused learning on university campuses. This information was used to form the basis of a guide to best practices for arts integration in U.S. research universities, with the goal of identifying models, obstacles, implementation strategies, costs, and impact. The study informs future practice and research and educates individuals as well as private and public entities in guiding the future development of the research university. Working together under a shared vision, many university leaders have sought to transform the research university through the infusion of the arts. This effort has been sustained by a formal national network led by **ArtsEngine** at the **University of Michigan** and later by a2ru (the Alliance for the Arts in Research Universities), strategic alliances, expanded participation, and other assets and activities necessary to achieving this goal.

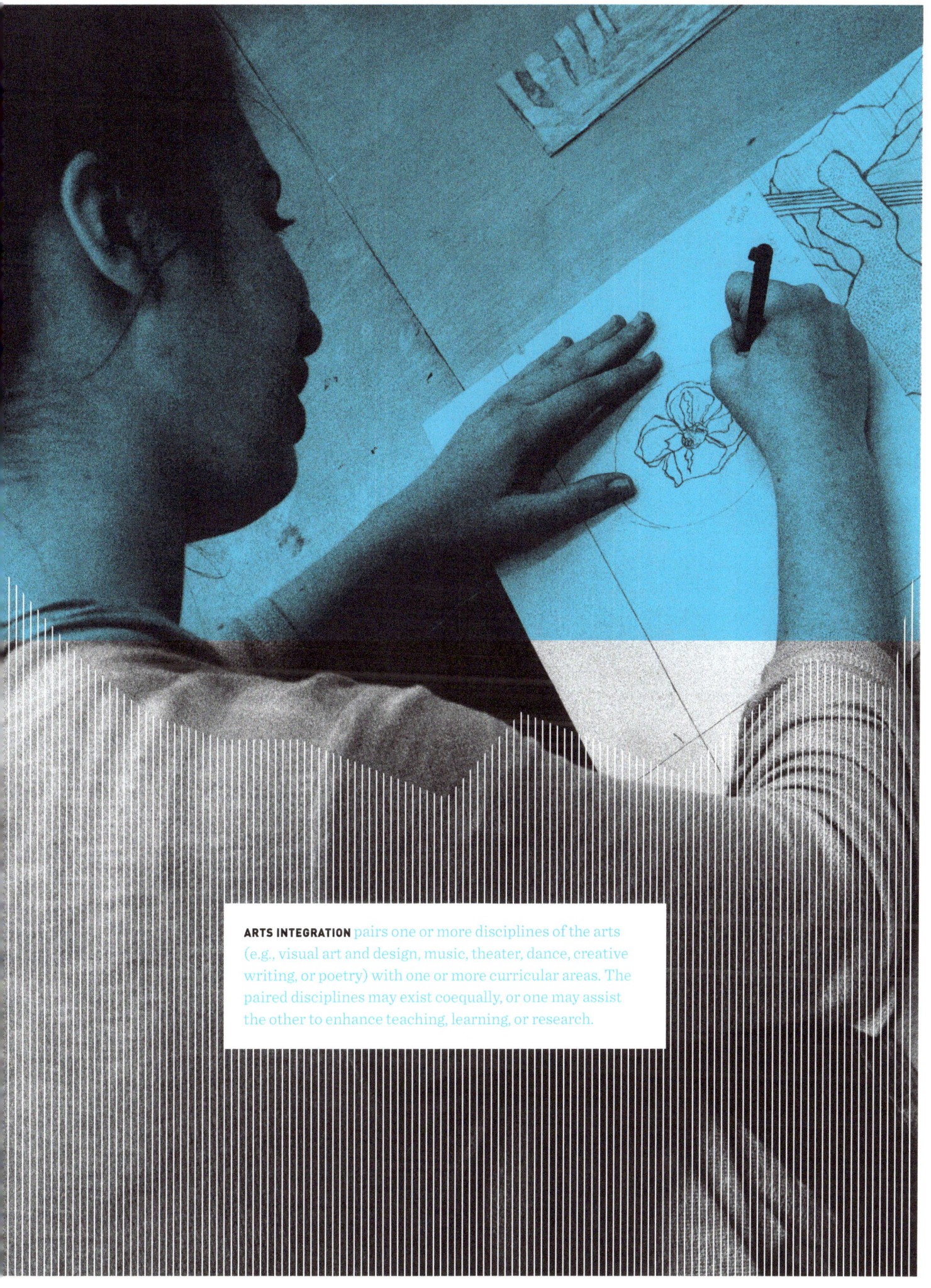

ARTS INTEGRATION pairs one or more disciplines of the arts (e.g., visual art and design, music, theater, dance, creative writing, or poetry) with one or more curricular areas. The paired disciplines may exist coequally, or one may assist the other to enhance teaching, learning, or research.

THIS PROJECT ORIGINALLY ENVISIONED
THREE PRIMARY EMPHASES (ARTSENGINE).

EMPHASIS 1: The Mellon Research Project will accumulate a coherent body of research to explore the value of arts and design practice to other knowledge areas, to assess the value to students, and to enhance the competitive position of the university, in accordance with the following initial goals:

GOAL 1: *Gather and publish evidence of student outcomes.*

GOAL 2: *Gather and publish evidence of impact on other knowledge areas.*

GOAL 3: *Gather and publish data on how art and design practice benefits communities and regions and aligns with national policy agendas.*

EMPHASIS 2: An agile, strategic, multifaceted set of mechanisms will deliver high-quality news and information to a range of influential people in order to build and maintain effective support for the efforts of this national agenda.

GOAL 1: *Develop a set of strategies and principles for enhancing internal communications within this network.*

GOAL 2: *Select and work with communications and marketing experts to lead a sophisticated initiative to create an identity and talking points for the "Arts Practice in the Research University" initiative.*

GOAL 3: *Create and launch a national advocacy organization – a "national academy," parallel to the National Academy of Sciences – to advance the role of arts and design to inspire policy and cultivate the imagination of America.*

EMPHASIS 3: As part of their core mission, universities will provide all students with regular opportunities for intensive, rigorous engagement in arts practice in all of its forms. This engagement will be both curricular and co-curricular, integrated across those domains when appropriate and useful, and regularly assessed and adjusted to enhance impact.

GOAL 1: *Promote campuswide conversation on the value of curricular and co-curricular arts practice.*

GOAL 2: *Develop/invent schemas for scaling arts practice courses for all students.*

GOAL 3: *Support and develop curricular and co-curricular interdisciplinary opportunities in arts practice.*

GOAL 4: *Catalog and share available courses/opportunities in arts practice on our campuses.*

GOAL 5: *Promote 100% participation in curricular and co-curricular arts practice among undergraduate students, increasing participation yearly.*

BACKGROUND

The Mellon Research Project traces its history to a conversation between academic deans at the University of Michigan: Paul Courant, Dean, University Libraries; Cristopher Kendall, Dean, School of Music, Theatre, and Dance; David C. Munson, Dean, College of Engineering; Monica Ponce de Leon, Dean, Taubman College of Architecture and Urban Planning; Bryan Rogers, Dean, School of Art and Design; and Theresa Reid, Executive Director, ArtsEngine, who realized the arts were notably absent in discussions about interdisciplinarity in research universities. This grew into a partnership known as Arts on Earth in 2006, renamed ArtsEngine in 2010. This initiative was intended to enhance creativity among students, faculty, and staff by integrating research, theory, and coursework in the visual, performing, and literary arts with engineering, architecture, and other academic disciplines. This group reached out to like-minded academics at other universities, hosting the first Michigan Meeting in May 2011, titled "The Role of Art-Making and the Arts in the Research University." At this event, 150 presidents, provosts, deans, directors, faculty, and administrators from 41 RU/VH[1] universities across the U.S. came together under a shared vision for recognition and advancement of university support for art-making and the arts as a matter of national cultural importance. Participants met in work groups to address advocacy structures, case-making, co-curricular programming, curricular models and impact, funding models, national network design, and research agendas. Each group sought a national commitment to art-making at all levels of education to match the current commitment to STEM (science, technology, engineering, and math) education. These working groups produced goals and action steps, leading to the establishment of four task forces – Research, Curricular Models, Co-Curricular Programming, and Advocacy – each of which was guided by three overarching principles (Reid):

FOCUS ON MAKING: Humanistic study of existing artifacts is already generally understood as essential to a complete university education. The distinct impact and value of engagement in original creative work in the arts is less well accepted. Making is a vital form of thinking and as such should be considered as important as writing or computation in the university years.

SET TERMS FOR THE ARGUMENT: Vast stores of data of many types demonstrate the importance of art-making and the arts in human intellectual, emotional, aesthetic, and moral life. Ongoing work should assume and build upon this position of strength.

STRESS THE UNIVERSITY'S UNIQUE RESPONSIBILITY AS A CULTURAL LEADER AND SHAPER: Integrating art-making and the arts enables the university to fulfill its responsibility to society by producing new generations of leaders adept in the use of all their creative and cognitive faculties and by providing an incubator for original creative work in the arts that is not constrained by market economics. Only the university can fulfill this vital social role.

THE TASK FORCES SUBSEQUENTLY GENERATED KEY QUESTIONS SHAPING THEIR WORK.

• RESEARCH TASK FORCE

1. How do artists benefit research in other disciplines?
2. What are the costs and benefits of integrating art-making in the research university?
3. How is original creative work in the arts different from creative work in other disciplines?

• CURRICULAR TASK FORCE

1. What do we mean by "integrating art-making and the arts" into curricula?
2. What efforts are currently underway to integrate art-making into curricula, and how well are they working?

• CO-CURRICULAR TASK FORCE

1. How well are research universities supporting co-curricular art-making, and what are the benefits?

• ADVOCACY TASK FORCE

1. How do universities resource art-making now? What general principles for resourcing art-making can we articulate?
2. What are the most persuasive arguments for integrating art-making into the research university?

A second Michigan Meeting in March 2012 initiated the idea of seeking funding for a project to:
1) gather and publish evidence of the impact of the integration of arts practice on students and faculty and
2) study the relationship between the arts and research, practice, and teaching in other knowledge areas.

---

4 According to institutional designation in the Carnegie Classifications system (The Carnegie Classification).

That same month, ArtsEngine applied for and later received a three-year research grant from The Andrew W. Mellon Foundation. The grant provided support for a professionally led, collaborative research project with the goal of generating an authoritative guide to best practices in the integration of the arts in U.S. research universities.

ArtsEngine at the University of Michigan provided a home for the three-year project, supervised by ArtsEngine's Executive Director. During the initial phase of the Mellon Research Project (2012-2013), the National Network transformed into a2ru – the Alliance for the Arts in Research Universities. Leaders organized four standing committees. The first two committees – the Research Committee and the Curricular and Co-Curricular Committee – were carried over from the former National Network. Two new committees were established – an Executive Committee to provide oversight and conduct strategic planning for the organization and a Program Committee to plan national conferences and other meetings. At present, a2ru encompasses 31 partner institutions that share a mission of ensuring "the highest standard of institutional support for arts-integrative interdisciplinary efforts that engage the whole university and beyond" (a2ru).

The Mellon Research Project launched in September 2012 with the hiring of the Research Project Director. Initially, the investigation centered on art-making, which was among the primary emphases of the Michigan Meetings and its task forces and working groups. Investigators refined project goals and emphases to align with the language of the Mellon grant, seeking to develop schemas for diversifying and scaling opportunities for arts-infused learning on university campuses by identifying models, obstacles, implementation strategies, costs, and impact. The resulting document addresses future practice and research, informs individuals within private and public institutions, and disseminates useful information to a broad educated audience.

DEFINITION OF TERMS

Definitions of key terms and an explanation of how these apply throughout this study may be useful to the reader. The following section presents a conceptual progression intended to maximize clear communication, examining the core ideas of best practice; disciplinarity; arts integration; and fusion, infusion, and diffusion.

The phrase **best practice,** as utilized in this study, refers to exemplary instances of arts integration rather than a hierarchical or systematic ranking of exemplary institutions, programs, or individuals. The study encompasses a wide variety of institutions, including public and private not-for-profit institutions ranging in size from fewer than 100 students to nearly 100,000 students, including institutions designated in the Carnegie Classifications system as RU/VH, RU/H, Master's, and Spec/Art (**The Carnegie Classification**). A vast array of factors affect every aspect of policy and practice in higher education; these factors include funding models, physical resources, historical precedents, campus climates, and a host of other considerations, making comparative classification infeasible. This study utilizes subjective ethnography based entirely on interview participants' narratives. Rather than indicating which programs, projects, institutions, or individuals are "the best" in any given category, "best practice" generally indicates examples meeting the following conditions. The characteristics below earn consideration as "best" because they successfully address challenges or prevent problems frequently occurring in arts integration efforts.

PARITY: *Within the given instance of arts integration, no individual or discipline exists as subordinate to another: the arts maintain an equal footing with partnering disciplines rather than merely playing a supporting role.*

SUSTAINABILITY: *Strategies, policies, procedures, and funding facilitate ongoing operations rather than one-time efforts.*

INSTITUTIONALIZATION: *The program, project, course, or organization has become a normalized component of the institutional environment, not just a temporary feature.*

REPLICABILITY: *The program, project, course, or organization, or aspects thereof, could be reproduced at another institution, bearing in mind each instance remains specific to its location and subject to conditions which may not be present in other settings.*

Named exemplars meet these four criteria unless otherwise stated. The size, structure, status, or affiliations of named institutions had no bearing on their selection. In a few cases, the same institution or organization appears more than once because it was especially notable or met one or more of the criteria exceptionally well. Although most of the programs,

FIGURE 1.
DISCIPLINARY CONTINUUM.

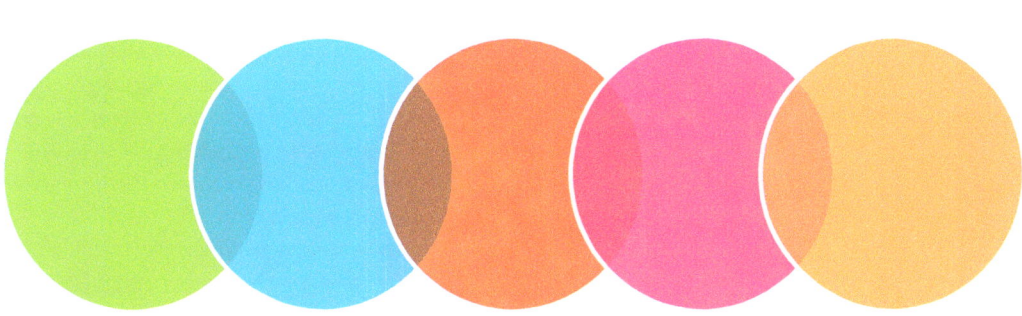

MONODISCIPLINARITY   INTERDISCIPLINARITY   TRANSDISCIPLINARITY   POST-DISCIPLINARITY   ANTI-DISCIPLINARITY

projects, organizations, or institutions involved in this study met at least one or two of these criteria, the most successful exemplars achieved all four of these important aspects of arts integration. Therefore, the term "best practice" does not indicate achievement of objective status as "the best" in any given category, but rather it denotes instances of arts integration in which

1) one discipline is not placed at a disadvantage compared to another;
2) there is demonstrable stability and sustainability;
3) arts integration efforts are recognized as integral to the university; and
4) arts integration efforts are reproducible at other institutions.

"Disciplinarity" has a number of meanings and definitions, but for the purposes of this study, it indicates the extent of adherence to or rejection of the domains, methods, literatures, standards, or norms of a particular discipline or set of disciplines. **FIGURE 1** presents a spectrum ranging from the most traditional or conservative view of disciplinarity to the most innovative or radical. A variety of terms describe these approaches, but for the purpose of the present discussion, the figure includes only five.

Rigorous adherence to the principles and characteristics of a single primary academic discipline and acceptance of its constituent norms as common sense, natural, and inherently correct characterizes the philosophical basis of "monodisciplinarity," also called "strict disciplinarity." A well-known theory of creativity promoted by Malcolm Gladwell, R. Keith Sawyer, and others states that achievement of proficiency in a specific discipline

requires at least 10,000 hours (10 years) of engagement, with mastery identified as a prerequisite to creativity within the discipline. This theory provides an argument for those opposed to interdisciplinarity, where some see the focus of a particular discipline as diluted or mitigated if combined with a partnering discipline or disciplines. Next on the continuum, interdisciplinarity sometimes refers to activities conducted across two or more domains or fields with some degree of epistemic compatibility. Collaborations between women's studies and philosophy, or between electrical engineering and computer science, for example, would constitute an interdisciplinary activity under this definition. The more common understanding of this term, however, indicates a configuration of two or more disciplines in which each retains its own identity. Although the term "interdisciplinarity" possesses the aforementioned meanings, in most instances it becomes a catchall for any partnering of two or more disciplines, regardless of the actual level of collaboration or configuration of the partnership. Therefore, this term appears throughout this study simply for the sake of brevity, not as indicative of preference for any particular configuration of disciplines or valuation of one approach or another but merely as a strategy to avoid unnecessary wordiness engendered through a more inclusive phrasing or an awkward construct such as "hyphen-disciplinarity."

In one sense, the term "transdisciplinarity" can apply to collaborations across fields with little apparent commonality such as engineering and dance, music and robotics, or visual arts and mathematics. According to another perspective, the "trans" in "transdisciplinarity" indicates a transformation rather than merely a crossing of disciplinary boundaries. As a faculty member in design noted, "Transdisciplinarity is about admitting that no one discipline can answer problem X and taking the risk to transform and make something new emerge." Transdisciplinarity most commonly refers to collaborations in which two or more disciplines, regardless of their similarity or difference, combine to form a new whole, relinquishing something of their disciplinary distinctions in order to achieve a desired result.

Definitions of interdisciplinarity, transdisciplinary, and similar terms resist standardization. For example, a 2004 report, *Facilitating Interdisciplinary Research*, prepared by the National Academy of Sciences, the National Academy of Engineering, and the Institute of Medicine, defines interdisciplinarity as two disciplines which "join together to work on [a] common question or problem. Interaction may forge a new research field or discipline" (29). Multidisciplinarity, on the other hand, represents disciplines which "join together to work on [a] common problem" but "split apart unchanged when work is done" (29). Participant responses in the Mellon Research Project, however, suggest that the term "interdisciplinarity" is used more in this latter sense, typically to refer to temporary partnerships between two or more disciplines retaining their disciplinary identities. For these participants, the term "transdisciplinarity" indicates deeper levels of collaboration possibly resulting in more lasting change.

Moving along the continuum, proponents of the term "post-disciplinarity" embrace "disciplinarity" when useful and abandon it when not, adapting their disciplinary identities as their work requires. Post-disciplinarity links to the term "silo-agnostic," meaning the holder of this philosophical view expresses neither faith nor disbelief in a particular disciplinary position. A faculty member in computational music noted that post-disciplinarity "is not the invention of something new so much as repairing centuries of damage since da Vinci." He explained, "We're talking about achieving a goal with creativity, not art or sciences. The ratio of art to science applied to how the goal is achieved doesn't matter so much as that [the goal] is achieved."

At the opposite end of the disciplinary continuum from strict disciplinarity, the term "anti-disciplinarity" indicates a conscious rejection of disciplinary categorization. The MIT Media Lab adopts a deliberately anti-disciplinary approach to collaboration, examined in chapter 5. Those holding an anti-disciplinary perspective see little benefit in maintaining disciplinary distinctions, focusing instead on particular projects.

An associate provost added an observation about "hyper-disciplinarity," or the dynamic combination and re-combination of disciplines, saying, "For me, [hyper-disciplinarity] came up in reaction to those who argue that we find ourselves in a post-disciplinary moment. At some point, we are going to have to deal, on several levels, with the 'growth by accretion' of 'new' disciplinary fields and directions." Hyper-disciplinarity closely links to arts integration, seen in hybrid fields such as electronic art and intermedia. However, this aspect of the disciplinary spectrum remains a topic for further study as it was not included in the interview question scripts nor was it directly addressed by the interviewees.

The spectrum of disciplinary perspectives exhibited by the interview participants impacts curricular paradigms, views of scholarly activity, and attitudes informing the courses offered and learning objectives defining them as well as the participants' willingness to engage in collaborative work outside of their primary area of scholarship. Disciplinary systems evolved over many centuries, and although much has happened to begin to move beyond them, fundamental structures governing hiring policies, progress toward promotion and tenure, expectations for how faculty will spend their time in research or creative activity, teaching, and service continue to favor the monodisciplinary traditions and practices of the 20th century.

Furthermore, some interview participants argued for the value of attaining expertise within a single discipline prior to attempting to engage in interdisciplinary or transdisciplinary collaborations. Those who excel in a collaborative partnership generally excel in a primary discipline, regardless of where their philosophy of disciplinarity may fall along the continuum. Even those who adhere to an anti-disciplinary mindset usually possess demonstrable expertise in a primary field. Ideally, students or faculty members should not become "a jack-of-all-trades but a master of none," as the antiquated figure of speech suggests. Rather, they usually seek attainment of a level of expertise beyond requirements for mere competence, empowering them to apply a specific body of skill and knowledge in an unfamiliar setting toward the achievement of a new result.

Countering this view, the director of an interdisciplinary institute strongly disagreed with an emphasis on acquiring disciplinary expertise prior to interdisciplinary engagement. He also advocated for inclusion of a greater focus on individual interdisciplinarity as opposed to the prevalence of collaborative or team-based arts-integrative work featured in this study. Both hybrid scholars and those pursuing collaborations participated in the interviews, and although arts integration through partnerships emerged as more common than individual interdisciplinarity, both approaches exist and deserve recognition.

Each approach to disciplinarity merits inclusion in higher education, whether for teaching, learning, or research. For good or ill, "interdisciplinarity" has become a buzzword in higher education, remaining an important aspect of this study. Aggregate analysis of participant responses leads to an emphasis on moderation: neither abandoning all disciplinary identities nor isolating each discipline within the walls of its silo is wise. Rather, recognition of attainment of disciplinary excellence not only is compatible with interdisciplinary activities but is an important prerequisite that can be enabling for students and faculty across the landscape of programs and curricula. Each participant in a collaborative venture must have something of value to bring to the table, whether through disciplinary expertise or as a hybrid scholar. As with many things in life, seeking harmony and balance between the points along the disciplinary spectrum and recognizing the purpose and place of each will allow for intellectual and creative growth.

ARTS INTEGRATION pairs one or more disciplines of the arts (e.g., visual art and design, music, theater, dance, creative writing, or poetry) with one or more curricular areas. The paired disciplines may exist coequally, or one may assist the other to enhance teaching, learning, or research.

Arts integration is inherently interdisciplinary since it necessarily involves the inclusion of the arts with another academic area; thus, the term "interdisciplinary" sometimes serves as a synonym for arts integration in cases where the overall discussion involves pairings or partnerships with the arts. Since this study specifically concerns arts integration, these terms share a strong conceptual link. Of course, not all interdisciplinarity includes the arts, but the terms "interdisciplinarity" and "arts integration" appear somewhat interchangeably within this text.

Furthermore, the Mellon Research Project presumes a core belief in the value and benefit of arts integration within higher education, particularly in research universities, will remain an implicit premise of the work of the Michigan Meeting, ArtsEngine, and a2ru. However, none of these entities conducted a review of scholarly literature regarding the value of arts integration, nor does the present report. A meta-analysis of existing literature about arts integration would certainly be a worthy enterprise, but such activity exceeds the scope of the present study. Appendix 1 provides a list of recommended readings for those interested in further study. Although participants expressed a baseline belief in the value of the arts to students' education and career success, the purpose of the Mellon Research Project was not to gather evidence upholding this belief but to document best practices in arts integration since external studies have covered this topic previously. For example, a 2013 study conducted by Michigan State University considered a group of its 1990-1995 honors college graduates who had majored in STEM disciplines. "Of those students," said the study, "the ones who owned businesses or filed patents had eight times the exposure to the arts as children than the general public," leading researchers to conclude that sustained arts exposure in childhood provides a driving force behind innovation and invention (Parker, Roraback, and LaMore). Mariale Hardiman, of Johns Hopkins University, created an educational system for K-12 called "brain-targeted teaching," which incorporates the arts as a key component of instruction (Hardiman).[5] The bulk of research into the value of arts education that applies to students exists in K-12, not higher education. Such assumptions were also prevalent among interview participants.

Whether conducted through arts integration or in monodisciplinary settings, the arts have long provided students with opportunities to develop further their capacity for creative expression. Experience in the arts cultivates students' ability to see the world differently through creative and critical analysis, fostering divergent thinking, increasing students' tolerance of ambiguity, and expanding their capacity for creative problem solving.[6] Therefore, arts integration may provide a viable approach for the development of future citizens and leaders, strengthening their ability to cope with the challenges posed by the

---

5   See also Rinne, Gregory, Yarmolinskaya, and Hardiman.
6   For additional information, see appendix 1: Preminger; Smith; Tyler and Likova; and Zull, "Arts."

ever-increasing complexity of a rapidly changing technological world that is experiencing a period of massive cultural integration, a natural result of enhanced communication and media-sharing opportunities.

Co-curricular student organizations, clubs, or faculty-led activities provide important means of engaging students in the arts. Even though these often take a monodisciplinary approach, co-curricular opportunities integrate arts engagement into students' overall university experience, providing outlets for creative expression that might not be possible within strictly curricular or research settings.

Emerging research into the positive effect of direct participation in the arts on student learning advances the importance of the study of arts integration. Although most scientific studies on this topic focus on K-12,[7] each of the arts presents a unique set of potentially advantageous experiences for students' intellectual and creative development.

Certainly, not every student needs to become a professional artist, musician, dancer, actor, or writer to experience the benefits of participation in the arts. Regardless of whether one presumes a view of human nature seeing creativity as inherent rather than learned or considers creativity to require supported

FIGURE 2.
FUSION, INFUSION, DIFFUSION.[8]

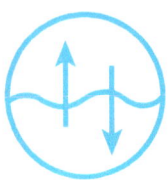 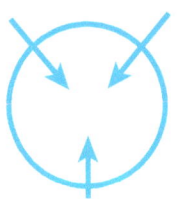 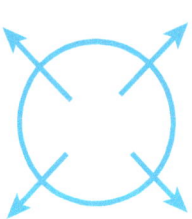

FUSION   INFUSION   DIFFUSION

instruction in order to flourish, educational engagement in the arts can both unlock students' creative potential and serve to hone existing talent in this area. Participation in the arts can awaken new interests and open doors to further personal engagement in arts practice. Furthermore, an arts-integrated course provides students with opportunities to experience the arts while releasing them from difficult choices

about perceived compromises from taking courses outside of established departmental requirements.

Arts-integrated coursework exposes students from diverse academic areas to experiences encouraging them to think outside of their primary learning modalities. Such courses also help students gain a fresh perspective on their approach to tasks, enhancing their potential for career success, regardless of their major field of study. In well-known 2010 and 2012 studies conducted by IBM, CEOs prioritized proficiency in communication, collaboration, flexibility, and creativity as highly valuable traits – characteristics closely associated with the arts (IBM, "Capitalizing," and IBM, "Leading"). Arts integration presents a unique opportunity to engender these traits in students from all academic majors, providing invaluable experiences with the potential to contribute to students' career success by fostering the skills necessary in the 21st-century workplace.

Arts-integrated academic experiences do not only benefit non-artists: encouraging students of the arts to participate in collaborative work with other academic disciplines expands their horizons and provides content traditional monodisciplinary programs might not otherwise supply. Furthermore, collaborations involving students from varied disciplines facilitate formation of professional networks, particularly if projects involve outside partners or organizations, thus also enhancing students' potential opportunities. Several programs visited had vital, innovative collaborations involving students and faculty members from a range of academic disciplines, often working on a project for a sponsor, industry partner, or community group.

Connections to the world outside of the university provided mechanisms enabling student exposure to circumstances not found in a typical classroom or studio, introducing non-arts students to the creative process and arts students to the rigors of science and business – a mutually engaging and eye-opening situation for all participants.

The terms *fusion, infusion,* and *diffusion* refer to key concepts used throughout the study. During a September 2012 ArtsEngine planning meeting, John Marshall, a committee member and professor of design at the University of Michigan's Penny W. Stamps School of Art and Design, proposed the following visual model categorizing approaches to arts integration (see **FIGURE 2**) in order to illustrate the varied relationships

7   See appendix 1: Burnaford, Aprill, and Weiss as well as Burton, Horowitz, and Abales.
8   Figure developed by John Marshall. See Reid 33.

taking place between the arts and other disciplines. Those present at this meeting found this to be an interesting and useful visual representation; the model quickly gained acceptance within the project and took hold as a model for the investigation.

By way of explanation, "fusion" refers to the complete integration of arts practice with other disciplines: courses, research, and projects equally incorporating one or more disciplines of the visual and performing arts with science, engineering, or another non-arts field or fields. In contrast, "infusion" indicates the addition of arts practice to other another discipline in order to demonstrate, illustrate, or provide examples or experience. Finally, "diffusion" describes disciplinary courses in the arts offered to non-majors, or traditional arts activities such as exhibitions or performances bringing the arts to a campuswide audience. All three of the categories in the model frequently exist at research universities, and none of the universities visited adhere to a single model. Infusion, diffusion, and fusion might be understood as different scales, or depths, of curricular arts integration efforts, with fusion standing as the highest degree of integration and the most innovative, and diffusion as the least integrative and most traditional. Individual instances of arts integration tend to occur on a continuum rather than falling neatly into any one of these three categories. The model simply provides a means of understanding different approaches to the combination of academic areas. Participants in the ArtsEngine National Network initially advocated for fusion approaches over infusion or diffusion; however, the data collected in the Mellon Research Project revealed both benefits and challenges present in each model of arts integration. These benefits and challenges will receive additional exploration throughout this study.

The reader should note that these terms exist solely within this study and in discussions within ArtsEngine and a2ru, not in external literature about arts integration nor within other scholars' research. Contributors have suggested other terms, such as "weak," "light," and "strong," as an alternative to "diffusion," "infusion," and "fusion." However, because the fusion, infusion, diffusion model has been present in this project from the beginning and because these terms have acquired specific connotations not present in alternative verbiage, their continued use in this study stands. Certainly, no other scholars should feel obligated to adopt this as the official language of arts integration if they are more comfortable with other designations.

Models of arts integration such as fusion, infusion, and diffusion do not directly correspond with the varieties of disciplinarity defined in the previous section. In general, we might recognize fusion as a more post-disciplinary or anti-disciplinary approach, whereas infusion tends toward interdisciplinary and diffusion toward monodisciplinarity. Each project, course, or program will utilize individual approaches to both arts integration and disciplinarity, thus making correlations between these essential concepts more difficult. Individual courses, projects, or programs manifest characteristics across these identities, further complicating categorization.

Arts integration applies equally to research as to curricular endeavors, providing a context in which artists and other scholars work together on a mutual project to develop new knowledge. Such collaborations take many forms, and artists often participate in research projects by supplying data visualization, sonification, or other embodiment. This phenomenon receives further explanation later in this study, both in terms of the remarkable enhancements artists can provide in the communication of research and in the challenges arising in such situations where the research team chooses not to include artists from the beginning of the project.

Inclusion of the arts in research centers or institutes represents yet another incarnation of arts integration in the research university. Several participating universities have developed such structures, providing artists with unprecedented advantages compared to a strictly disciplinary approach; these new structures are identified as examples of best practice in several areas. Arts and artists affiliated with centers and institutes sometimes partake of funding available through STEM disciplines not typically accessible to the arts, lending enhanced status or prestige to participants or affiliated disciplines. Centers and institutes may also receive funding from sponsored projects conducted on behalf of or in affiliation with corporate or governmental entities. Such projects not only engage in interdisciplinarity and arts integration: they also give students the benefits of both direct participation in the arts and genuine work experiences, including opportunities to establish professional networks with potential employers.

Whether it occurs in a curricular, research, or co-curricular context, the idea of arts integration remains integral to the Mellon Research Project, apart from citation of external sources of valuation or explanation. This observable theory and practice unifies this study, supporting each of the following chapters.

METHODOLOGY

The Mellon Research Project utilized a mixed methodological approach, blending ethnographic, quantitative, and qualitative methods. Interviews provide the majority of project data, requiring the approval of the University of Michigan's Internal Review Board (IRB) due to the involvement of human subjects. Researchers recorded the interviews using digital audiovisual equipment, and the IRB required each participant to vocalize his or her consent to the recording at the beginning of an interview session. To ensure anonymity, researchers refrained from identifying participants by name in any published materials without first seeking their express permission. Therefore, this study refers to individuals only by position title, departmental affiliation, or academic discipline. Institution names receive similar anonymization except when serving as positive exemplars; in those cases, this study uses institution names only with specific permission. In this same way, this study avoids descriptions providing clues to institutional identifications such as "West Coast university" or "Ivy League institution," preventing preconceptions about the various institutions from coloring readers' perceptions.

Among the findings of this study, researchers discovered that misconceptions or lack of specific knowledge about research practices outside of one's own academic discipline could complicate understanding of or appreciation for the research conducted by others. Although discussed at greater length later in this study, the following explanation may serve to clarify the research processes underlying the Mellon Research Project.

The project utilized both qualitative and quantitative methods in seeking to arrive at its research goal. Briefly, qualitative methods typically rely on interviews and review of documents or artifacts. They employ inductive processes to formulate theory and appear more subjective than quantitative methods, describing a situation from the point of view of those experiencing it rather than maintaining a detached or external stance. Quantitative methods, on the other hand, rely on surveys and structured observations yielding numerical information, usually relying on deductive processes used to test predetermined concepts and hypotheses. Quantitative methods maintain an emphasis on observation and objectivity. Results tend to be more generalizable than qualitative methods, typically more specific to the context of the study.

TABLE 1[9] outlines these methods as applied within the Mellon Research Project, providing a broad generalization in order to situate the present study rather than establishing inflexible rules or categories. Other studies will likely exhibit different characteristics, and proponents could argue for or against any given criterion when applied to different situations.

For clarification and greater specificity, it may be helpful to provide a more extended explanation of the concept of ethnography, as this idea forms the conceptual basis of the interviews utilized in the Mellon Research Project. A qualitative research methodology originating in cultural anthropology, ethnography supports projects intended to provide detailed description of cultural phenomena featuring observation of social practices and interactions (Hoey). Ethnography investigates culture by seeking the perspective of participants, allowing meaning to emerge through the ethnographic encounter and attempting to avoid imposing meaning derived from existing models. Ethnographic studies sometimes, but not always, involve long-term engagement in a field setting; this is known as participant observation. Formerly, this type of research applied primarily to settings external to the researcher's own environment, most often outside of the U.S., but ethnographic studies increasingly take place within the communities or environments where the researchers themselves live or work. Ethnographers both describe and interpret the words and actions of the human subjects of a study and the environment in which these interactions occur. Ethnographic studies take a holistic view, considering the histories, present practices, and future possibilities of a community, spanning temporal and physical boundaries.

Ethnographers primarily collect data through interviews comprised of open-ended questions, resembling a conversation between the interviewer and the subject. Open-ended questions refrain from limiting subjects' responses to predefined choices, distinguishing ethnographic techniques from quantitative or demographic methods relying on surveys or multiple-choice questionnaires. Researchers may collect other data sources specific to the goals and aims of individual projects, including artifacts, news articles, government reports, and so on. Using the ethnographic method, the Mellon Research Project collected course syllabi, institutional policy documents, research project data, grant application materials, and other supplementary documentation.

9   This information is based on Creswell.

TABLE 1.
COMPARISION OF QUALITATIVE AND QUANTITATIVE RESEARCH
METHODOLOGIES UTILIZED IN THE MELLON RESEARCH PROJECT

	QUALITATIVE	QUANTITATIVE
DATA COLLECTION	Ethnographic study featuring interviews utilizing open-ended questions, generating rich conversations between the interviewer and subjects Collection of documents such as course syllabi, grant proposals, institutional policy documents, and publications	Survey results; compilation of numerical information regarding participating universities such as enrollment figures and numbers of co-curricular programs; numerical information mentioned by interview participants
REASONING	Inductive, seeks to determine best practices in arts integration through the statements made by interview participants	Deductive, seeks data to support the theory that arts integration is beneficial to the research university
INFORMATION TYPE	Textual-verbal description and analysis	Numerical data generated through statistical analysis and anecdotally within individual interviews
VIEWPOINT	Subjective personal accounts gathered through participant interviews	Objective observations gathered through external program analysis
GENERALIZABILITY	May apply to a limited group of higher educational institutions or to specific programs or situations	Determination of best practices with potential applicability to a broad range of higher educational institutions

Qualitative research, such as the ethnographic approach utilized in this study, need not adhere to standards of objectivity common to quantitative research, nor must it maintain an empirical stance. As mentioned previously, this project began with general goals rather than a defined research question, does not contain a literature review, and takes a narrative approach to the presentation of its findings. The basic presumption of the value of arts integration in the research university remains unquestioned because all interview participants volunteered for the study based on their interest or involvement in arts integration. Arts research as a whole represents an emerging field with few precedents for a study of this kind. Therefore, the reader should not expect this study to follow a presentation format already familiar to academic audiences.

TABLE 2.
INSTITUTIONS PARTICIPATING IN
THE MELLON RESEARCH PROJECT

Arizona State University

Boston University

Carnegie Mellon University

Dartmouth College

Goldsmiths College, University of London, UK

Harvard University

Indiana University

Iowa State University

James Madison University

Johns Hopkins University

King's College, London, UK

Lancaster University, UK

Louisiana State University

Massachusetts Institute of Technology

New York University

The Ohio State University

Otis College of Art and Design

Pennsylvania State University

School of the Art Institute of Chicago

Stanford University

Syracuse University

Texas Tech University

Transart Institute

Tufts University

The University of Alabama (Tuscaloosa)

The University of Alabama at Birmingham

University of California, Berkeley

University of California, Santa Barbara

University of Chicago

University of Colorado Boulder

University of Florida

University of Illinois at Urbana-Champaign

University of Iowa

University of Kansas

University of Manchester, UK

University of Maryland

University of Michigan

University of Nebraska

University of Southern California

University of Utah

University of Virginia

University of Wisconsin-Madison

Vanderbilt University

Virginia Commonwealth University

Virginia Tech

Washington University in St. Louis

PROJECT HISTORY AND DATA COLLECTION

Work on this project began in September 2012. The Research Project Director began visiting sites and conducting interviews in November 2012, concluding in February 2015. The study spans 41 institutions of higher education in the U.S. and 5 in the UK (see **TABLE 2**). Researchers issued formal invitations to institutions participating in the former Michigan Meetings and member institutions in a2ru and also extended invitations to additional institutions based on participant recommendations. A table of participating universities is included as appendix 2; this table includes the institutions' 2010 Carnegie Basic Classifications,[10] their identification as public or private not-for-profit institutions, and their student enrollment.

Prior to the Research Project Director's visit at each site, participating institutions received a letter of introduction and copies of the interview scripts.[11] Each institution was asked to seek the support of a designated contact person to forward these materials to prospective interview participants and to coordinate a schedule for these interviews, including access to a conference room or other quiet space conducive to audiovisual recordings.

In total, 965 individuals from across the spectrum of higher education participated in the interviews, including:

30 university presidents or vice presidents

42 provosts, vice provosts, or associate provosts

189 deans, associate deans, or assistant deans

129 directors, chairs, or department heads

386 faculty members

189 students or fellows

---

10   The Carnegie Classifications are updated every ten years, and at the time of this writing, the 2015 data had not yet been published. See The Carnegie Classification.
11   Complete copies of the interview scripts are located in appendix 3.

Participants represented a broad spectrum of academic disciplines, including but not limited to those listed in **TABLE 3**.

Of these 965 interviews, 881 were digitally recorded,[12] resulting in a collection of over 1,100 hours of video, necessitating a minimum of 3 hours of processing per hour of video or greater than 3,300 hours all told. The project documented approximately 8,650,000 words and thousands of pages of analysis, with a final database comprising roughly 75 terabytes of stored video, text, and documentation. This database as well as ongoing communication with the interview participants serve as the primary source material for this study.

LIMITATIONS

This study operates under an assumption of arts integration as beneficial and desirable. Participation in the project interviews was voluntary, attracting participants who engage in arts integration activities, presuming a bias toward arts integration. Individuals with opposing viewpoints did not volunteer for interviews. Similarly, sites visited drew from institutions participating in the Michigan Meetings, ArtsEngine National Network, or a2ru – institutions known to support arts integration.

A bit of philosophical exposition might help to clarify the foundational assumption regarding arts integration present in this study.[13] According to the norms of philosophical argument, statements making a descriptive claim (a statement of fact) sometimes omit key information because it seems obvious and uncontroversial to the speaker and his or her presumed audience. General conversation typically involves such statements. Imagine a pair of students working on a project, each using a laptop computer.

TABLE 3.
ACADEMIC DISCIPLINES
OF INTERVIEW PARTICIPANTS

Anthropology	Entertainment technology	Museum studies
Architecture	Environmental design	Music
Art education	Ethnomusicology	Music composition
Art history	Film archive	Music theory
Arts management	Gaming	Musicology
Arts research	Holography & spatial imaging	Neuroscience
Biochemistry	Human development	Performing arts and cinema
Chemical engineering	Human-computer interaction	Policy and governance
Chemistry	Humanities	Political science
Cinematic arts	Industrial engineering	Psychology
Computer animation	Interactive media	Religious life
Computer science	Landscape architecture	Scenic design/theater
Computer visualization	Library science	Social sciences
Construction and planning	Literature	Sociology
Critical studies in drama	Material engineering	Student affairs
Dance	Material science	Technology
Dance ethnography	Mathematics	Theater
Design	Media studies	Theater engineering
Digital humanities	Media and game studies	Theater lighting
Digital media	Media arts	Urban studies
East Asian studies	Medicine	Video and media design
Education	Molecular biology	Visual arts
Engineering	Multimedia	Women's studies
English	Multimedia literacy	Zoology

12　Eighty-four interviewees declined to be recorded; this is less than 10% of the total number of participants.
13　For further information, see Hasan and Fumerton as well as McKeon.

Student A says, "My computer's about to die," to which Student B replies, "There's a charger on the desk over there." This conversation implies, but does not explicitly state, the following facts: 1) Student A's computer problem is due to a low battery; 2) Student A does not possess a computer charger at the present time; 3) Student B is aware of this fact; and 4) Student B indicated the location of the charger in an attempt to assist Student A in solving the problem. None of these suppositions is controversial, and all are obvious.

Just as we presume the two students in the example possess a fundamental understanding allowing their conversation to omit relevant knowledge details, the majority of participants in the Mellon Research Project interviews possess an implicit understanding of the value of arts integration, forming the basis of their subsequent statements during interviews and their observed actions. Therefore, unlike traditional methods of inquiry relying on a review of existing literature to contextualize the subsequent research, this study presumes the value of arts integration based on the interview participants' statements and actions. For the purposes of this study, statements about arts integration in the following paragraphs draw upon the body of interview data and observations of practices in place at participating higher educational institutions. As generalizations, few of these statements derive from a single scholarly source but rather arise from multiple participants' statements and observation of widespread practices among this group. From a philosophical standpoint, such assumptions provide a basis for achieving a common understanding, although perhaps more uncommon among research in other disciplines. Further, individuals already engaged in arts integration, including administrators, faculty, and staff, form the target audience for this report – a group likely to possess existing background information about arts integration.

Time affected the study in several dimensions. First, the active data collection phase lasted from November 2012 to February 2015, allowing two months of preparation prior to the beginning of site visits and four months after the conclusion of research travel for the writing of this study. Next, by the time of publication, reports of arts integration activities may no longer reflect present practices due to the nature of these activities and routine changes occurring in higher education (i.e., projects reach completion, course offerings change from one academic year to the next, and programs begin and end).

DELIMITATIONS

Given the vast amount of data collected, this study could reasonably have become three separate projects, examining research collaborations with the arts, curricular arts integration, and co-curricular arts programming as separate entities. Interview scripts delimited data collected, as did the language of the grant proposal. These scripts, included as appendix 3, shape interviewees' responses through the specific verbiage of the questions, yielding subjective narratives. Questions sometimes grouped multiple data points, leading to participant responses possibly omitting salient information. For example, in one instance, participants were asked: "What difficulties did you encounter in terms of operations, university structures, and others in the process of development? How did the obstacles affect your implementation, planning, and strategies?" In responding, interview participants sometimes addressed just one aspect of this multi-part query. If an interviewee spoke about how a problem with the university's funding structure affected her research in that she could not procure necessary equipment, we cannot presume she encountered only the one problem simply because she chose to relay a single story regarding difficulties. Such incomplete responses prohibit formulation of a data set suitable to generating numerical information that might be preferred by many potential readers of this study.

Grant language required disaggregating participants' narratives in order to address specific areas of interest such as challenges, impact, and measurements of success. In the early stages of the Mellon Research Project, this seemed logical and appropriate, but as the catalog of collected interviews grew during the first round of the research site visits, the value of participants' whole narratives became increasingly evident. Quoting portions of participants' interviews addresses pre-established informational categories, but much of the power of these statements rests in the context of the full story rather than in selected quotes. The recently awarded second Mellon Grant will allow ArtsEngine to relay these stories in their entirety, providing greater cohesion and comprehensibility by presenting participants' statements in their original context.

Participant interviews provide the primary informational source for the findings contained in this document. Two other data collection tools were planned but not executed due to administrative choices early in the project and personnel changes within the

TABLE 4.
KEY TERMS AND
CONCEPTUAL CATEGORIES

Key Terms and Conceptual Categories	Tally	%
Institutional structures and funding	**[308]**	
Bottom up	24	20
Center	15	13
Discord	5	4
Grants/external funding	69	59
Institute	8	7
Language of granting	13	11
Nonfinancial resources	35	30
Promotion/tenure	54	46
Revenue stream	25	21
Sustainability	32	27
Top down	27	23
Research and creative practice key terms	**[270]**	
Arts practice-focused	53	45
Arts reached out	45	38
Research/creative production impact and dissemination	69	59
Research-focused	47	40
Science/technology reached out	56	48
Attitudinal key terms	**[173]**	
Anti-post-disciplinary	18	15
Disciplinary hierarchies	52	44
Disciplinary vernaculars	38	32
Instrumentalization	12	10
Interdisciplinarity same as transdisciplinarity	29	25
Intrinsic value	20	17
Personal asymmetries	0	0
Strict disciplinarian	4	3
Curricular key terms	**[401]**	
Curricular arts practice-focused	48	41
Arts reached out	38	32
Buying time	9	8
Co-curricular	39	33
Co-taught	31	26
Contact hour	13	11
Curricular assessment	26	22
Curricular development	46	39
Curricular focus	26	22
Diffusion	1	0.8
Fusion	25	21
Infusion	15	13
Science/technology reached out	18	15
STEAM focused	22	19
Student research opportunities	44	38

ArtsEngine organization: a literature review and a detailed institutional and program analysis. External data were limited to those documents interviewees chose to provide, mostly consisting of course syllabi but not including sufficient, consistent, or detailed information such as grant proposals, project findings, institutional statistics, and so on. Likewise, university websites provide finite information unsuited to comparative analysis due to a lack of uniformity in what institutions choose to make public and the frequency with which published information is updated. Therefore, no database presently exists for making institutional comparisons of percentages of students involved in the arts, numbers of students participating in co-curricular arts programs, budgets of centers and institutes, or similar factors. Much more data would be necessary in order to formulate comparative analyses about institutions and programs, representing another area of opportunity for the second Mellon Research Project grant.

Finally, the spectrum of the arts includes such varied practices that no convenient language presently exists to address them inclusively. The term "the arts" unintentionally tends to connote the "fine arts" of music, theater, and visual art while seeming to omit design and architecture, creative writing and poetry, media arts, and a host of other creative practices. All of these fields, perhaps design most especially, play an integral role in arts integration. Omission of any area of creative practice should be understood as purely inadvertent, not as a deliberate or strategic choice on the part of the researchers or author.

ANALYSIS OF KEY TERMS AND CONCEPTUAL CATEGORIES

During the interview process, participants responded to questions regarding their experience with arts integration, encompassing models, obstacles, implementation strategies, costs, and impact on students and faculty and on research, practice, and teaching. The language and ideas conveyed through participants' responses represent issues related to arts integration efforts at the sites visited. Research assistants searched interview recordings for key terms and conceptual categories conveying these issues, examining video files of 117 individuals at 8 institutions and identifying 1,152 instances across 39 designations – or an average of 9.8 items per interview. These eight institutions provide a cross-section of the full body of research sites in the

project. Seven of the eight institutions examined in this sample earned the RU/VH designation. Three are private institutions, and five are public universities. Five are located on the East Coast, two in the Midwest, and one on the West Coast, with enrollments ranging from under 6,000 to over 50,000. Participants included administrators and faculty members, with participation per institution ranging from a low of 3 interviewees at one of the smaller universities to a high of 26 at one of the larger institutions. This diversity in size, location, and classification provides a representative sample likely to be reflective of the institutions involved in this study. In order to avoid creating a comparative ranking of these institutions and to preserve anonymity, researchers intentionally avoided correlation of identifying characteristics and chose not to separate participant responses by institution or individual. This analysis provides a tool for understanding characteristic responses and identifying frequency of terms in order to generate categorical comparisons. **TABLE 4** provides a tally of responses and a percentage of the tally figure in comparison to the 117 total interviews undergoing this analysis. Figures in brackets represent total instances of terms within a given category.

The following figures illustrate points of interest in this analysis (see figures 3-7). Although future examination of interview transcripts might produce differing results, these figures may help to shed light on the general types of information contained within the interview recordings.

As seen in **FIGURE 3**, key terms occurring in 30 or more of the sample interviews reveal participants' areas of concern, involvement, or interest. Of the top 5 terms, 59% of participants spoke about grants and external funding; 59% mentioned impact and dissemination of research and creative production; 46% of interviewees discussed promotion and tenure; 45% spoke about arts practice; and 44% cited disciplinary hierarchies.

Within the Mellon Research Project, investigators utilized three categories of arts integration: 1) fusion refers to a course fully merging one or more academic disciplines with one or more areas of the arts; 2) infusion indicates collaborations in which the arts support teaching and learning in another discipline; 3) diffusion refers to courses in which non-arts students engage in immersive study in the arts. As can be seen in **FIGURE 4**, of the 41 identified instances in this sample, investigators categorized 62% of their curricular

FIGURE 3.
FREQUENCY OF TOP TERMS

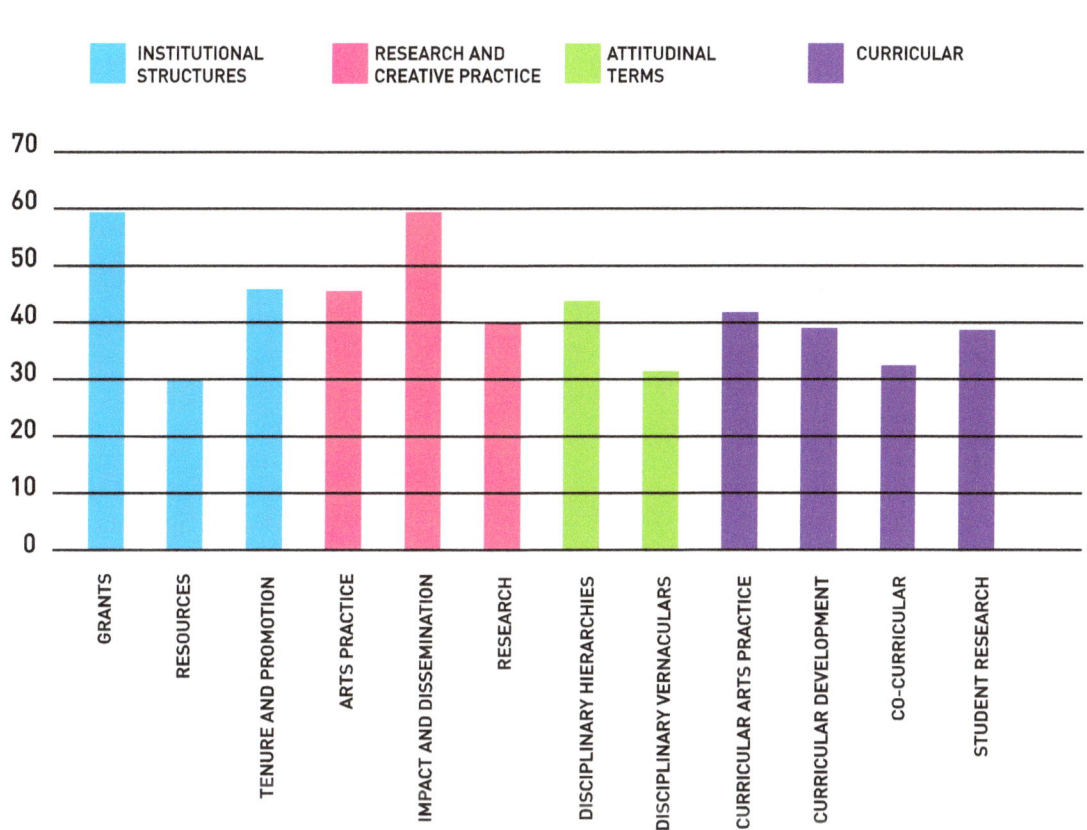

FIGURE 4.
TYPE OF CURRICULAR ARTS INTEGRATION

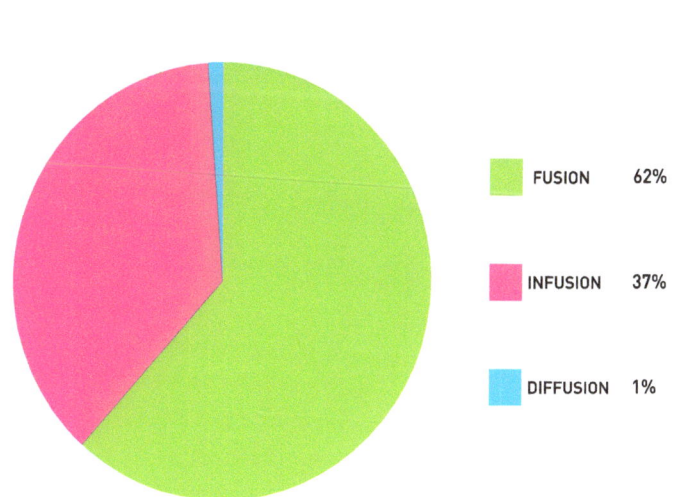

collaborations as fusion, 37% as infusion, and only 1% (one instance) as diffusion. These categories receive a more comprehensive treatment in chapters 1 and 2, with the best practice identified as fusion in chapter 5.

The focus of participants' remarks demonstrates distribution across the conceptual areas of the Mellon Research Project. As can be seen in **FIGURE 5**, curricular development provided a focus in 12% of the sample interviews, and 24% centered on arts practice. Participants discussed arts curricula in 22% and research in 21% of interviews. Co-curricular discussions appeared in 12% of interviews and STEAM (Science, Technology, Engineering, Arts, and Mathematics) considerations in 10%. With a data range of just 14%, these categories reflect the relatively even attention paid to these areas of interest throughout the research process.

Discussion of partnerships indicated which participant initiated the collaboration (see **FIGURE 6**). In instances of arts-integrated research, the partnering discipline reached out to the arts most frequently, with 56% of collaborations initiated by the non-arts discipline. In curricular collaborations between the arts and another discipline, the arts reached out to the other discipline in 68% of identified instances. Further, 101 participants spoke about initiating research partnerships, while 56 interviewees mentioned curricular partnerships. From this comparison, we can observe the arts as taking a lead in initiating collaborative projects, with 83 instances, while another discipline initiated the collaboration in 74 instances.

As **FIGURE 7** shows, interview participants' views on disciplinarity indicate 18 individuals as holding anti-disciplinary or post-disciplinary views, 29 as holding interdisciplinary or transdisciplinary view, and 4 individuals adhering to strict disciplinarity. Disciplinary identities may influence participants' willingness to engage in arts integration or the types of arts-integrative activities in which they choose to participate. As these figures reflect a relatively small percentage of the whole – comprising 12% of all interviews and 17% of all institutions included in the full Mellon Research Project – we should be cautious of drawing conclusions based on this representative sample. However, we might identify characteristics among participants' responses and the relationships of key terms and conceptual categories serving to illuminate the subsequent discussions in this study. Full transcription of all recorded interviews will help to re-aggregate these terms and concepts into the participants' narratives, providing greater contextualization of issues faced with arts integration.

FIGURE 5.
INTERVIEW FOCUS

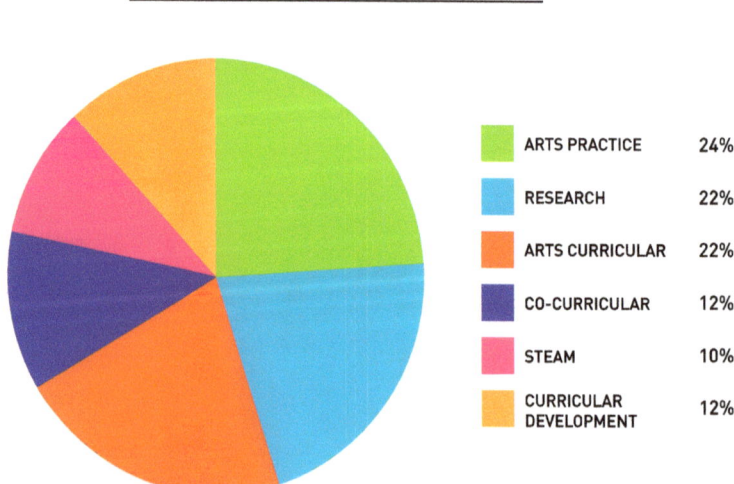

ARTS PRACTICE	24%
RESEARCH	22%
ARTS CURRICULAR	22%
CO-CURRICULAR	12%
STEAM	10%
CURRICULAR DEVELOPMENT	12%

FIGURE 6.
INITIATION OF PARTNERSHIP

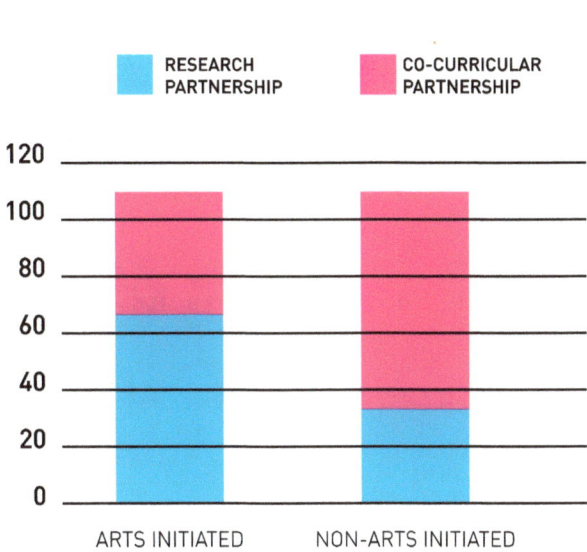

FIGURE 7.
DISCIPLINARY IDENTITY

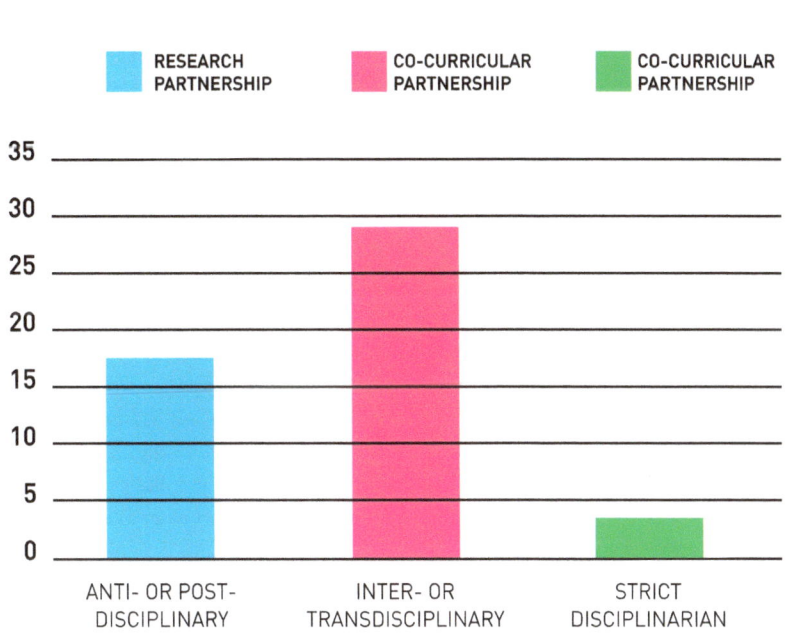

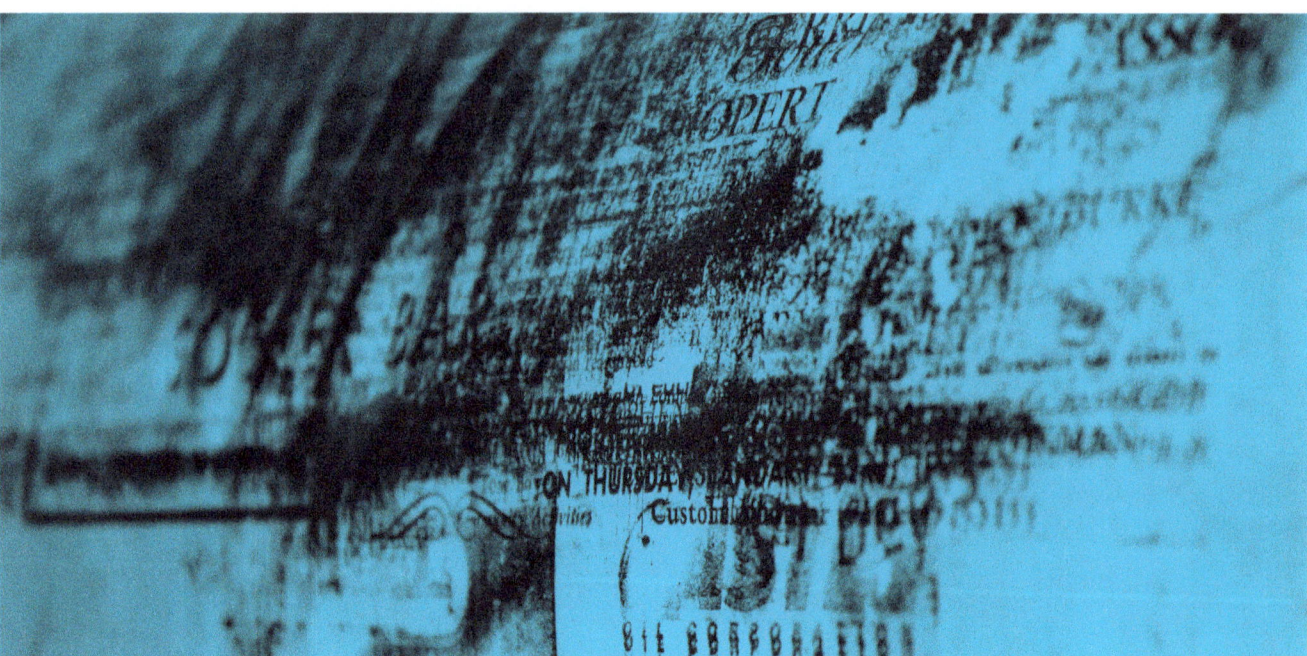

FINDINGS

Data gathered through the interviews, site visits, additional materials, and ongoing communications span general categories of student needs and perceptions, curricular integration, collaborative research, and co-curricular programming. A brief summary of each category follows.

STUDENT VIEWS AND EXPERIENCES

Students place high value on collaboration and expect opportunities for interdisciplinarity and arts integration to be easily available. Although realizing the importance of disciplinary training, they often prefer interdisciplinary engagement. Disciplinary vernaculars create discord and miscommunication among both students and faculty members, and interdisciplinary students express the need for a community to assist in gaining interdisciplinary skills and connections.

CURRICULAR INTEGRATION

Participants reported their institutions as highly valuing their arts-integrated curricular efforts, although inequities in funding and status present continuing challenges. Policies for promotion and tenure tend not to encourage curricular experimentation, remaining focused on traditional standards for disciplinary achievement rather than rewarding innovation. Rigorous and promising, dominant practices to evaluate student success within courses reflect the creative processes the instructors intend to teach.

COLLABORATIVE RESEARCH

Participants reported success with research collaborations and indicated support and affirmation from their institutions, believing these efforts have significant value despite obstacles such as resistance from their disciplinary peers, lack of funding, or challenges in gaining peer acceptance of collaborative work toward promotion or tenure. Data visualization and sonification represent the most common link between arts practice and research in other disciplines, a situation with both advantages and drawbacks for the artists called upon to provide these services. Overall, research collaborations present mutual benefit for all parties, evidenced by successful projects.

CO-CURRICULAR PROGRAMS

Students reported positive experiences surrounding their participation in co-curricular programs offering arts opportunities beyond classroom and research settings. Primarily anecdotal and qualitative, available data regarding the impact of these programs on students and on the campus culture diverge from the interdisciplinary or collaborative approaches typically found in the research or curricular aspects of this study.

BENEFITS TO THE ARTS

Individuals, particularly those in the arts, may be reluctant to participate in collaborative or arts-integrative work due to concerns that their efforts will be of secondary importance within a research project or that the arts will be devalued when linked to another discipline. However, such work possesses demonstrable benefits for all participants, providing improved creative practice, personal development, enhancement of professional standing, and enrichment of student learning.

CHALLENGES AND ADMINISTRATIVE CONCERNS

Change, regardless of how welcome or necessary, happens slowly in higher education. Researchers found several themes emerging with regard to challenges to arts integration, whether this related to research, to teaching and learning, or to co-curricular programming, primarily in the categories of support, development and planning, funding, impact, assessment, considerations of implementation or logistics, sustainability, and promotion and tenure. Participants identified strategies and solutions for managing these problems but seldom reported their experiences as trouble-free.

SUPPORT. Some faculty members reported enjoying significant support from their administrators or institutions in the form of public recognition, awards, publicity, or provision of necessary resources. However, others spoke of administrators who were unaware of their accomplishments, of struggling to work with inadequate facilities or equipment, and of opposition by their departmental colleagues. Some institutions have established strong systems of support such as centers or institutes, but others provide little recognition of faculty efforts in arts integration. Institutions vary widely in this area, from university-wide arts integration initiatives to sporadic efforts by individuals or departments.

DEVELOPMENT AND PLANNING. Collaborative or interdisciplinary work generally occurs outside regular expectations for research, teaching, and service. Developing resources through grants or other sources of funding and planning for collaborations or interdisciplinary curricula are activities that require a significant investment of personal time and energy beyond a faculty member's normal duties. This can impede collaboration, as can a lack of institutional encouragement or the absence of structures supporting such preparatory efforts.

FUNDING. Decreased investment remains a perpetual obstacle in the cultural sector. Some institutions enjoy generous funding, especially those placing a systemwide priority on arts integration or interdisciplinarity. At other institutions, faculty report notable struggles to secure the financial resources necessary to sustain their work. Partnerships between the arts and STEM seem to be more advantageous than those between the arts and humanities, mainly due to the more abundant funding available in STEM, as well as to administrative or cultural prioritization of such projects.

IMPACT. Where arts-integrative projects or courses studied were ongoing or classifiable as works-in-progress, few data were readily available to measure their impact. In other cases, participants provided anecdotal reports of impact such as verbal feedback from student participants or professors' recollections. Participants did not mention formalized or systemic mechanisms for evaluating impact, rendering this issue problematic.

ASSESSMENT AND EVALUATION. Widespread discussion of assessment and evaluation occurs across the academic landscape, from broad measures of institutional effectiveness to instructor evaluations. Surveys measuring student engagement, student satisfaction, and perceived gains are common in higher education. Assessment often concerns student learning, whereas evaluation usually refers to institutional outcomes or goals. Comprehensive measurement of the success of arts integration efforts remains difficult to achieve due to the breadth of these considerations and inherent variation in meaning depending on the situation and type of assessment or evaluation under consideration. Much like the issue of impact, evidence gathered was mainly qualitative, yielding little by way of numerical data or suggested measures with the potential for broad application across institutions or programs.

CONSIDERATIONS OF IMPLEMENTATION. When individuals from different disciplinary backgrounds decide to form a partnership, several factors can produce complications and challenges. The process of becoming a professor involves the acquisition of particular disciplinary habits of mind, development of a specialized vocabulary, and membership in a departmental culture. These characteristics influence the professor's approach to collaboration, work habits, and teaching style, which vary widely from one department to the next. Communication between individuals from disparate departments or disciplines can prove to be challenging because a common word such as "color" or "content" can have vastly different meanings depending on the academic area under consideration. Furthermore, faculty members teaching in the studio arts operate under different systems for credit hours and contact hours than do faculty teaching lecture-based or lab-based courses; this affects participants' availability to work with those from outside of their home departments. Status and rank may affect collaborations, with senior faculty finding less incentive to pursue projects requiring more work and little potential reward, while junior faculty may harbor concerns that engaging in interdisciplinary ventures may not be credited toward their pursuit of career advancement or may be looked down upon by their departmental colleagues. Therefore, finding common ground for collaborations, whether research-based or curricular, presents significant challenges on a practical level.

SUSTAINABILITY. Even when participants plan, develop, fund, and launch an arts-integrative project or course, the issue of sustainability arises. Grants and gifts allow innovation to blossom, but even the most laudable program may close without stable, ongoing funding. Some interviewees reported ingenious methods of ensuring their project or course could continue indefinitely, but others were not as successful in achieving this goal.

PROMOTION AND TENURE. Of all the challenges to arts integration studied, the issue of promotion and tenure held the most significance for participants. Naturally, faculty members seek recognition for their work, and they strive to progress through departmental ranking systems toward the achievement of professional status. Policies and procedures governing the evaluation process tend to rely on tradition and specific disciplinary norms. Furthermore, faculty members and administrators comprising promotion or tenure boards may view situations through specific disciplinary lenses, affecting their perception of candidates' achievements outside of expected standards. If, for example, a professor of music composition publishes an article in a science journal or if a professor of mathematics presents a sculpture installation at a juried arts festival, how should their promotion and tenure committees judge this work? What standards of excellence apply? Activities diverging so widely from typical research or creative practice can complicate the process, rendering career advancement more difficult for interdisciplinary scholars.

CONCLUSIONS

This document is the tangible outcome of the Mellon Research Project, providing a review of best practices in the integration of the arts in higher education, articulating models, obstacles, and impact on students and faculty as well as on research, practice, and teaching in other knowledge areas.

This study serves to inform future practice and research, providing examples and strategies interested individuals or organizations could utilize in order to implement research, curricular, and co-curricular programs integrating the arts across diverse academic divisions.

PREVIEW

The following chapters examine each of the ideas and themes presented in chapter 1. Chapter 2 presents models of arts integration, exploring some of the exemplars discovered at the 46 participating institutions. Chapter 3 features student needs and perceptions. Chapter 4 examines challenges and administrative concerns, while chapter 5 features best practices based on information gleaned from the models in chapter 2 and lessons learned from the ways in which institutions and administrators have met the challenges in chapter 4. Finally, chapter 6 presents a summary of findings from the previous chapters and suggestions for future research.

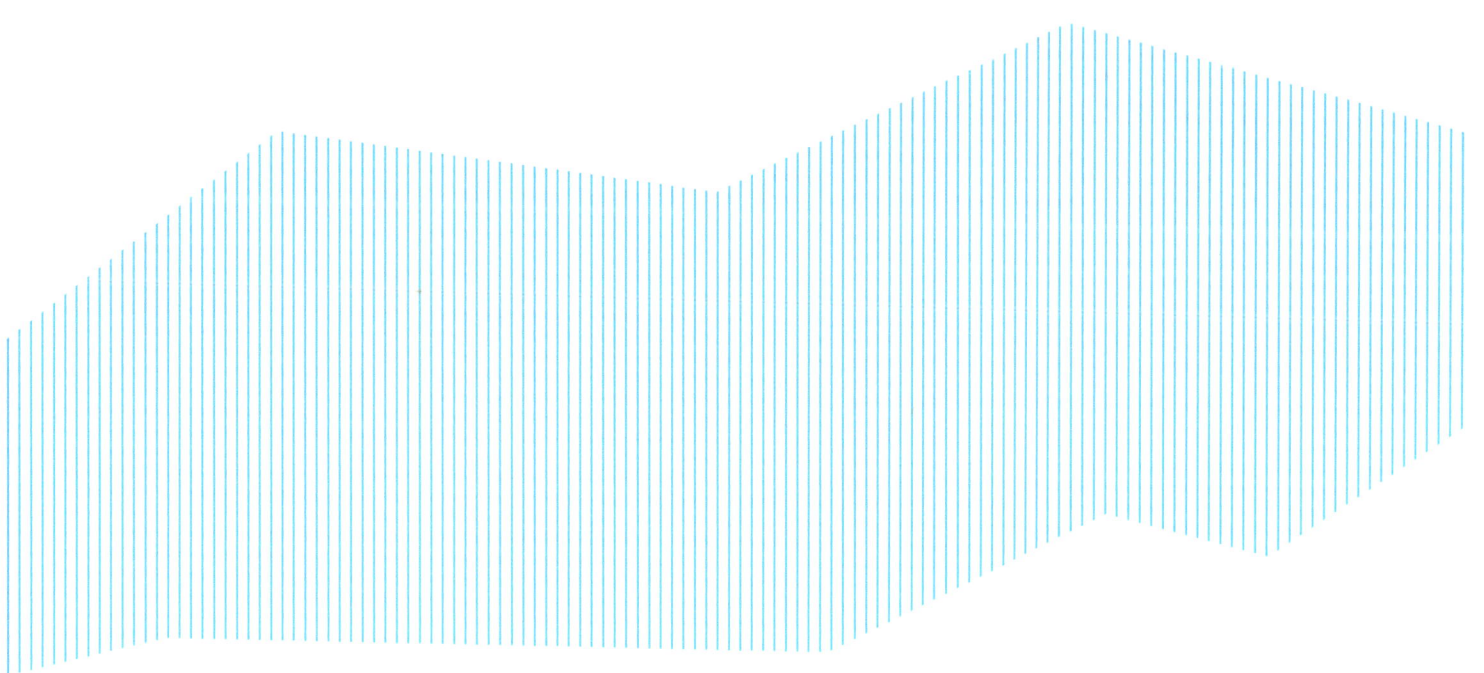

CHAPTER TWO

MODELS OF ARTS INTEGRATION

The Mellon Research Project identified models of arts integration at the institutions of higher education visited, organizing these into three general categories: curricular integration, collaborative research, and co-curricular programs. In most cases, these models depend upon individuals or groups of faculty and administrators, interdisciplinary degree programs, centers, or institutes incorporating the arts with other academic areas.

This chapter draws upon the Mellon Research Project's Interim Reports previously disseminated through a2ru and ArtsEngine: Curricular Integration (Kolenic and Mackh), Collaborative Research (Mackh and Kolenic), and Co-Curricular Programs (Mackh and Baefsky), revising and updating the information contained in these reports for inclusion in this study.

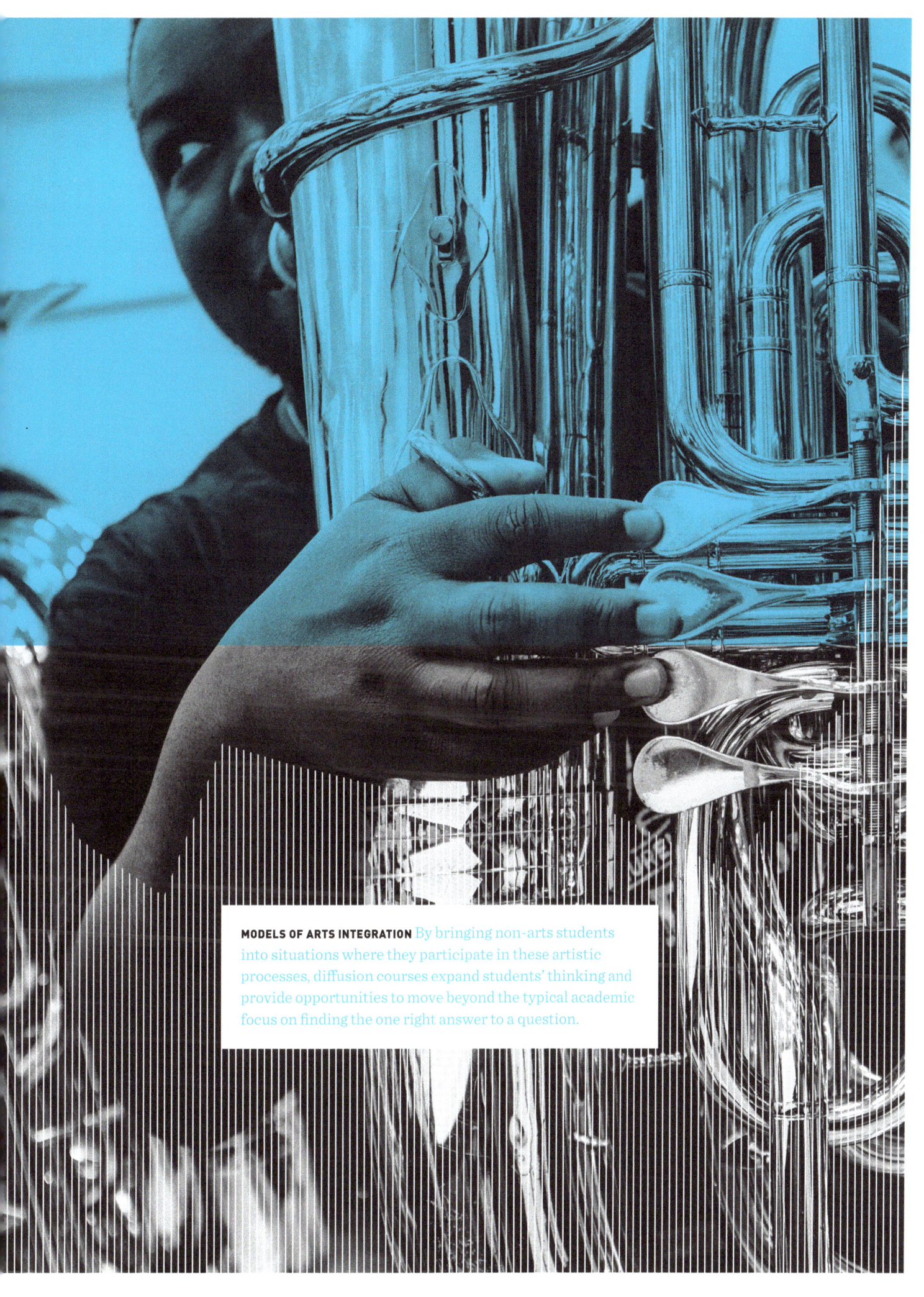

MODELS OF ARTS INTEGRATION By bringing non-arts students into situations where they participate in these artistic processes, diffusion courses expand students' thinking and provide opportunities to move beyond the typical academic focus on finding the one right answer to a question.

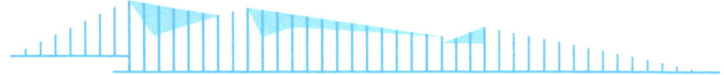

CURRICULAR INTEGRATION

Curricular integration of the arts found at each of the partner institutions employs innovative pedagogical and andragogical methods. As defined in chapter 1, fusion courses fully integrate the arts with another academic discipline; infusion courses add the arts to another discipline for the purpose of illustration, example, or experience; and diffusion courses provide arts experience to students not majoring in the arts, integrating the arts with students' overall program of study.

The choice of which arts-integrative approach is used in a course's design depends on a faculty member's individual level of disciplinary adherence, contributing to a course or program's construction and its constituent learning objectives. Infusion-based courses, for example, may expose students from areas such as engineering or biology to arts practice, or they may introduce studio arts students to computer science, attempting to provide an experience in an alternative mode of critical or creative thinking as well as instruction in the partnering discipline. Diffusion courses might involve non-art students in an immersive arts experience, while in fusion models, the epistemology and practices of the arts permeate the course featuring learning in a partnering discipline. The following section presents examples of each type of curricular approach to arts integration.

INFUSION

Infusion-based curricular offerings tend to be brief or temporary, employing one subject in the instruction of another for the purposes of illustration, example, or experience. This might occur in only one or two class periods by means of guest speakers, performances, or demonstrations. Arts faculty tend to be wary of instrumentalization or marginalization of their subject by other curricular areas; they reported their reluctance to participate in situations with less than a full partnership, beginning with a course's ideation and extending through its implementation. Learning objectives of infusion courses relate to the anchor discipline of the course, sometimes including mention of an arts exposure component. Interviewees stated that arts exposure through infusion broadens the base of possible applicability, shifting the angle at which students view course content and introducing other possible avenues for the transmission of skills and knowledge. A faculty member in microbiology, for example, spoke of dedicating a week of her semester-long course to using bacteria as an art medium. Students were to read articles on relationships between microbiology

and the arts, attend a guest lecture, and at the end of the week, make works of bacterial art by creating aesthetic patterns or images in their petri dish canvases. Students expressed positive feedback. According to the professor, "At first they're a bit perplexed: 'We're really allowed to do that?' It is uncommon that they would be rewarded for being creative. Their faces, motivation, excitement, the fun they're having. So much more than textbook information in and spitting it back out at me."

The director of a business school offered another successful example of infusion, saying, "Business students are not creative at all – they have to learn to be creative." So he invited the director of a dance company (in residence with the school of dance) to teach business school students how to become creative and how to become entrepreneurs. "A lot of the students became interested in dance," he reported. "We also brought someone from the board of the dance company to speak to the entrepreneurial students."

In this same vein, a vice provost with background in the arts describes arts integration as the "ability to tap into the full robustness of the arts across all curriculum." He continued:

Arts are not a separate appendage or add-on experience. And [they] don't have to manifest in traditional formats like dance, music, theater, but there are components that are rooted in the creative enterprise, and that's the common denominator across all fields of knowledge – so you tap into that as a means of sharing arts across all parts of curriculum.

Infusion examples extend beyond individual classrooms to programs and university-wide efforts. A participating university offers grants to encourage faculty from non-arts fields to bring artists into their classrooms, providing similar opportunities for faculty members in the arts to bring in non-arts faculty. Some university museums of art supply space and programming to faculty members both in and out of the arts. Museum staff members contact various departments to determine ways in which interactions with the museum can expand or support their curricula, such as creating exhibits serving as touchstones or examples for students in fields like mechanical engineering or aeronautical sciences.

Participants reported positive experiences with arts infusion enriching students' understanding and enlivening non-arts courses. As the professor of microbiology said, "We integrated the arts into [the lab project at the end of the course], and it drastically changed the output as well as the students' attitudes toward their work.... It's very rare that such a thing would be integrated into a purely science class." This professor found her experience with arts integration to be "extremely positive. Some students have nominated me for teacher of the year. Truly outstanding feedback. I expect more people to understand that arts and science are completely connected even through one day of exposure."

DIFFUSION

At the opposite end of the spectrum from infusion, where students study in a particular non-arts discipline accompanied by additions of arts exposure or experience, diffusion courses focus on providing students with an immersive experience based on sustained engagement with arts practice throughout the course. Diffusion courses vary in the depth of arts experience, ranging from learning experiences still largely disciplinary in nature but including applications of a skill set for the arts or, alternatively, those imparting new meaning or approaches to students' curricular experiences by contextualizing or practicing them within an arts context. For example, a learning objective stated in the syllabus for a course entitled "Programming as Art" positions the course as an "introduction to computers and programming within the context of artistic practice."

As another example, a diffusion-based graduate course primarily populated by computer science students features the creation of digital environments for aesthetic and experiential purposes, requiring students with advanced knowledge of computer programming to learn unfamiliar skill sets such as narrative creation and storytelling. Students must negotiate epistemological disjunctions between the worlds of computer science and the creative considerations to which their prior skills and knowledge apply – an interaction among the intended learning outcomes of the course.

A similar course titled "Media Experiments in Art and Technology" invites students to engage in a real-world engineering experience while learning to think creatively and analytically in order to create engaging works of art. The course prioritizes collaboration and creative methodologies to further lifelong creative practice for engineers and artists including training in MakerBot, basic electronics, the Arduino prototyping platform, visualization and communication techniques, systems troubleshooting, and integrating technical knowledge with artistic vision.

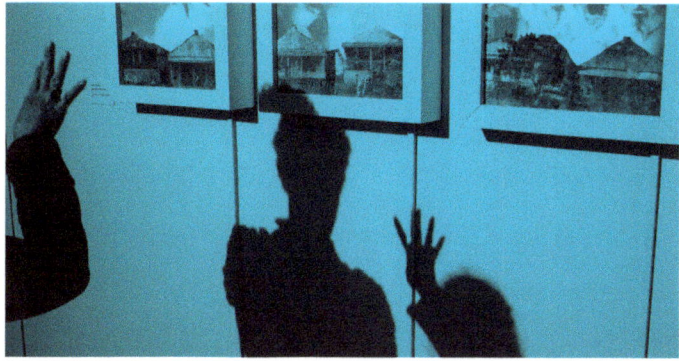

Yet another example comes from a "Senior Reflection" course, intended to facilitate biology students' learning how to use art in science and how to use science in artistic production. Students approach their interest in biology through a sequence of quarters during which they engage in arts practice and create works of art, whether musical, theatrical, or visual, among others. The first quarter entails brainstorming and exploring media, developing proposals for specific projects, and identifying faculty mentors with whom the students might work in both biology and an arts discipline. The second quarter includes an intensive focus on creative execution of students' projects. The third and final quarter entails polishing the projects, making final adjustments, and preparing for a final exhibition. According to student testimonials, this course has yielded dramatic shifts in their thinking. For example, a student made a sculpture resembling a large wooden cube with strings attached and running through its center, demonstrating the curve of a mathematical model he had created in his studies. During the process of construction, the student realized that only theoretical space allows lines to intersect without occupying physical space and disrupting each other's trajectories.

Diffusion courses, especially those involving design, frequently place students in interdisciplinary teams; thus, faculty members evaluate a team's work rather than individual projects. In such instances, students must negotiate their own strengths, weaknesses, personality dynamics, and disciplinary barriers while working toward the completion of a shared task. Furthermore, instructors often require project documentation by means of a sketchbook or lab book, forcing students to engage with the uncertainty and ambiguity of the creative process, to record the journey from ideation to prototype or completed object, and to expose the iterations punctuating the work as well as capture their interdisciplinary

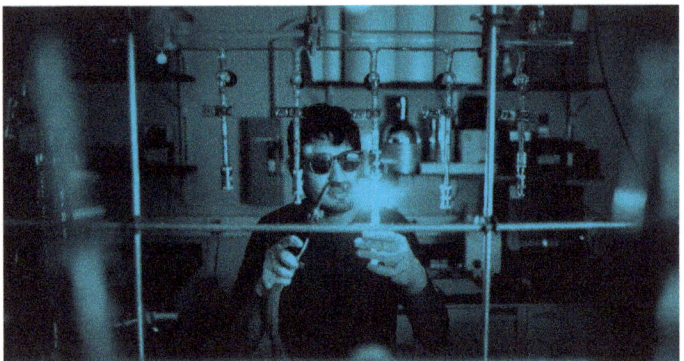

teams' successes and failures. A syllabus for a course titled "Analogous Thinking in the Arts and Sciences" informed students: "All investigations, experiments, research, drawings, diagrams, photos, writings, etc. will become part of review and presentation. . . . How you make what you make, your process, techniques, material choices, and insights are part of the meaning of the final work."

This emphasis on process over product appears markedly different from a typical university course requirement to turn in only the result of students' efforts, such as a research paper or completed exam. However, the arts find emphasis on process integral to students' efforts, whether through preparation for a musical performance, a theatrical production, the creation of a work of visual art, or the design process. Artists of all types engage in heuristics, trying new approaches to their creative problems until arriving at a final product or performance. By bringing non-arts students into situations where they participate in these artistic processes, diffusion courses expand students' thinking and provide opportunities to move beyond the typical academic focus on finding the one right answer to a question.

FUSION

Fusion courses provide similar opportunities to experience the creative process, with fusion fully integrating two disciplines in a single course, whereas a diffusion classroom tends toward primary emphasis on the arts. The Kennedy Center for the Performing Arts provides the following definition of arts integration, which encapsulates the fusion model identified in this study: "Arts integration is an approach to teaching in which students construct and demonstrate understanding through an art form. Students engage in a creative process which connects an art form and another subject area and meets evolving objectives in both" (Silverstein and Layne 1).

Universities sometimes limit these courses to students in certain programs or majors, such as a course admitting only lower-level undergraduates from engineering, art and design, music, theater, dance, architecture, and urban planning. Such restrictions usually serve the purpose of constructing evenly distributed interdisciplinary teams. In other cases, universities open courses to all students, transcending the boundaries among majors or between undergraduate and graduate designations. These courses demonstrate a range of constructs, from interdisciplinary teaming to independent study.

Faculty members espousing anti- and post-disciplinary philosophies gravitate toward fusion courses, identifying themselves as hybrid scholars. Co-teaching promotes collaborative relationships between those who do not fit easily into disciplinary silos. As one such professor said, "I work with other hybrids; I tend not to seek specialists." This professor prefers to work with scholars whose work exhibits similar difficulty to pinpoint within a single discipline.

Learning objectives and structures of fusion courses largely mirror these hybrid, post-disciplinary or anti-disciplinary philosophies. In a creative process course explicitly concerned with "debugging" modes of learning that define standard K-12 curricular and knowledge testing, the professor said, "This is talent meeting passion, versus the mindless 'worker bee' ethic." Presumably, arts-integrated courses could generally make this claim, but the language present in fusion course syllabi differs perceptibly from infusion or diffusion syllabi, which tend to focus on a particular discipline. Learning objectives of fusion courses reveal goals such as "igniting curious minds," "developing fluid and critical thinking," promoting an "ecology of cooperative production," and learning to harness the "power of play." The syllabus for a "Creative Process" course outlines a goal of seeking to "position abstraction as a way of life," teach students to "embrace failure," and approach problems and interdisciplinary work with a sense of "openness." To these ends, the objectives of fusion courses tend to emphasize removing students from their comfort zones while encouraging them to discover a personal "sweet spot" of interest and passion. Instructors may also position their goals for student learning within an understanding of growing corporate emphases on interdisciplinarity, collaboration, and teamwork.

As an example of a fusion approach, a dean discussed the creation of a new interdisciplinary course:

The faculty just came together on their own, which blew my mind away. [The new course is] called Creative Living 101. It's a freshman course. Six professors coming together creating one course – [that's] truly transdisciplinary. In the past for an intro class, each major has three weeks, divided by module. No. We are starting with the user. What does an 18-year-old need to know about living? What can you contribute to that perspective? Personal finance perspective, design perspective, etc. Everyone brings their perspective to the user. . . . [There's] lots of excitement among faculty members. They are having so much fun. You have to put money where you say something is important. And this was important.

The dean's affirmation of allocating financial resources in support of priorities underscores an important point echoed by other interview participants. Faculty appreciate their administrators' verbal expressions of support, but tangible backing clearly demonstrates administrators' priorities.

Another course example involved a pairing of biology, specifically landscape ecology, and painting; the course was led by a professor of visual arts. The professor wanted to create a course allowing visual arts majors to meet a science requirement while also allowing science majors to meet a visual arts requirement. Held at the university's remote science center as a two-week residency, the course produced unexpected results:

[Based on submitted student reflections], we saw that the artists on the team caused the research output to be different. The artists weren't just doing what the scientists were doing: they were interacting. The scientists also walked away with a new respect for artists. Frankly, the arts are looked at as we are children and we play. But scientists found out that there are rules we follow, and we think conceptually. So that was exciting. Also because the science courses are usually so big, they had never had such close interaction with the other students and the faculty. It helped them in their communication skills. At the end of this, we had an exhibition. The scientific research and paintings of the scientists were displayed. I hope I can find another partner to do this with because it was very beneficial, however very laborious.

This professor's full narrative, included as appendix 4, provides an intriguing story of the rewards and difficulties of initiating an arts-integrated course. The final example in this section paired physics, theater, and medicine. The theater professor explained the course as using the lens of live performance to examine the cultural representations of science, scientists, and ethical issues, focusing on "real science rather than science fiction. [The course] opens up lots of interesting dialogue between physics, theater, and medicine." She discussed her motivations for creating the course:

We wanted to model and create a space for students from different disciplines to come together. This comes back to [having a] large research university where faculty and students are siloed – encouraged to declare majors as soon as possible. So the students are not developing relationships with other students as much. So we wanted to develop a place for this exchange to happen.

An emphasis on developing relationships between students from differing disciplines appeared in this example (as well as the previous course cited) among the desirable outcomes of arts-integrated courses and student priorities mentioned in chapter 3.

Evaluation of student learning in such courses takes a number of forms. Because these courses tend to have significant art-making or performing components, participation requires more emphasis than in standard curricula, including active engagement in critique sessions. Instructors record observations of individual students' work both in and out of the defined class period, along with review of journals or sketchbooks documenting students' processes, failures, team dynamics, and other concerns as they grapple with arts practice throughout the course. Fusion courses tend to feature project-based learning, often incorporating the norms of design, in which students define the purpose and problem within the context of the project and work toward answers, filling their sketchbooks with these processes and iterations. Semesters frequently culminate in a presentation or exhibition, with projects sometimes becoming prototypes for marketable products or presented in a later juried art exhibition.

Assessment mechanisms in fusion courses attempt to evaluate the development of students' critical thinking, willingness to engage in iteration, the level of an idea's completion, and attempts to break out of prior comfort zones. Potential assessment questions synthesized from multiple course syllabi include:

- *Did this student conduct significant background research in the development of her ideas or clone a previous idea?*
- *Did this student explore multiple possibilities, or did she have an initial idea and carry it out without continuous reconsideration?*
- *Is the idea fully realized, and did it manifest in the way the student had hoped?*
- *Did the student attempt to become more vocal/ participatory/invested in the team dynamics?*

Methods to measure these various elements, however, remain largely informal and particular to individual courses or instructors, limiting the transferability of methods from one instructor or course to another. Assessment tools suited to evaluating a sculpture, for instance, might not be useful if applied to the script for a one-act play or to the score for an original musical composition. Studies have been conducted at K-12 regarding arts assessment, such as the National Endowment for the Arts report, *Improving the Assessment of Student Learning in the Arts – State of the Field and Recommendations* (Herpin, Washington, and Li). Although interviews conducted by the Mellon Research Project yielded little in the way of concrete assessment mechanisms, examining work in this area under consideration by K-12 represents an area of study potentially applicable to higher education.

When asked how they determined the success of their courses overall, faculty reported use of informal assessment, such as "buzz" about the course on campus. They also relied on standard course evaluations, informal assessments such as verbal feedback from students, and measurement of course enrollments over time. Student interview participants frequently indicated these courses were transformative, saying they wished they had had the opportunity to take more such classes throughout all stages of their undergraduate careers. As with student evaluation, determining the success of arts-integrated courses will require additional study in order to determine effective assessment methods.

PROGRAMMATIC ARTS INTEGRATION

Arts-integrative curricular initiatives increasingly appear within programmatic frameworks. The **University of Florida**, for example, developed a minor in the arts specifically designed for engineering students and a reciprocal minor in engineering for students in the arts. **Stanford University** recently recast its general education requirements as a series of general education electives from which students must satisfy a "making and doing" requirement through courses focused on creative expression in an arts context. To develop the new breadth requirements (including those courses in the "creative expression" requirement), an administrator explained that Stanford conducted a battery of student surveys, town halls with students, focus groups, and dorm storms. Stanford included dozens of students and faculty in the process and also surveyed CEOs, who valued skills in creativity and collaboration.

Programs integrating the arts with other disciplines may employ varied approaches to curricular offerings rather than maintaining a preference for fusion, infusion, or diffusion of the arts. Interdisciplinary majors, double majors or additional minors, individual courses, or full degree programs conducted through centers or institutes integrating the arts offer students plentiful options for pursuing an arts-integrative educational experience. The complexity and diversity of such efforts prevents a full exposition in this chapter. However, chapter 5 will provide an extended examination of exemplary centers, institutes, and degree programs, highlighting instances of best practices in these areas.

PEDAGOGICAL FRAMEWORKS

Infusion, diffusion, and fusion approaches to curricular arts integration provide a framework for arts-integrative practices, which share methods allowing for development of connections between contrary, diverse, and sometimes opposing disciplinary epistemologies. The interweaving of different pedagogical experiences creates value in arts-integrated curricula by reframing students' interactions with the course material through two or more disciplinary lenses. In arts-integrated settings, instead of "doing an assignment," students frame their work as a relationship with a problem or set of problems, working through them by aesthetic manipulation. Such a difference requires students to approach an intentionally underdefined problem – not just its potential solutions – by integrating typically segregated modes of knowing. One might claim that such courses seek to integrate the thinker/learner/knower so that different epistemologies of knowing, thinking, and problem solving might serve one another rather than remaining separate and distinct. A professor teaching such a course said he includes a disclaimer in the syllabus noting the course "is not for the faint of heart."

Arts-integrative courses frequently introduce non-arts students to critique sessions, a standard practice in a studio art, design, or architecture course or seminar. Definitive of arts practice, critique punctuates the majority of courses that fall under the diffusion and fusion categories. Critique sessions require periodic presentation of works in progress as well as the finished project. Students accustomed to the norms of non-arts fields may find critique methodology unfamiliar and uncomfortable at the outset. Participation requires students to be willing to hear and evaluate criticisms of their work, negotiate potentially competing criticisms, and curate the input best serving their proposed outcomes. In critique, students interact with one another to respect the work and ideas of peers from diverse viewpoints and backgrounds. In all cases, students must articulate their creative process, narrating their approach to problems or a specific line of inquiry.[14] A dean of arts and sciences said:

I think the practice of peer critique, although somewhat evident in other fields, is an aspect of education in the arts that all other disciplines can learn from. This is practiced at the graduate level in all disciplines but lacks emphasis at the undergraduate level. This is one area of arts-informed practices that could have pan-university benefit, particularly teaching how to work in teams, which is all the buzz these days. Meditative vs. interactive learning.

A professor of architecture discussed the pedagogical practices of team-based work and critique, which are fundamental to architectural and design education, and the ways these have begun to extend into other curricula, particularly in business and engineering:

Students learn from each other as much as from the instructor. Learning doesn't just occur in teams but also is produced and disseminated in a public way, as opposed to students writing a paper that the instructor reads and then is never made public. In studio-based learning, the work is presented publicly. Work is critiqued as if they were clients. Also, students learn how to re-ask the question that the client is asking – often the right question is way better than the right answer.

The professor also discussed arts-based curricular integration as an effective way to foster prototype thinking:

Every exercise is given as a "What if" question, or given these constraints, "What would you do?" It's a cycle of answer, review, refine. It's this iterative process, which results in innovation as opposed to something "new." Innovations are the things that the client did not have before coming to you – they already had the problem. They may have had the wrong problem. Change that, and it gives something they didn't have before. Innovation does not exist before the problem is engaged. "New" is answering the problem as given, and innovation is redefining the problem in order to surface and produce things that don't occur in the problem itself.

As Nobel Prize-winning scientist Albert Szent-Györgyi said, "Discovery lies in seeing what everybody has seen and thinking what nobody has thought" (qtd. in Today). The iterative cycle of answer-review-refine remains an integral part of design thinking and of the creative process. Arts integration allows students to participate authentically in experiences that allow them to develop skills and competencies with this crucial process.

Each of the higher educational institutions participating in the Mellon Research Project contains curricular integration of the arts, supported by faculty members from across the disciplinary spectrum and representing curricular areas literally ranging from anthropology to zoology. Participants overwhelmingly reported success with their work in this area, and although they spoke of challenges and impediments, they discussed viable solutions to overcoming the problems they encountered, discussed at greater length in chapter 4.

RESEARCH INTEGRATION

Collaborative research occurred at each partner institution, generally falling into one of three categories: the arts enhance inquiry in another discipline; the sciences or humanities support investigations in the arts; or disciplinary areas exist interdependently. Examples of each of these types of research collaboration follow, providing illustrations of the larger body of activities conducted at the institutions visited.[15] This section presents an overview of interview participants' statements about their engagement in arts-integrative research in order to establish a conceptual framework for the varieties of research encountered throughout the project, but a detailed, comprehensive accounting of all instances of research

---

14 For additional information on critique, see Bayles and Orland; Buster and Crawford; and Elkins.
15 Interview participants were not asked to classify their research according to the three types identified in this report. Identifications were made by the researchers.

activities remains well beyond the scope of this study, providing avenues for future research. Similarly, this section relies on the words of the interview participants themselves rather than making connections to external scholarship regarding arts-integrative research.

ARTS PRACTICE ENHANCES INQUIRY IN OTHER DISCIPLINES

Perhaps the most common way to link arts practice with research in other disciplines involves data visualization, although embodiment or sonification of data through theater, dance, music, poetry, and other artistic expressions also occurs. Several interview participants offered commentary similar to this associate provost of undergraduate affairs:

[Artistic presentation] adds a dimension or component to basic science research projects. Often the arts provide a new way of communicating findings, a visualization component. . . . Many of our projects have been outstanding as a result; we find that the arts component brings a unique perspective that complements and gives new insight or connections to things outside of the science areas. That gives rise to unique advances in new knowledge because it provides the scientist another way of looking at things. The artist also learns a lot of science in the process. This is complementary, not at odds. It exposes the technical expertise and creative imperative of both artistry and science and can lead to new materials and ideas. There is a synergy between arts and science that benefits both.

Increasing demand by funders and authorizers for public dissemination of research data has prioritized visualization, sonification, and other artistic presentations of research, drawing upon the ability of the arts to translate such information into presentations accessible to broader audiences within civil society. For example, at the time of the interview, a professor at one of the study locations was in the process of creating a National Science Foundation (NSF) proposal for a research center in materials science and engineering. He planned for graduate students conducting lab-based projects in science and engineering to pair with graduate students from the fine arts as part of the center's outreach education programs for students in grades K-12. In each pairing, the science graduate students would create a poster about their work, and the art students would create artistic interpretations of the work. The two representations would be featured together. The professor hoped that couching this partnership in

terms of public outreach might increase its eligibility for scientific funding while allowing the science to reach the public in an accessible and engaging way through the arts. Federal funders, such as the NSF, consider educational and public dissemination of research to be important, bringing the value of their investments to a broad range of people.

Another professor, with joint appointments in information sciences and technology and women's studies, received an NSF grant to communicate the results of research on underrepresentation of various groups of people in computer-related careers. Seeking a new way to convey the results of her study, she wrote a play about young women in high school who were becoming aware of career possibilities in computer science and making decisions about their futures. She said: "When you write a paper, you get an opportunity to give quotes, at best, but it lacks the feeling of it all. . . . This is where art excels – dealing with the emotional and implicit. . . . . Arts are what make people human: they nurture humanity and creativity. Math is a tool to do analysis; arts are a tool to do creativity and human emotion."

These examples begin to illustrate artistic presentation of data, but far more instances exist. **The Cube** at Virginia Tech and the **AlloSphere** at the University of California, Santa Barbara create multi-sensory presentations of data, discussed in detail in subsequent chapters. Not all situations in which artistic presentation of data enhances inquiry in a partnering discipline involve public outreach, but this function remains among the contributions made by the arts to the larger enterprise of research.

OTHER DISCIPLINES SUPPORT ARTS PRACTICE

Scholars in the arts sometimes work with partners in other academic disciplines in order to seek new knowledge in their artistic fields. A specific example comes from the pairing of drama and robotics, in which a professor of drama worked with computer scientists in order to create a robotic character that could interact with humans in stage productions. This relationship has lasted for more than ten years, with mutually beneficial results. The director explained, "As the conversation [with computer scientists] went forward, we found we had a lot to offer each other. Over the years, our character development expertise has changed their views, and their technical know-how has drastically changed ours."

Computer science proved to be a valued partner for research in the arts and design, appearing in varied collaborations. For instance, several interviewees in theater, drama, and dance spoke of projects employing the technologies of film or computer science to assist with motion capture. Likewise, music and computer science combined to produce gesture recognition software to analyze a conductor's movements, develop software for digital accompaniment, or create a laptop orchestra.

Chapter 5 addresses additional examples of partnerships in which another discipline supports arts practice, featuring instances of best practice. A more complete analysis of this aspect of arts research could prove an intriguing topic for future study.

INTERDEPENDENT, MUTUALLY BENEFICIAL PARTNERSHIPS

Similar to the fusion approach to curricular partnerships, some research collaborations present mutual benefit for all parties involved. This category also involves research conducted at centers or institutes providing a shared space for collaborative investigations in which partnerships begin on an equal footing within an environment conducive to interdisciplinarity. The following paragraphs present a few examples of such collaborations in order to provide examples of the variety of activities included in this category, but these statements do not provide detail about the investigations themselves beyond the interviewees' commentaries.

MECHANICAL INVENTION THROUGH COMPUTATION. A professor of computer science and MacArthur Genius Grant awardee combines computer science, paper folding, mathematics, and mechanical invention. He leads one of the most notable of these models of arts-integrated research, working alongside an architect with a background in art and design. He uses his classroom as a laboratory, with undergraduate students taking on the role of lab assistants, thus exposing them to formal research early in their academic careers. The professor and his students investigate the development of transformable objects, optimizing their creative process through mathematical analysis and computation. An exhibition copresented by the computer science laboratory and center for art, science, and technology displayed the prototypes produced in these investigations. This professor has achieved professional distinction in both science and art: his folded paper sculptures are part of the permanent collections of the Smithsonian Museum and the Museum of Modern Art, and he has won awards from the National Science Foundation, the European Association for Theoretical Computer Science, and a John Simon Guggenheim Memorial Foundation Fellowship. This collaboration meshes the research and curricular aspects of the professor's work, just as it integrates mathematics and paper sculpture, creating opportunities for students to experience undergraduate research as well as produce works of art suitable for formal exhibition in the university's museum.

HUMAN-COMPUTER INTERACTION. A dean with a background in information sciences discussed ways his institution has interwoven aspects of the arts with technology. For example, he mentioned data sonification as an attempt to understand how human hearing can enhance comprehension of data and anomalies. Data visualization often brings computer science together with visual art, and it can similarly encompass performance studies involving human beings and computers, including robotics, medicine, and entrepreneurship. The dean sees the arts as integral to learning. He said, "There are components of art in all sciences. I don't think that has been explicitly discussed much yet, but it's certainly happening." His department investigates haptic interfaces – systems allowing a user to touch data and information inside of computers – and applies this knowledge to improvisation and acting, the visual arts, and other fields. He continued, "We are continually looking at the interactions of information, technology, and humans, and we need to understand humanity very well in order to do our work."

These interactions provide a rich source of research possibilities, not only at this university but also across other sites visited in the Mellon Research Project. The arts and design provide a means of linking human beings to technology, adding a dimension of sensory experience to complex technological information. Music and neuroscience. A research program investigating the role of music in human cognition involves neuroscience and neuroimaging, using functional MRIs in order to identify and study the parts of the brain involved when experiencing music. The professor of music who initiated the project seeks to enhance understanding of music through scientific methodologies: "The value of partnering with the sciences is this: the sciences work to refine a body of knowledge over time. . . . I believe it's important for music, and the scientific method allows me to do that in a way I feel comfortable."

The pairing of music and neuroscience emerged in other instances, such as the research conducted by a professor of music and expert in cognition and expression, working with a neurologist from the university's medical center. This project measures how surprises in music stimulate the brain.

Technological advances facilitate scientific understanding of music and the human brain, such as MRIs conducted by researchers at **Johns Hopkins University**, in which researchers scanned the brains of jazz musicians while they played improvisationally, revealing new information about how the brain processes both music and language (Johns Hopkins Medicine). The relationship between music and neuroscience represents a growing field of scientific and artistic research, and additional information will be included in the discussion of best practices in chapter 5.

MUSIC AND COMPUTING. Connections between music and technology exist outside of the health sciences as well. For example, a professor of computer science with courtesy appointments in the school of art and school of music works at the intersection of music and computation through sound synthesis, analysis, music representation, and music theory. He values the conceptual linkages between music and mathematics. He explained, "Music has strong abstract theory behind it that is close to mathematics and computation. Modern electronic musical practice is computational, so huge connections [exist]." His research involves creating computer accompaniment, designing a computer that can listen to a live performer, following along and synchronizing with the musician much as a human accompanist might, and adjusting the accompaniment to the instrumentalists' performance. This includes creating programming languages for representing music that can read input quickly and produce results using "temporal semantics," that is, recognition of timing as an essential part of the program's accommodation of musical performance. This professor reported that he "started with music; computer science came later. My most important work has been driven by musical experience, at the very least inspired by it." This investigator demonstrates that research in a single discipline can often lead to explorations in other areas as the direct result of observed similarities between the two practices or phenomena.

ONLINE SALON COMMUNITY. Computer science, textual information, and visual media merge in an online "salon," a virtual discussion group for examining texts and artifacts fostering intellectual development through depth and engagement. The founder, a computer science professor with an interest in texts, commented that in the sciences, scholars tend toward convergent thinking, whereas those in the humanities exhibit more divergence. His goal was to create a place where scientific thinking in pursuit of a single right answer could mesh with humanistic thinking seeing infinite possibilities. This free online community, ClassroomSalon.com, has over 15,000 participants, testifying to the success of the collaboration. In this instance, research between computer science, textual studies, and visual media produced a resource surpassing not only the initial project but the researcher's university as well, reaching participants from around the world.

Although comparatively fewer collaborations involving the humanities appear in this section of this study, more were mentioned in the full set of interview data gathered. During the second Mellon Grant, a2ru will compile a more thorough catalog of these collaborations. Examples here merely serve as illustrations of selected instances of research collaborations that maintain a balance between partnering disciplines.

MEASUREMENTS OF SUCCESS

Interview participants consistently viewed their collaborative research endeavors as successful, impactful, and valuable, but they provided little concrete evidence beyond anecdotal statements. Responses similarly did not yield any differences in measures of success among the three types of collaborations identified in this chapter. In fact, interviewees seldom shared information regarding any specific methods used to assess their work.

Perhaps the lack of concrete data regarding measures of success for collaborative, arts-integrative research is due to the relatively brief existence of projects since they have not been in place for sufficient time to gather adequate data in interviewees' current work. Projects may be ongoing, or investigators may not yet have created appropriate assessment mechanisms for their studies. Findings in this report rely only on the participants' responses, which simply did not yield much about their methods of assessing collaborative research. Participants may well employ methods to assess their work since research design typically includes evaluative measures. However, interviewees did not typically choose to share this information with the researchers.

Of those who mentioned measurement of their research, participants' responses fall into three broad categories specific to the individual project: the products of the research, whether the project met its stated goals, and collection of data through experiments. A very brief explanation of these categories follows.

ARTIFACTS. Producing a physical artifact as the result of research provides a tangible opportunity to conduct objective assessment of a project's success. Several participants mentioned this method of assessment; these participants included faculty members from design, engineering, and technology. As one example, a faculty member at a center for arts, science, and technology said, "We like to see things that have a chance at being prototyped and used or created to show out in the world.... If the works are successful, we hope to get them into the [university] museum as part of an exhibition." Prototyping, exhibitions, performances, or demonstrations can each provide a means of validating research products. Interview participants did not elaborate upon how artifacts demonstrated a project's success. For example, evaluation according to audience reaction, the possibility of monetary reward, or positive critical review serve as very different indicators of success, and one may not align with the other. Artifacts receiving critical acclaim do not always demonstrate profitability, for example. Further investigation into participants' evaluative measures for these artifacts could prove valuable.

PROJECT GOALS. Each project has different goals and objectives, with assessments of success typically involving an examination of whether or not researchers achieved these goals. A professor of mechanical engineering working in 3-D printing explained, "The resources we've been asking for have been aimed at creating momentum to do something big; the last several years have been building this momentum.... This is about achieving the goal...." Perhaps because research design tends to include such measures as a matter of course, interview participants may take this important aspect for granted, partially accounting for participants' lack of explanation during the interviews.

EXPERIMENTS. Several interview participants engaging in scientifically based research said they relied upon the results of their experiments to gauge the success of their projects. A clinical neuroscientist reported using norm-referenced tests common to a psychology clinic along with direct observation of interactions between parents and children and social engagement during a structured activity occurring as part of her research. Assessment of experiments, according to a professor of critical studies in a school of dramatic art, "is really easy. We are working scientifically in my collaboration, which means crunching statistics." Interview participants using these structured assessment mechanisms seemed to be more comfortable discussing measurements of success, but their specificity to individual projects prevents generalizability or application to other contexts or researchers.

CONCERNS. Some participants, especially in the arts, vocally resisted measuring the success of their work. A professor of critical studies reported:

> *[The] disturbing thing about the sciences to me is their metrics for assessment, which are being forced into humanities, social sciences, and the arts (number of citations, prestige of a journal, etc.)... The arts can produce lasting work, and if you support experimental work in the arts, it can last forever, having a major impact.... We don't have these elaborate structures for validating ourselves.... We need to let something breathe long enough to find its importance, which is outside the scientific model.*

According to this professor, the arts approach the task of assessment differently than the sciences. We might see this as a difference in departmental cultures, examined at greater length in chapter 4. Furthermore, measurements of success provide a source of frustration to some scholars. A professor of theater and chair of a school of performing arts, who conducts research in association with her classes and projects, said:

> *The challenge of measurement drives me crazy. I don't know how to measure any of it, and as an actor and theater practitioner, I tend not to care about measurement. My communicating science project is what I'm most struggling with right now; all we have are measurements of change, interviewing and surveys pre and post. That's all I have: it's narrative, it's subjective, and it's the kind of justification and proof that a university like ours tends not to take very seriously. And I get that. As an administrator, I want to know about the bottom line – how much it's going to cost and how much it's going to make. But as an artist and teacher, I don't care because I see it and I know the difference in students, just like a doctor can identify some elements of an illness without any instruments.*

The theater professor's statement that she tends not to care about measurement as an actor or theater practitioner, although she does care about measurement as an administrator, illustrates the conundrum in which artists working across disciplines may find themselves. Quantifiable measurement in the arts, such as the size of an audience or numbers of tickets sold, cannot apply to critical reviews or an audience's enthusiastic reception of a performance or exhibition. As the professor of critical studies mentioned, the impact of an artistic product or performance might require a greater amount of time than is usual for other disciplines. Works of art sometimes meet with rejection and condemnation at first, only to earn the status of masterpieces later on. Playwright Tony Kushner's *Angels in America*, composer Igor Stravinsky's *The Rite of Spring*, and the paintings of Vincent van Gogh all met with strong rejection at first. Religious groups staged boycotts of theaters where performances of *Angels in America* were scheduled (Healy). The audience walked out on the first performance of *The Rite of Spring* (Kelly). Van Gogh died penniless, unable to sell paintings now worth millions of dollars and revered throughout the art world (Artble). Yet few would contest the success of these works today. Measurement of research collaborations involving the arts links the expectations of the partnering discipline with those of the arts, sometimes producing uncomfortable frictions between the desire for immediate, measurable results and acceptance of results as less concrete and occurring over time, as expressed by these interview participants. On the other hand, a dean of arts and sciences cautioned that sciences also experience shifting views over time, especially "when overcoming longstanding dogma. New and challenging ideas never have an easy path to acceptance, given the buy-in to the dogma on which so many conventional careers were based."

IMPACT OF RESEARCH

Evaluating the impact of a research project differs from assessing its success, emphasizing a wide range of considerations beyond the project itself. As with measurements of success, interview subjects did not provide concrete or numerical data in support of their statements about the impact of their research.

Of those who addressed impact, interview participants sometimes cited multiple dimensions. As a professor of human development and family services said, "On one level, it's grant dollars, how much investment there is, how much return there is on grant monies. On another, publications, products, and quantifiable

things like that. And another is the intangibles: how many people we inspire or the ways in which informal conversations about the group or topic occur."

A professor of music working with human cognition reported measuring the impact of his research by "the number of graduate students on campus engaging in this, the number of publications coming out of this university within this area, and the amount of funding we're seeing for our study." A professor of interaction design said the impact of his research was found in "citations (people taking up my work and building on it), ability to publish in the best venues, the quality of work, being invited to do keynotes or be on editorial boards and review programs, etc. And of course, the amount of money you can get a granting agency to give you."

Although funding emerged as a factor noted by the interview participants, several individuals cited the less quantifiable ability of their work to inspire others or effect change. A professor of music composition and technology who serves as the director of a center for media arts and performance said: "A sizable amount of professional activity [springs] from these collaborations. . . . The faculty research and [artistic] production has also become highly collaborative and successful." A professor of art education and women's studies used audience members' reactions to measure the impact of a play presenting the results of a research project in computer science. She noted, "People kept saying, 'Everyone needs to see this play.' When the script is out there and schools are enacting this performance within their schools and the resources are out there with it, it's the ultimate impact."

A professor of public and internal affairs working with theater as the director of an institute on policy and governance said the impact of research lies in changing the internal culture of the university as well as quantifiable factors such as the number of theses, dissertations, or other publications arising from his work. He said, "We've galvanized a different way of asking about community change. . . . We have some traditional scholarly measures. Still, those don't get to how to change the zeitgeist in the university." He went on to explain, "The arts can open up the frame of culture's intense permeation in every aspect of life. You can often reach a cultural tipping point at the individual level all the way to the top. . . . The arts can be a catalyst for framing these changes and making them possible."

Clearly, interview participants measured the impact of their research differently, yet some common themes

TABLE 5.
INTERVIEW PARTICIPANTS' MEASURES
OF IMPACT OF COLLABORATIVE RESEARCH

Ability or potential of research to acquire funding or maintain acquired funding

Ability to create excellence within a field

Ability to have academic institutions compete for an individual scholar, allowing the potential to demand the terms of employment, providing discretion and negotiation power regarding the balance between teaching and research commitments

Ability to influence or guide public policy; ability to guide decision makers in private and public sectors

Ability to monetize research in patents, for-profit entities based on research, art sales, or ticket revenues

Ability to realize new faculty collaborations

Capacity of research to increase professional status through:
- Success at conference submissions and representation in refereed symposia
- Specific invitations to attend conferences and symposia, to serve as a keynote speaker, or to participate on boards and panels
- Opportunities to publish in peer-reviewed journals and/or respected outlets
- Citation in reviews and/or media and the press
- Ability to acquire expert consulting opportunities in order to disseminate research, whether this includes commentary for mainstream media outlets or specific consulting contracts with government or private industry

Changing university cultures (e.g., promoting a more accepting climate for collaborative research)

Citations by other scholars

Creation of new works or works considered to be original contributions to the field/discipline/discourse

Graduate applications to work with specific faculty

Incorporation in education, in terms of materials included in course curricula or events/products included as educational content or tools

Increased ability to attract research collaborations to a field of study

Increased peer respect for their fields of study or increased interest by students in the field of study

Increased personal artistic or scholarly productivity or trajectory – or enhanced quality of personal work

Patents or copyrights

Recognition of excellence through awards and honorifics

Social change (e.g., creative place making, changing attitudes related to a social or cultural situation)

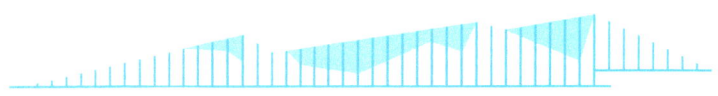

emerged. Combining the statements above with other commentary gathered through the interviews, **TABLE 5** synthesizes the measures participants cited in evaluating the impact of their work. The table presents information alphabetically, not in order of prioritization, which remains to be determined through future research.

We might understand the idea of impact as the power to make a difference, whether large or small. This difference may apply only to the individual researcher, such as enhanced ability to seek career advancement, or it may have wider applicability to the department, college, or school, as with bringing increased attention to a discipline. The impact of arts integration might produce benefits for the university as a whole, for the field of study, for the surrounding community – or perhaps create a positive benefit for human life in general. Arts-integrative medical research, for example, might yield such broad impact, as with the pairing of dance and neuroscience producing demonstrable improvement in Alzheimer's patients (discussed in chapter 5). Further research into the impact of arts-integrative collaborative research could elaborate upon these impacts, not only through additional analysis of the existing database but also through mechanisms such as surveys or collection of artifacts or documentation.

INSTITUTIONAL VALUATION AND SUPPORT FOR COLLABORATIVE RESEARCH

Notable differences exist between the sites visited in terms of institutional valuation and support for collaborative research. At some institutions, especially those where arts integration remained a comparatively small part of the institutional culture, little evidence of support could be identified. Other universities embraced systemwide arts integration, at least in their public statements or initiatives. Ongoing efforts toward securing funding for research, finding ways to publicize or promote ongoing work, establishing internal structures, and reconsidering traditional attitudes about scholarship, especially in matters of promotion and tenure, take place at each of the participating universities, although at different levels. Participants' experiences with institutional valuation of their research ranged from testimonials of enthusiastic university support to noting they had received little validation of their work. Universities' primary means of expressing belief in the value of collaborative research comes through providing funding and other resources. A professor of musicology working with theater arts and a media lab explained:

There were internal funding calls for big money for science, engineering, and tech, and [when] the university realized that this was short shrift for the arts and humanities, they made monies available to us, too. [This was] more money than I would have had access to where the arts and humanities were larger or where their interactions with the sciences and each other weren't as valued. I've been able to get funding from the NEH and other institutes because of how much the scientists are able to do with me. I don't have those kinds of restrictions in funding that are so common to the humanities and arts, especially when it comes to competitive funding.

Some institutions offer remarkably generous support. A professor of sculpture and the head of a school of art said, "My colleagues around the country are jealous: I get to teach what I want and they give me money." In addition, a professor of human development and family studies remarked that his institution provides excess resources, "sometimes pushing ideas forward or even more money than we need."

Naturally, this level of validation does not occur at all universities. Participating institutions exhibit a vast range of differences, from Penn State, with a combined student body of nearly 100,000 (Penn), to Transart Institute, with fewer than 100 students (Transart).[16] Institutions report to different accreditors and authorities (e.g., states, private boards, public boards, and so on), they have different purposes (e.g., land grant, urban research, art schools), and different funding mechanisms (e.g., endowments, tuition, state funds, alumni support). We might therefore expect to find significant differences in terms of institutional ability to support arts-integrative research, even based on financial wherewithal alone, not to mention other factors. Administrators may wish to promote or support arts integration but lack the means to put this desire into action. At present, correlations between institutional factors and demonstrated support for arts integration remain uninvestigated, representing yet another possibility for additional study.

Absence of administrative support emerged as a significant problem for several interviewees. Some participants reported that they had received little in the way of funding, recognition, or encouragement, even when administrators acknowledged the value of the projects. According to a professor of clinical neuroscience, "Most people aren't particularly aware of [our research]. . . . My chair sent me a congratulatory

---

16 Transart Institute does not publish student enrollment figures. The figure here represents an estimate based on student profiles available on the Transart website.

email when I got the award. Beyond that, most people are either unaware or generally myopic." A professor of drama reported: "My boss doesn't know a lot about my robotics work.... In 25 years, I've never had a sabbatical. It'd be like manna from heaven.... People are quite supportive of my work, but in terms of time and dollars, never quite as much as one would want." Administrators and faculty members appear to have different approaches to the issue of recognition, with faculty hoping their administrators will positively acknowledge their arts-integrative work and administrators expecting faculty to bring these efforts to their attention. Faculty members participating in arts integration – whether curricular, research, or otherwise – mentioned concerns with practices in promotion and tenure. Addressed further in chapter 4's analysis of administrative challenges, these concerns remain a primary area of consideration at the institutions participating in this study.

Examination of participants' responses revealed a number of specific institutional demonstrations of provision for collaborative research. **TABLE 6** provides a synthesis of these statements, outlining a variety of types of recognition or support.

These actions show great promise, but participants also identified opportunities for improvement, as might be expected. Chapter 4 provides further examination of these issues.

INSTITUTIONAL ARTS INTEGRATION

Curricular and research collaborations thrive in environments created by establishing institutional support such as interdisciplinary degree programs, centers, or institutes. The pages that follow provide several examples from among the institutions visited, but inclusion of these examples should by no means indicate a prioritization of these institutions. With such a large and diverse group of institutions, not every example could be presented, even though others were equally worthy. Further research by a2ru could present a comprehensive reference of programs, creating an open source archive that will allow institutions to upload and share exemplar programs to provide a more thorough accounting of efforts across the country. The following examples feature interdisciplinary degree programs and programmatic arts integration taking place at centers and institutes.

TABLE 6.
TYPES OF INSTITUTIONAL SUPPORT
FOR ARTS-INTEGRATIVE RESEARCH

Allocation of physical space and equipment

Buying faculty members' time from another department

Consideration of interdisciplinary research or curricular efforts, including community engagement occurring outside of a faculty member's primary discipline, in matters of promotion and tenure

Establishing structures such as institutes and centers for collaborative research

Faculty awards, within schools or the university as a whole

Funding for conferences and events

Internal funding for projects

Limited funds for employees and student workers

Presenting a "listening posture" and willingness to embrace innovative work

Publicizing research in partnership with university communication strategies and communications teams, including recognition on university, school, and department web pages

Showcasing speakers, scholars, projects, or programs at events

Support for seeking grant funding

INTERDISCIPLINARY DEGREE PROGRAMS

As previously mentioned, institutions participating in this study vary widely, including the degree programs they make available to their students. Unsurprisingly, most students pursue degrees in a specified major, but two of the participating institutions offer opportunities for interdisciplinary majors allowing students to create their own arts-integrated program of study.

THE UNIVERSITY OF ALABAMA'S NEW COLLEGE, TUSCALOOSA, ALABAMA. Founded in 1971, the New College at the University of Alabama offers students the opportunity to personalize their undergraduate education within an interdisciplinary and integrative liberal arts program. In consultation with a faculty mentor, students build a course of study that includes community-based learning, traditional coursework, undergraduate research, and self-directed study, leading to either a BA or BS in Interdisciplinary Studies with a self-designed concentration. Given its four decades of operation, the New College enjoys robust support from the university administration and campus community, distinguishing it from other interdisciplinary degree programs.

Students admitted to the University of Alabama may then apply to the New College, which seeks self-directed, motivated, creative, and ambitious individuals. However, the New College opens courses to students from across the university.

Four primary assumptions guide the program:
- *Students are capable of accepting much of the responsibility for their own learning.*
- *Each individual is unique; therefore, educational programs can be developed that reflect and expand on each student's interests and capabilities.*
- *Significant learning can occur outside the traditional classroom; to that end, students may receive credit for such outside learning experiences.*
- *Problem-focused, interdisciplinary educational experiences are highly desirable in a fast-changing society. (New College, "History")*

Students choose from among courses organized under three areas of emphasis: Creativity and Culture; Environment, Sustainability, and Conservation; and Social Problems and Social Change. The purpose of seminars in the Creativity and Culture emphasis relate most closely to the Mellon Research Project's focus on arts integration:

These seminars explore the world of the mind, specifically the realms of human thought and expressive practice. They interrogate beliefs, values, and dispositions that comprise culture, and focus on essential questions about what it means to be human. Seminars focus on the following issues: the urge to create and to appreciate creativity; perspectives on class, gender, race, and place; historical memory's role in identity formation, politics, and ethics. (New College, "New")

Course offerings in the Creativity and Culture emphasis for Spring 2015 include diverse seminars on Creativity; Experimental Music; Gender, Sexuality, and Pop Culture; Documenting Justice; Concert Series Management; Zen Buddhism and Radical Approaches to the Arts; History Gamers; Creativity and Computers; Monsters; and the Psychology of Awakening. The program adds new seminars each semester depending on student and faculty interest and participation. Dedicated to building strong relationships between faculty mentors and students, the program provides students with active engagement in learning. For example, New College sponsors the Sonic Frontiers Concert Series, which features experimental music, and publishes *New College Review*, an annual nonfiction magazine entirely written and produced by students.

Several New College students participated in interviews for the Mellon Research Project, sharing their experiences with interdisciplinarity. They reported increased interest in their studies through their participation in this program and an enthusiasm for arts integration. A journalism student said: "When you think about the work of Creative Campus, we have partnered with virtually every single group. We brought these groups together and integrated the arts into different communities. It's our job to keep shaking the 'salad' of Tuscaloosa. The arts is the dressing. We are constantly shaking them together."

One of the students, a nonprofit management and community arts development major, described a course in which an instructor choreographed a dance to illustrate cellular biology, saying: "When you read it on paper, it's boring, but when you understand that cells are alive and they move ... it helps you learn so much better because you understand that it's important."

New College students take the emphasis on interdisciplinarity and arts integration to heart. "To be interdisciplinary is the true meaning of education," said a journalism student. "You're not going to be able to innovate radically if you stay on the same path.... Being interdisciplinary is going to be with us for the rest of our lives. We are always going to be seeking new things."

New College presents an innovative approach to interdisciplinary majors conducive to students who seek to integrate the arts into their undergraduate program more cohesively than simply adding a minor to their degree plan, as might be more typical at most universities. The varied menu of seminars offers alternatives for study featuring inherently interdisciplinary content, providing engaging options for students seeking an alternative to a traditional monodisciplinary undergraduate degree.

VANDERBILT UNIVERSITY, NASHVILLE, TENNESSEE.
Students in the College of Arts and Sciences at **Vanderbilt University** have the option of participating in established interdisciplinary programs or creating completely individualized plans of study. As at other universities, Vanderbilt offers over 18 interdisciplinary majors, including:

AFRICAN AMERICAN AND DIASPORA STUDIES

AMERICAN STUDIES

ASIAN STUDIES

CINEMA AND MEDIA ARTS

COMMUNICATION OF SCIENCE AND TECHNOLOGY

ECONOMICS AND HISTORY

ENGLISH AND HISTORY

EUROPEAN STUDIES

FRENCH AND EUROPEAN STUDIES

LATIN AMERICAN STUDIES

LATINO AND LATINA STUDIES

MEDICINE, HEALTH, AND SOCIETY

NEUROSCIENCE

PUBLIC POLICY STUDIES

RUSSIAN AND EUROPEAN STUDIES

SPANISH AND EUROPEAN STUDIES

SPANISH, PORTUGUESE, AND EUROPEAN STUDIES

WOMEN'S AND GENDER STUDIES

Clearly, these interdisciplinary choices span more than just arts-integrative options. Students who wish to pursue an individually designed interdisciplinary major develop a written proposal for a minimum of 48 hours of study, which must reflect a defined academic purpose, drawing upon the academic resources of relevant departments and schools.

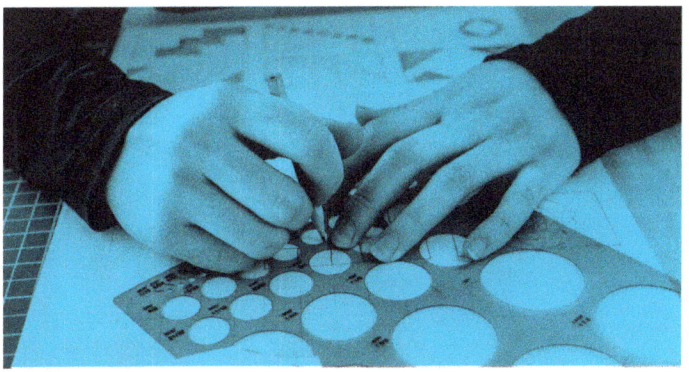

The Committee on Individual Programs must approve the student's plan, which represents a contract between the student and the university. Students may combine an interdisciplinary major with a traditional major or create a personalized course of study.

Students must accompany this plan with a two-page written statement describing why existing majors do not meet their needs and providing a rationale for why the area they wish to pursue offers a valid and relevant subject for study within the context of the liberal arts and sciences. The statement must include an explanation of the relevance of particular courses, a discussion of how the proposed courses cohere, and a discussion of how this major will prepare the student for post-graduate study or long-term career goals.

In a post on Vanderbilt's admissions blog, admissions counselor Carolyn Pippen makes a case in support of interdisciplinary majors: "The fact is, today's society demands that students graduate from college with a broad base of knowledge and skills in order to succeed in almost every profession" (Pippen). College majors, she writes, cannot always reflect careers in which students may find themselves after graduation, so preparation for the workplace may necessitate broadening one's course of study beyond standard majors or minors, depending on the student's personal goals.

Vanderbilt's university-wide emphasis on interdisciplinarity opens the door to students' pursuit of study outside a single focus, permeating even the schools of law and medicine, which each offer joint-degree, specialized, and interdisciplinary programs. This approach stands in marked contrast to traditional monodisciplinary degree plans and reflects university Chancellor Nicholas S. Zeppos's 2013 goal of fostering trans-institutional programs in order to "pave the way for new undergraduate curriculum, enrich and make better our graduate programs, guide our faculty and capital investments, and allow Vanderbilt to ask and answer questions in new and better ways" (qtd. in Patterson).

Home to the **Curb Center for Art, Enterprise, and Public Policy,** Vanderbilt promotes arts and creativity through research and teaching (The Curb). The Curb Center offers undergraduate creativity grants, promotes a Creative Campus initiative, and sponsors the Curb Scholars Program in which students engage in creative leadership salons and creative practice workshops, and develop a portfolio of their contributions to Vanderbilt's creative campus initiative. They also conduct case studies exploring the challenges of creative enterprise and public leadership, including interviews with top policy makers and leaders working in the arts, entertainment, and media industries. The program provides a summer public leadership internship, and seniors develop a creative project contributing to the campus community.

Students interviewed at Vanderbilt spoke of the value of the university's interdisciplinary mindset and their participation in such courses or programs. One Curb Center scholar, who is an interdisciplinary major, said, "Research is about attempting to discover truth. Art is about expressing some sort of truth, so they go hand in hand." A student with a self-designed major in creative enterprise studies noted, "If you're an artist, you automatically integrate art in what you do – sort of an untapped part of human society." Vanderbilt students working across disciplines tend to embrace arts integration, seeing it as a natural outgrowth of their personal and professional interests. The director of Vanderbilt's Curb Center explained that the Creative Campus mission aligns with arts integration through an extensive effort to bring the arts to every discipline on campus, including sciences, engineering, medicine, and law. The engineering school established an initiative to include the arts as one of its four principal thrusts, while the business school supports a program called Design for America, incorporating design into various aspects of business culture.

Interdisciplinary majors, individually designed majors, the university-wide Creative Campus movement, and the arts-integrative emphases promoted by the Curb Center combine to establish Vanderbilt University as a leader in the arts integration movement. Other universities offer comparable interdisciplinary programs but rarely achieve the level of campuswide emphasis on the arts as Vanderbilt.

PROGRAMMATIC INTEGRATION

Arts integration may exist within a single center or institute, or it may become a driving force across an entire university's campus. The following examples, selected among many partner institutions striving to raise the arts to a position of greater prominence in academic life, illustrate models of successful arts integration.

THE UNIVERSITY OF SOUTHERN CALIFORNIA, LOS ANGELES, CALIFORNIA. The University of Southern California (USC) offers a distinct program whose attributes speak to the question of arts vitality and strategies for arts integration. Among these features, the Institute for Multimedia Literacy (IML), an organized research unit, investigates the shifting terrain of literacy in an increasingly networked society, promoting scholarly production through multimedia tools (USC Cinematic Arts, "Institute"). IML's curricular aspect offers an Honors Program in Multimedia Scholarship; a Multimedia in the Core Program, allowing all USC students to utilize multimedia labs; and the Multimedia Across the College Program, in which upper-division courses pair with multimedia instruction.

USC's International Artist Fellowships program promotes cultural diversity, offering graduate scholarships to international artists, particularly those from the Pacific Rim, Latin America, or Southeast Asia, allowing them to study in any of USC's six arts schools (*USC International)*. Arts students in general enjoy a vibrant, robust campus community.[17]

The Brain and Creativity Institute at USC explores the relationship between cognitive functioning, brain processes, and human creativity and emotion (*Brain)*. Studies have yielded applications to the diagnosis and treatment of neurological and psychiatric disease, to education, and to increased understanding of the brain's functioning in the creative and performing arts. State-of-the-art neurological imaging facilities share a building with a classical auditorium for musical and theatrical performances, scientific presentations, or literary readings, bridging the arts and neuroscience.

USC's new Jimmy Iovine and Andre Young Academy for Arts, Technology and the Business of Innovation provides an environment in which "[s]udents learn to think seamlessly across disciplines and to leverage the theories, concepts and vocabulary of each to imagine and develop bold new ideas" (*USC Jimmy Iovine*

---

17 For more information, see a short video from USC's website (USC Cinematic Arts, "DADA").

and Andre Young Academy, "The Academy"). The program offers a BS degree combining art and design, engineering, and computer science, in which students select two emphases from among courses in visual design, technology, mechanical engineering, venture management, audio design, and communication. In a student's fourth year, a "Garage Experience" takes student teams through the process "from concept to creation, vision to prototype" *(USC Jimmy).*

USC enjoys an enviable geographic location in the heart of one of the U.S.'s most influential urban cultural centers as well as comparatively plentiful physical and financial resources. It has leveraged these strengths in support of the arts, producing exemplary results.

THE DA VINCI CENTER, VIRGINIA COMMONWEALTH UNIVERSITY, RICHMOND, VIRGINIA. Centers or institutes (such as those featured at USC and in many other locations) provide opportunities for arts integration by establishing structures that formalize relationships between disciplinary areas, by fostering collaboration through research and curricular partnerships, or by providing an academic home for hybrid scholars. The **da Vinci Center at Virginia Commonwealth University** (VCU) is a collaborative venture between the Schools of the Arts, Business, and Engineering and the College of Humanities and Sciences; the center advances innovation and entrepreneurship through interdisciplinary collaboration. The center offers several programs, including a certificate in venture creation, a master's degree in product innovation, an undergraduate certificate in product innovation, the VCU INNOVATE Living-Learning Program, and the Venture Creation Competition. In addition, the da Vinci STEM Scholars Program offers scholarships to qualified undergraduate students majoring in engineering who seek to earn a Master of Product Innovation.

Interdisciplinary student teams led by a faculty advisor work on projects for corporate, university, or government partners, with current tasks underway for Altria (user experience with electronic handheld devices), Kimberly-Clark (applicator tool for the airplane industry), Pfizer Consumer Healthcare (product and packaging design), and VCU's Department of Mechanical & Nuclear Engineering (nuclear energy exhibit at the Science Museum of Virginia). Past projects have included partnerships with DuPont, TKL guitar boxes, Dominion maintenance tools, and United Group chair designs, among others. Such corporate and industry partnerships constitute a

typical feature of design education, especially with product development and human interaction design.

The director spoke of the value of students developing both breadth and depth through interdisciplinary collaboration. He has found that one of the most important skills necessary for communication across disciplines involves teaching engineering students how to draw, which students first find to be uncomfortable, then emancipating. Students echoed the importance of arts integration in their studies, feeling that an immersive environment holds the greatest benefit for learning. They found seeing people learn how to think differently to be inspiring and noted that "lots of communication" was needed. A student of painting and printmaking, who is working with biology and botanical studies, said, "It was difficult in the critiques to discern what was art, biology, research, or otherwise . . . , but the debate was a big part of the class. It resulted in learning that you can really integrate them all."

The da Vinci Center exemplifies programmatic arts integration through curricular and research activities, offering undergraduates and graduate students opportunities to engage in the pursuit of innovative technologies through creative problem solving in real-world design contexts.

THE ARTS RESEARCH CENTER, UNIVERSITY OF CALIFORNIA, BERKELEY, CALIFORNIA. In another example, the **Arts Research Center at the University of California** (UC), Berkeley – known as ARC – serves as a "think tank for the arts," bringing people together for collaboration and community building "across the arts and beyond the arts" *(Arts Research Center).* As an incubator for scholarship and new creative activity, ARC serves as a center for interdisciplinary arts research, sponsoring conferences, symposia, fellowships, curriculum development grants, faculty seminars and salons, online discussion forums, and artists' residencies. ARC "champions the centrality of the arts at our public university and in public life," promoting inclusion and support of the arts through campus and community initiatives *(Arts Research Center).*

ARC provides online resources for students, faculty, and staff, such as a directory of campus arts and resources, a monthly, curated list of arts events on campus and in

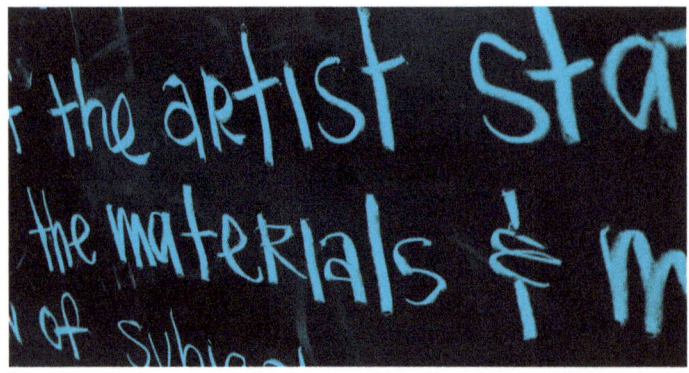

the Bay Area, and an online space where audiences can connect with content before and after ARC-sponsored events. ARC currently supports three areas of research. Inter-Arts Inquiry involves projects centered on the theme of time zones, featuring time-based art and international contexts. According to ARC's website, the Art and Social Change focus examines two key questions: "1) how best to advance the role of the arts in addressing issues of social inequity and 2) how best to create a social and economic ecology that sustains the arts and cultural sector" (*Arts Research Center*, "Research"). Finally, the Art + STEM focus fosters cross-disciplinary experiments and endeavors such as cultivating general student literacy about the arts and STEM fields, highlighting scientific breakthroughs using the arts as a platform for public engagement, or featuring artistic practices utilizing sonic, visual, or embodied forms to communicate understanding of biological or technological concepts. ARC cosponsored the 2014-2015 Art, Technology, and Culture Colloquium, a free year-long public lecture series considering contemporary issues and critical perspectives on aesthetic expression, cultural histories, and emerging technologies.

ARC offers fellowships for UC, Berkeley graduate students and faculty designed to foster collaboration across disciplines, and it promotes a community for artists and arts scholars with similar interdisciplinary interests. Fellowship candidates apply jointly as advanced graduate student and faculty partner pairs, advancing through the program as teams. These pairs may comprise a graduate student and his or her faculty mentor, or students may partner with a faculty member from a different department or program. ARC provides interaction with a cohort of colleagues engaging in interdisciplinary research and a research grant of $2,000 per student-faculty pair ($1,000 per person).

ARC also works with the Berkeley Arts Connect program, placing students in nine-month internships with one of ten Berkeley-based arts organizations, providing experience in fund development, communications, and marketing. Interns learn nonprofit management and forge connections with Bay Area arts organizations. A significant partnership between the university, students, and the Berkeley arts community, Arts Connect provides administrative support and professional development for nonprofits, engaging students and established arts professionals in critical, expansive conversations about the role of the arts in civic life.

As a research unit, ARC reports to the dean of arts and humanities. According to the center's associate director, it provides "a place where artists and many others can talk about arts and community, where we aren't weighting one above the other, creating a place for various perspectives to be voiced. We want to see the arts thrive, broadly defined." The center's director shares this vision; she went on to say:

I want us to be a place that also produces leaders in the arts, not only arts practitioners, but arts thinkers, working in policy, cognizant of big questions around the arts even if they aren't going to be the genius artists themselves. We're fairly well positioned to become a place that can provide that. We're also a very artistic place, here at Berkeley. I'd like us to recognize the entire making going on here and name it. I'd like the Bay Area and the nation to recognize Berkeley as a collaborator and innovator of the artistic landscape, to recognize artistic organizations working with the university and using the arts to help all boats rise for our students and the community.

ARC serves as an exemplary model for an interdisciplinary research center because it actively engages the vibrant arts community of Berkeley, encourages interdisciplinary research with the arts across the center's three research emphases, and fosters a community of scholars in which arts integration thrives.

Featured centers and institutes merely provide representative samples of innovative programing discovered during the Mellon Research Project. Other laudable structures exist at institutions including but certainly not limited to:

→ ARTS IN MEDICINE PROGRAM,
CENTER FOR ARTS IN MEDICINE, UNIVERSITY OF FLORIDA
→ ARTS INSTITUTE,
UNIVERSITY OF WISCONSIN-MADISON
→ FINE ARTS DOCTORAL PROGRAM,
TEXAS TECH UNIVERSITY
→ HIGH IMPACT HIRES INITIATIVE,
IOWA STATE UNIVERSITY
→ INSTITUTE FOR VISUAL STUDIES,
JAMES MADISON UNIVERSITY
→ MEDIA LAB *and the* CENTER FOR ART,
SCIENCE, AND TECHNOLOGY,
MIT
→ OPEN CURRICULUM *model,*
SCHOOL OF THE ART INSTITUTE OF CHICAGO
→ STUDIO|LAB,
PENN STATE UNIVERSITY

Each of these locations prioritizes arts integration, establishing structures and programs allowing the arts to flourish in a climate of research and curricular innovation, enriching the university and providing students, faculty, and staff with incomparable opportunities to engage in interdisciplinary, integrative academic work.

CO-CURRICULAR OPPORTUNITIES

Research universities have long provided students with opportunities to engage with the arts through campus organizations or groups outside of standard programs of study. Co-curricular activities tend to be more monodisciplinary than the collaborative research or interdisciplinary curricula presented earlier in this chapter, allowing students to integrate arts engagement with their overall student experience, even if their major or program cannot accommodate interdisciplinary or arts-integrative coursework. For example, an engineering student might not be able to undertake a minor in music due to strenuous program requirements in her major, but she could join the marching band in order to maintain her engagement in music performance.[18]

The term "co-curricular" recognizes that such involvement supports and enhances student learning and students' overall experiences in higher education, indicating a broad range of activities occurring beyond the classroom, including performances by curricular or faculty-led groups, community service, or student employment, as well as participation in clubs, groups, or student organizations. Although it is sometimes challenging to distinguish between curricular and co-curricular designations depending on the group or organization under consideration, co-curricular activities usually do not involve a grade and tend to be voluntary, although exceptions exist, such as a requirement for instrumental music majors to participate in a non-credit, faculty-led music performance group like a symphony orchestra or marching band. Curricular activities, on the other hand, assign grades and become part of the student's permanent academic record.

Researchers, including George D. Kuh, show a positive correlation between student engagement in activities outside of the classroom and students' collegiate experience (Kuh).[19] Universities support these activities and promote student participation. For example, the Johns Hopkins University "Parents' Advising Handbook" offers this message for families of incoming students:

Co-curricular activities complement traditional education by offering a range of experiences that help students hone and develop interpersonal and work skills, as well as explore creative, cultural, physical, societal, and spiritual ways of connecting with and learning more about themselves and others. All of these are necessary for students to become successful individuals and contributing members of the larger community . . . Studies have consistently found that students who are involved outside the classroom are happier, especially if they are involved in something that allows self-expression and teaches skills such as time management. (Johns Hopkins University)

Parents may fear that spending time on co-curricular activities could distract their children from their college studies, but co-curricular involvement can provide positive engagement with peers and opportunities to reinforce learning.

A study conducted by Richard J. Light, professor in the Harvard Graduate School of Education, found that students who were active participants in co-curricular programs reported the highest levels of satisfaction

---

18 Although co-curricular programming supplements students' academic experiences and occupies a key position in campus culture, it does not substitute for curricular arts courses providing students with the ability to pursue majors in the arts, nor does it support faculty research in, through, or with the arts. A director of an interdisciplinary institute cautioned against promoting student involvement in co-curricular arts activities as not adequately fulfilling students' needs to engage in the arts, saying universities would never suggest students deepen their STEM skills through a "science appreciation club."

19 Appendix 1 provides recommended reading for a more in-depth examination of this subject.

with their college experience; this was especially true of those involved in performing arts groups. In *Making the Most of College: Students Speak Their Minds*, Light presents a multi-year study involving interviews with students and faculty members at Harvard University and other institutions, finding involvement outside of the classroom could be powerfully transformative for students. He writes:

The evidence shows that . . . learning outside of classes, especially in residential settings and extracurricular activities such as the arts, is vital. When we asked students to think of a specific, critical incident or moment that had changed them profoundly, four-fifths of them chose a situation or event outside of the classroom. (4)

Students find their co-curricular involvements to be the most memorable, most valuable, and most transformative of their college careers. Furthermore, Light's finding that those involving the arts proved especially impactful appears consistent with information collected from our partners and with other published research on the benefits of student involvement in co-curricular programs. The National Survey of Student Engagement (**NSSE**) is administered to first-year and senior students at participating higher educational institutions. Since the survey was first given in 2000, it has encompassed more than 1,400 colleges and universities. The 2013 survey indicated that just 25% of all students completely eschew all out-of-class engagement, meaning that at least 75% of a given student body participates at least to some extent in co-curricular activities if these are considered to the broadest extent possible, including employment, internships, faculty-led and student-led organizations, and so on (Zehner).

Mellon Research Project interviews corroborated this message. For example, a program director emphasized student engagement as more than membership in clubs, groups, and organizations:

You could argue that any part of the residential university experience that is not directly related to classwork or credit-bearing activities is co-curricular because every part of that student's whole experience at the university is part and parcel of their developmental path. . . . All of those efforts support, inform, and are informed by and supported by the curricular experience. . . . You're recognizing that some experiences outside the classroom can be as transformative or more transformative – as great a learning experience or a greater learning experience – than those that

may be gotten curricularly, and the other piece of this to recall is that students spend most of their time outside of class, even in a residential university.

Co-curricular programs exist at all but one of the institutions participating in the Mellon Research Project,[20] and their value to students is supported in both academic literature and students' anecdotal accounts. The Mellon Research Project's findings confirm existing literature, further validating the arts as occupying a key position in this important aspect of campus life. This study groups co-curricular programs into broad categories offered at most institutions studied:

- *On-campus cultural events/presentations by groups or individuals from outside the university*
- *Student-led clubs, groups, and arts organizations, both formal and informal*
- *Faculty-led clubs and organizations*
- *Non-curricular learning opportunities in the arts (classes, lessons, instruction)*
- *Off-campus trips to cultural events or locations*

The discussion of best practices in chapter 5 provides illustrations of each of these types of co-curricular programming categories through specific examples identified during the Mellon Research Project site visits and interviews.

MEASURES OF CO-CURRICULAR PROGRAMS' SUCCESS.

Several interview participants spoke of the popularity of their institutions' co-curricular programs, citing high attendance rates and enthusiastic participation by stakeholders. Other measurements included qualitative assessment, achievement of program goals, student feedback and valuation, and longitudinal studies of student involvement.

ATTENDANCE AND PARTICIPATION. Event attendance and numbers of student participants provide metrics for measuring the impact of co-curricular programs at most institutions. The following list of examples provides representative samples of interview participants' evaluation of co-curricular programming.

ARTS SHOWCASE. The head of an arts program (also an associate dean in the College of Engineering) reported that the College of Engineering held an event in the campus art museum showcasing artwork created by faculty and students. She said, "Over 900 people showed up that night. We took over the place with

---

20   Transart Institute, as a low-residency graduate program in the visual arts, offers no co-curricular activities to its students.

musicians, dancers, paintings, and sculpture." This interviewee indicated delighted surprise that so many people chose to participate in this event, which, for her, demonstrated the success of the evening's activities.

MUSIC ENSEMBLES. A professor of music explained that only 50 of the university's 6,500 students major in music but that 1,000 students participate in music ensembles, all of which are co-curricular. In other words, far less than 1% of the students major in music, but 15% of students participate in co-curricular music ensembles – a fairly dramatic difference that demonstrates demand for these programs.

CAMPUS MUSEUM. Three administrators of a campus museum and film archive described a kick-off event called the Pizza-Poster-Palooza to welcome incoming first-year students, giving away posters, free pizza, and iced tea; the event was funded by a philanthropic organization. The director explained that measuring success "is a question we're dealing with. In our case, we used questionnaires. We also count how many people show up for events, and sometimes even the consumption of the food bought is a good way to measure." Although a "pizza index" for measuring student attendance seems rather lighthearted, free food remains an effective strategy for promoting student participation. Campus museums, in general, utilize sophisticated metrics for evaluating program effectiveness, but interview participants did not provide information about other evaluative measures.

CULTURAL EVENTS. A dean reported, "Over the course of the year, over 12,000 students out of 40,000 students on campus come to an event sponsored by [our office], so we know that's the number we're working with." Knowing that 30% of university students attend cultural events at this university creates the impression that its programs seem to be reaching students, as evidenced by their popularity.

The dean went on to explain that the department collects feedback from students, saying they often spoke of events as being personally transformative or inspiring: "It's not assessment in any disciplined way, but in the world of religion and spirituality where there's much emphasis on narrative and feeling, this counts."[21] Student feedback, therefore, provides an important measure of success in co-curricular programming, particularly in the absence of grades or formal assessment mechanisms. Students interviewed for the Mellon Research Project expressed enthusiasm about their participation in these programs, an observation also made by Richard M. Light, Andy Zehner, and other researchers. (See appendix 1 for a list of recommended readings, including these and other resources.)

PROGRAM GOALS. Co-curricular arts programming tends to promote broad, holistic, and long-term goals apart from explicit systems for measuring the attainment of these objectives. The following example of stated goals at Boston University demonstrates this type of philosophy:
- *Raise the visibility of and bring recognition to the breadth and excellence of the arts at BU.*
- *Increase student access to the arts at BU and the Boston area, so that students develop an active and participatory role in the arts as a meaningful element of their BU experience.*
- *Support student, faculty, and staff initiatives that engage our community in the practice of and intellectual dialogue around the arts and art making.*
- *Encourage meaningful opportunities for the BU community and the Boston area community to connect via the arts. (BU)*

Boston University's goals demonstrate similarity with other institutions. For example, the University of Michigan's **Arts at Michigan** program seeks to "actively engage undergraduate students in the arts as a meaningful way to build connections between academic and co-curricular experiences and engage student life overall. . . . Arts at Michigan fosters creative learning, multi-disciplinary approaches and global perspectives by providing the resources students, faculty, and staff need to utilize the arts as tools for learning" (Arts at Michigan). This program's goals include increasing student access to the arts, promoting arts as a tool for student learning and development, supporting students' creativity and arts initiatives, and serving as an informational resource.

All of these goals represent worthy aspirations for co-curricular arts programming, although rarely quantified through concrete measurement. Future research could include identifying frameworks allowing for assessment, but we might also consider the advantage of co-curricular programming remaining free from university imperatives for assessment, allowing more rapid and dynamic means of meeting students' needs and interests. Such freedom cannot occur through curriculum precisely because co-curricular programs

---

21 The Office of Religious Life on this campus operates a program called "Spirituality and the Arts." The dean described the program: "Concerts and artists that brought together the musics that inform their faith traditions, focused on similarities and forms of expression. We bring world musicians that specialize in musics that have devotional strands. Also, [the university] does not have an ethnomusicology department, so we often supplement that lack by bringing in people and programming in this way. We do things around spoken word, student art exhibitions, plays, and theatrical performances."

lie outside of curricular reporting requirements, logical models, and formal evaluations. Therefore, although measuring goal attainment could prove interesting in future research, so could the absence of pressures brought about by such assessments.

STUDENT VALUATION. Student interviewees highly valued their participation in co-curricular arts programs, with the most enthusiastic responses coming from students majoring in fields outside of the arts. A student leader cited a conversation with a new member of his group, who expressed some dismay about his upcoming choice of major: he was interested in organizational studies, economics, and music but did not know how to integrate these into a degree plan. By majoring in economics and participating in the music group, he was able to envision future employment as a music industry executive. The pre-med student, who was also a member of a co-curricular singing group, emphasized: "Co-curricular studies would be such an important aspect of any school because you can have a finite number of majors and you can have a finite number of departments, but when you add in co-curricular choices for people, then you have an infinite number of possibilities and an infinite number of careers."

Another student – a biopsychology, cognition, and neuroscience student who is president of the council of co-curricular a cappella groups – emphasized the role the arts had played in his overall experience as a student and his career plans:

Music is very important to me as a pastime but also as a creative outlet. Sciences all drive toward a particular answer, but music gives you the opportunity to find a million different answers to the same question: "How do I want this to sound?" I definitely wanted to have music be part of my life despite the fact that I'm in the sciences. I'm interested in integrating the knowledge that I'm gaining through this extracurricular activity into my research doing music therapy.

Other students also readily made connections between their co-curricular involvement and their major fields of study, reporting that the arts allowed them a creative outlet, provided opportunities to form relationships with other students, and afforded access to cultural arts they would not otherwise have experienced. As a doctoral student in nuclear engineering said, "There's always five things you should be doing, so getting out to do something that's good for your soul is easier when you're part of the group." Testimonials from other students further this case. A pre-med student who is a member of a co-curricular singing group said:

If I didn't have the opportunity to be involved in music, I wouldn't be where I am today – I wouldn't be as developed as I am as a person. Music has afforded me more opportunities than I can count to mature as a person, such as the community you get from being in a group of people that are creating something together – it's really unlike anything I've experienced before. Without the people in my [group], I wouldn't have been able to deal with all of the emotional strife that I've had to deal with in college.... Without having a real musical outlet, I would have overloaded myself with all of the science classes that are necessary, and that's really true of any discipline.... If I didn't have anything to break up those science classes, I would have gotten way worse grades than I did.

A doctoral student in nuclear engineering said:

It's just thinking creatively and letting go of whatever boundaries you think are there.... It's a completely different way of thinking than the engineering mindset here. Engineers want to be precise and want to compartmentalize things, and everything goes in a little bucket, as opposed to blurring boundaries and being okay with not having answers and living in that sort of gray area. Science has right answers and wrong answers, but art can be anything you choose. They might be right answers and wrong answers to you, or to another person, but they can differ between people.

As a creative outlet, source of recreation, and provider of positive peer interactions, co-curricular arts programing proved highly valuable to students across academic disciplines. Conventional wisdom might suggest that students majoring in nuclear engineering or medicine would have little time to include the arts in their lives, but the opposite seems to be true: students engage in the arts through co-curricular involvement even when their course schedules lack opportunity for curricular arts engagement.

The University of Michigan completed a study tracking undergraduate participation in co-curricular arts activities, with complete findings expected in the near future. The investigator reported:

We just closed a 4-year longitudinal study where we followed 200 students looking at their arts engagement prior to coming to the university both in their childhood and at a high school level, what they did while they were here, and then what they expect to do afterwards.

Almost 50% of our students coming in as first-years say that they have an identity as musicians. We were very surprised by this. Will that many say that they're musicians when they leave? And are we good at maintaining that? And if we know that 50% of them are musicians and we know that there aren't enough places for them to play, should we then look for ways that we can beef up that kind of programming?

Universities supporting co-curricular arts programming tap into students' prior arts experiences, allowing students to continue their arts participation regardless of their chosen major. Further studies such as the one cited above could guide future program development and inform facility usage and resource allocation to best meet students' needs.

INSTITUTIONAL VALUATION AND SUPPORT OF CO-CURRICULAR PROGRAMS.

Administrators at the sites visited expressed their support of arts-related co-curricular programs. Levels of institutional valuation vary from systemwide initiatives to more localized efforts within student affairs or student programs offices.

Institutions frequently demonstrate valuation through financial support. For example, offices of student affairs or student life, specific schools or departments, philanthropic organizations, or alumni associations may offer grant funding for students or faculty members seeking to host an arts event or sponsor a club or group; these grants may range from $500 to $5,000. Faculty members donate 1% of their annual salary toward funding one especially notable grant program that carries the arts into neighborhood schools through lessons taught by university students. According to a dean, "It's good for our students and for the students at these neighborhood elementary schools. This can be a national model for civic engagement and engagement with the arts."

An administrator overseeing a program offering mini-grants of up to $1,000 for students seeking funds for performances and projects reported that this had had a significant impact for a wide range of students, stating:

Last year, we directly impacted more than 2,000 students. By directly, I mean they were involved in the film production, they were in the show, they were dancing the choreography, they were the production assistant, directly involved with the arts that they were presenting. More than 15,000 students were in

the expected audience. So when you're talking about impact, you're talking about those who were able to do this production, either at all because you gave them that money or in a way that improved that aesthetic outcome, that excellence, that connection to the arts. And then you have those that came, who would not have otherwise seen that production or wouldn't have seen the level of artistic expression in that production if that money hadn't been there. And that's a single arts granting program. . . . What's the impact past that? The idea that these kinds of opportunities are available at the university: does it impact recruitment? Does it impact retention? Does it have an impact that we can't even quite codify but we can imagine? So the individual student is developed, the campus climate and culture is changed, all because of a $500 grant, a $1,000 grant.

Several interview participants spoke of the value of personal engagement in the arts through music performance, poetry writing, or creating works of visual art. A campuswide initiative known as SEA Change at the University of Florida (UF) specifically seeks to integrate co-curricular, curricular, and research under one program, bringing the sciences, arts, and engineering together to cultivate and distribute strategies for research, teaching, and campus service. In "**Experimental Palette**," an article published in a UF magazine, author Donna Hesterman features SEA Change and the ways in which scientists and artists have collaborated on the UF campus. Among its more notable facets, SEA Change encourages faculty arts practice across all academic disciplines. "Most scientists who practice some form of art will tell you that it makes us better at our craft," reported an associate dean and professor of environmental engineering sciences. "I'm not a neuroscientist, but there is plenty of research that suggests scientific genius and artistic talent are closely linked" (qtd. in Hesterman). Interviewees from across this campus consistently mentioned this program as being a powerfully transformative influence on integrating the arts with other disciplines.

Hesterman reports that faculty members at UF see great promise in providing opportunities for students to experience the arts and says that the program occupies a key position in the university culture. As an associate professor said during an interview for the Mellon Research Project, "We're trying to tell our engineering students that it is not just okay to engage in these activities but essential." An associate professor of biology reported, "Studio artists get just the sort of training that researchers need to be successful. The arts have these well-developed models and practices for teaching the creative process, and students are expected from Day One to wrestle with open-ended questions. They also learn how to deal with setbacks and failures early on" (qtd. in Hesterman). Science students, on the other hand, do not receive similar experiences, which might hinder their early graduate school experience. The biology professor explained, "The hardest day for a new Ph.D. student in science is the one when he or she is given the keys to their cubicle and told go come up with a research project. The last time they did something that self-directed or creative was probably in the sixth grade science fair" (qtd. in Hesterman). While this might oversimplify student capacity to develop original ideas, this remark demonstrates diverse faculty views of arts and design training as a key resource for generative thinking.

Institutions continue to pursue these goals, although not every campus included in this study deliberately explores and experiments with the role of arts and design throughout their campuses. In some places, a certain degree of inertia may still exist. One interview participant described faculty and administrators as "not unsupportive of these programs; they're mostly inattentive to these programs." She went on to say:

They're pleased that they're going on, they know they're going on, but they really don't have the kind of firsthand understanding of the excellence, or the commitment, or the scale of students involved in the arts on campus. . . . There's often kind of a pleased astonishment at how many students are interested. There's also a sense that I've gotten from administration and other faculty members that whatever the students are doing, it's sort of playtime – that it's really not at the level of the things that we put on in the school of music, theater, and dance. . . . A lot of times, when you get a faculty member or administrator to come to one of these productions, they're blown away. They had no idea, even though they're sympathetic to the idea of student co-curricular art. They don't have a sense of how good these students are, how committed they are, how much they care about doing the highest level work they're able to do. . . . Their view is changed. They're surprised. They're changed. Kind of gobsmacked in a way how good they are, how much there is, and how they may not have seen that they might have a role in making that even better for the students.

Arts experience through co-curricular programs allows students whose major course of study does not allow for arts electives to receive the benefits of engagement in creative and performing fields. This study revealed models and best practices for co-curricular programs across the institutions visited, presenting a number of opportunities for those seeking to implement similar programs elsewhere. Interviews demonstrate participants' high esteem for co-curricular arts programs, providing statements underscoring the benefits of co-curricular arts engagement in personal, social, and academic development. Faculty members and administrators who maintain a creative practice in one or more of the arts, in addition to their primary academic and professional pursuits in disciplines outside the arts, also benefit from co-curricular engagements.

When asked to describe the most important thing to know about co-curricular programs, a program director adamantly explained:

They absolutely matter to the students, to their experience, and to their development. . . . Understanding how much they matter to the students, to the campus, to our diversity efforts, to our multicultural understandings, to our cross-cultural collaborations, to our global understanding of each other – I think that it matters to the students, it matters to our culture, it matters to our development as an institution of higher education, and that it needs to matter more than it does to how we support it within the university, for all of those reasons. It matters. It makes a difference.

While seemingly the least integrative or least interdisciplinary of the areas featured in the Mellon Research Project, co-curricular programs provide the greatest number of students with arts and design experience during their university years. Interviewees across the sites visited expressed commitment to ensuring students have access to such programs, encouraging their participation, and building opportunities specifically in the arts. At the same time, co-curricular programs face the same challenges with funding and resources as curricular or research endeavors, reflective of higher education funding in general.

CONCLUSIONS

Based on the testimony of individuals participating in the Mellon Research Project, arts integration thrives within our research universities. Researchers identified instances of curricular integration, research collaborations, interdisciplinary degree programs, centers and institutes, and co-curricular programs at these locations, supported by administrators, faculty, staff, and students committed to the value of infusing the arts into all aspects of higher education. While recognizing the grand potential of the arts on campus, stakeholders and institutional leaders remained wary of challenges inhibiting aesthetic development. According to the interviews, arts integration can stumble when faced with weak communications, uncertain promotion and tenure policies, and limited or inconsistent funding opportunities.

FINDINGS

- *Curricular arts integration occurs through a range of practices, from collaborations in which the arts or design support instruction in a partnering discipline (infusion), students engage in the arts or design through an immersive creative experience (diffusion), or the arts or design partner equally with one or more other learning areas (fusion).*

- *Research collaborations involving the arts also occur across a continuum, spanning equal partnerships, situations in which an non-arts discipline supports research in, through, or about the arts, or situations in which the arts support research in a partnering discipline, mainly through data visualization, sonification, or other embodiment.*

- *Institutional or programmatic structures for arts integration exist in interdisciplinary degree programs and in centers or institutes fostering research and teaching integrating the arts with diverse academic fields.*

- *Co-curricular programs integrate the arts with students' overall academic lives through direct participation in the arts or design. Such programs allow students to engage in the arts even when their programs of study might not accommodate coursework in the arts.*

- *Measurements of the success or impacts of arts-integrative activities resist generalization, manifesting differently in each specific instance. Further development of tools for assessment of arts-integrative activities represents an area for future study.*

CHAPTER THREE

STUDENT NEEDS AND PERCEPTIONS

Students have been an integral part of the Mellon Research Project since its inception, comprising 19.6% of interviewees. Additionally, researchers gathered information through written responses, formal small group discussions facilitated by a2ru staff and partner faculty and staff, informal discussions, and email exchanges between a2ru staff and students at the a2ru **Emerging Creatives Student Conference**, held January 30 to February 1, 2014, at Stanford University.[22] Student attendees at the conference represented 25 a2ru member institutions, evenly distributed between graduate and undergraduate students. Students' major fields of study were reflective of the diversity found throughout the Mellon Research Project. Small group questions opened dialogue during the conference rather than serving as data collection instruments, but they also helped to identify observations and issues relevant to the present study.

22   Portions of this chapter were previously published as a 2014 a2ru white paper (Thompson and Kolenic).

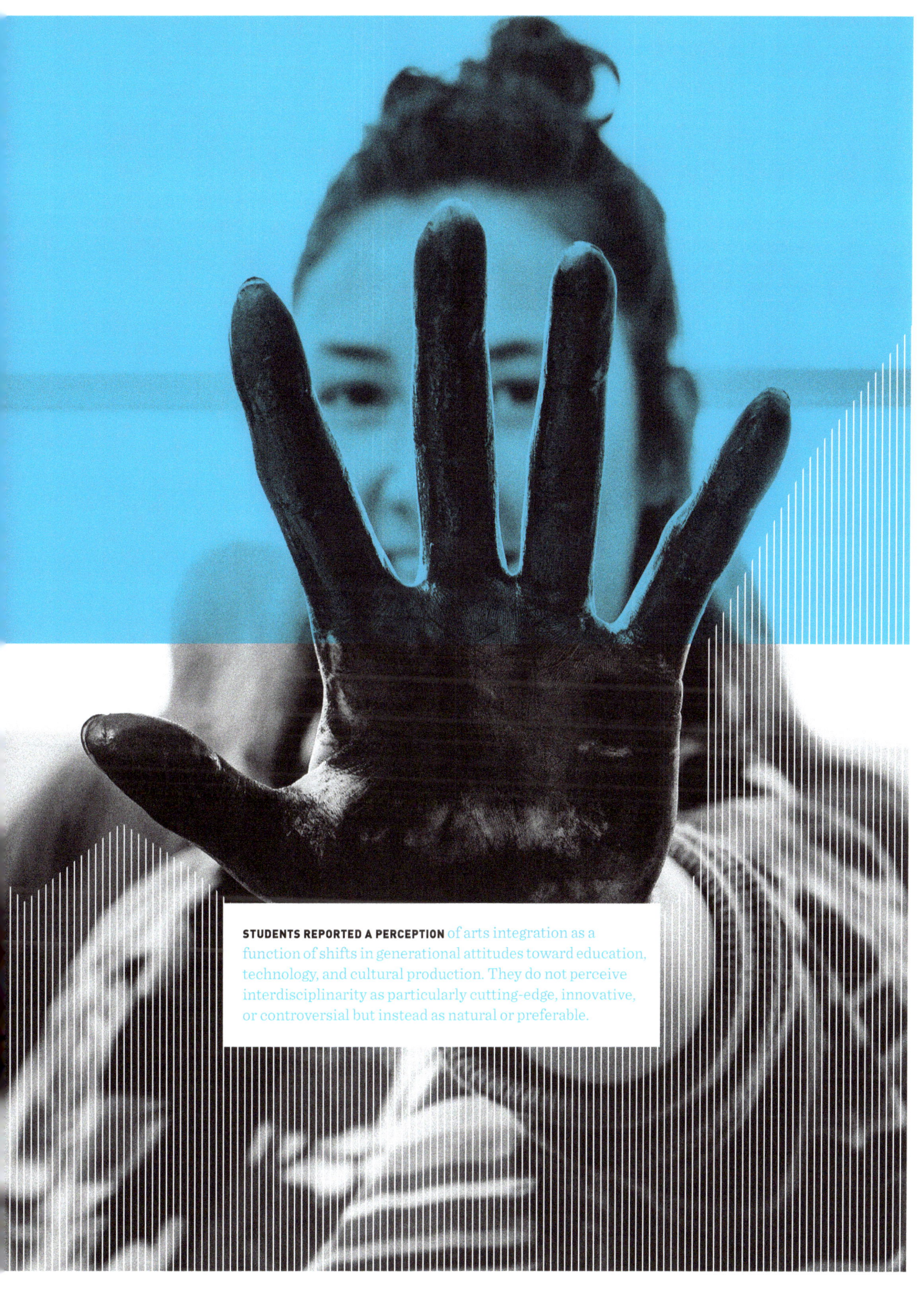

STUDENTS REPORTED A PERCEPTION of arts integration as a function of shifts in generational attitudes toward education, technology, and cultural production. They do not perceive interdisciplinarity as particularly cutting-edge, innovative, or controversial but instead as natural or preferable.

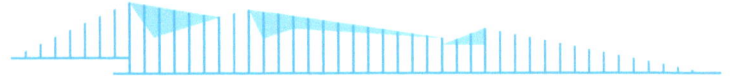

COMMON PERSPECTIVES

Whether at the student conference or through the interviews gathered at site visits, students expressed several common perspectives related to the importance of self-discovery during their college years and self-identification as being native to interdisciplinarity. They also emphasized a desire for greater depth and authenticity in their interdisciplinary or arts-integrative studies and a strong yearning to pursue study in areas with the potential to make an impact on the world.

IDENTITY FORMATION AND SELF-DISCOVERY

Several common perspectives on arts integration emerged among students, but these appear somewhat contradictory. First, students expect their university experience to impart more than just skills for future employment. They hope to learn more about themselves: they want to develop or discover new passions and gain an understanding of the types of lives they want to live beyond their employment or careers, thus laying the foundation for their futures as individuals, not just as members of the workforce. Higher education, for these students, involves discovering personal identity, not merely acquiring skills. Students see higher education as a means to becoming the best people they can be, in a broader sense, rather than a vehicle to career preparation. Students see college as a time to confront questions related to identity. What type of life am I looking for? What types of problems and work excite me? What fields interest me? To what extent do I want my career and personal life to overlap? What motivates me? How do I want to manage my time? How do I take advantage of opportunities in life? How do I push myself to be the most I can be? What philosophies or religious paths do I want to embrace? Students see college as the time to experiment, fail, try many things, and do the things they cannot do once they assume responsibilities in the workforce.

Some students advised peers not to worry about job placement but to use their time in college to focus inwardly, believing success will naturally follow. This sentiment occurred, in general, across majors. However, the discussion at the conference took place in relation to the role of the arts in the university. In fact, the arts may be a fitting metaphor for the journey of self-discovery typical in students' undergraduate years. A faculty member's comment helped to frame the student challenges:

I believe universities are all about, first and foremost, being a place where kids are becoming adults by ex-panding their universes, learning to critically think and engage, finding out what their passions are, learning to research and study. It's about what's available to your mind, providing the tools to be a perpetual student throughout life, to be successful at learning the things you want to learn. These two things are what make a university a university. There is no great culture that hasn't left a great art behind it. It's not realistic to think that you can produce an educated person without an appreciation and understanding of culture. The arts are inherently important to becoming a well-rounded person, and being well-rounded is what a university should cause. Things have more and more to do with churning people out and into the economy at a faster and faster pace, but that makes the arts even more important.

An arts dean's remarks extended this theme: "We spend an enormous amount of time trying to explain ourselves, as [the arts] have been under attack for at least 100 to 200 years. Our purpose is not just developing skills; we also help students understand who they are and who they want to be. All forms of arts are central to this."

The impact of the teaching and learning of art practice on students' personal or identity development surfaced in several interviews. Students learned (or perhaps relearned) something more than just facts or skills – something deeper affecting all areas of their lives. A former visiting artist and now faculty member recalled:

Today I gave my students a text – the first chapter of Malcolm Gladwell's Blink. The reason I got them to read it is because as a printmaker you always have blank canvas – and you always hesitate. But you have to trust your instinct. Make your mark. You always worry about making the wrong or right mark – that it isn't the right mark and will be there in perpetuity. What I'm saying is trust your instincts, let your hand guide you wherever it needs to guide you, and that will ease you into the process of making work because success comes through failure. We make things, experiment, something goes wrong, something falls over – that's when we discover something new. That's how you keep yourself fluid. One student said this conversation meant a lot.

In this case, art practice provided an opportunity to teach a much deeper lesson. Although this may not be limited to the arts, being common to all high-quality education, it clearly offers an effective means to this type of student growth. This faculty member elaborated upon the true meaning of art practice as requiring a student to confront, explore, know, and ultimately express his or her identity. High-quality art education addresses deep issues, allowing the student to find and use her voice. An arts dean commented: "Perhaps Paulo Freire puts it best: 'The teacher is of course an artist, but being an artist does not mean that he or she can make the profile, can shape the students. What the educator does in teaching is to make it possible for the students to become themselves.'"

Educational experience's impact on student identity may produce lasting, lifelong effects. For example, art education can broaden student interests or develop curiosity related to other fields. Not all art students become artists, but they may acquire benefits from their art experiences nonetheless. As another illustration, a professor in dance recalled a PhD student in chemistry who was so shy he couldn't present his work, saying he was the worst person in her dance class. She didn't know why he came back because it looked like such a struggle for him. Later, she received an email from him saying her class had made a huge impact on his career because, through his experiences in her classroom, he learned to be comfortable presenting his work.

Similarly, another faculty member remarked:

Students come in having to pick majors at 18 years old; we open up an interdisciplinary world to them and realize through art that they are interested in environmental studies and so on, so they may go back and get another degree or dual degree.... I think this is maybe even better than being a gallery artist; they can do things that are uniquely for our economy and culture. Our students can be smart thinkers; we just don't know it.

This last line reflects a potential mismatch between students needs' and faculty and university vision and course or program offerings. The quote also mentions the role of interdisciplinary exposure, another key need and expectation of students; this role is described next.

DISCIPLINARITY

Students reported a perception of arts integration as a function of shifts in generational attitudes toward education, technology, and cultural production. They do not perceive interdisciplinarity as particularly cutting-edge, innovative, or controversial but instead as natural or preferable. Statements such as "I don't think about being interdisciplinary; I just am," and "Interdisciplinarily is how I live every day," were common. One student remarked, "My work is inherently interdisciplinary. I am working in a place previously divided by academics, but I work in the boundaries I

create now." Another described his thought process: "I cannot really approach a project from one view because that does not exist in my head. If I want to create a glowing sign, I think about it in stages and incorporating people to help me make the sign. I cannot think in a way that is not interdisciplinary."

Students link arts integration and "open-mindedness," identifying this educational model and their expectations of access to it as a generational shift. They have a keen awareness of the benefits and limitations of interdisciplinarity and understand the need for deep disciplinary expertise. Students place a high value on collaboration, hoping to add "layers of experience" and expertise to their involvement in particular projects or problems. They also identified a need for "community," facilitated by campus cultures that engender sincere, collaborative interdisciplinary efforts and provide clear avenues and opportunities for students and faculty to engage meaningfully. A professor and director of an MA program in the humanities noted, "The university is slowly coming to recognition of training students for a new world where people jump boundaries all the time." So for example, the freedom to sample classes from various disciplines cannot substitute for students' desire for interdisciplinary approaches to learning and problem solving to become more deeply embedded in the university overall.

Students' interdisciplinary identities naturally relate to the role of the arts in the university. The director of an interdisciplinary degree program explained:

I think we are in a society where our kids have had more opportunities to have the arts present as part of their public education and lives much more than previous generations. So when these kids get to the universities, they don't want to check this at the door if they don't want to be an arts major. That's why we are finding that our courses are attracting students from the other [majors], because they don't want to leave the arts aside no matter what the practice is that they've decided to engage in.

A dean in the sciences noted:

We've found that many students that come here for a technical major are also musically or artistically talented and can pursue both here, which isn't true everywhere. You can come here and do two at the same time, and that's special about [this university]. We want to continue to welcome students for whom the full range of learning is crucial.

As the director of an interdisciplinary center remarked, "[It's about] becoming a T-shaped individual. Working with other disciplines makes you appreciate your own more." Interdisciplinary exposure allows students to gain both depth and breadth in their educational programs, moving beyond acquisition of skills and competencies emphasizing disciplinary depth alone. Further, an associate dean in a college of engineering remarked on student recognition of the arts as integral to good engineering:

Engineers are the appliers of science to improve the quality of life. We don't always hit that mark, but that's our idea. As such, there's always a place for the arts in engineering, sciences, medicine, etc. And there should be a nameplate for the arts in these houses because the arts are too easy to see as a luxury instead of part of the work we do in the sciences. Students see this much easier than faculty. Once we start embedding art and beauty in our technical lectures, we can begin to see the art and beauty in our equations much more easily. We see this with calculus instruction; there is beauty in mathematical formulas, in designing a bridge, etc. We too often get stuck in the practicality of those forms, though; that keeps us from seeing the beauty that does in fact live there. Like good religions, we're all seeking the same truth. We get too mired down when we sit in our silos. As we infuse more art, it tends to smack us right in the face and remind us that we should design things to make life better. That's what art does for me.

Similarly, a program director in the arts noted: "Students are more open. Faculty have so many responsibilities to their discipline, scholarship, teaching, etc., perhaps not extra time to explore or dig deeper across disciplines."

Such statements corroborate statements by interview participants, such as a professor of cinematic arts who commented, "[Students] come into the undergraduate system without the interdisciplinary boundaries that existed even ten years ago. [Joining] cinema and engineering is logical to them. . . . They pair artistic expression with analytic expression. We don't want an education system where we beat that out of them. Instead, we want to contextualize and further it."

This does not mean students find interdisciplinary approaches to be easy. "It's hard to find the joints between disciplines," commented one student. "You have to learn all kinds of knowledge from different places." Another said, "Millennials are generalists." These students enjoy pursuing a subject on their own terms, to the extent of their interest. They want the freedom to exercise their curiosity for a few hours or to develop genuine expertise over the course of years. They also want to be able to articulate what they hope to accomplish so others who possess a particular skill set can help them achieve their goals. A graduate student remarked that by dabbling in a given area, "You can learn what is possible and what is not possible [for one's own work]." Far from thinking they can know everything, these students indicate a recognition of the rapidly changing landscape of knowledge production in which they participate. One student mentioned that when thinking about a new project, he first asks, "Who knows more than I do?" This leads him to seek out those persons with greater knowledge in order to support his work.

Students recognize the danger in becoming a "jack of all trades and master of none" – that is, the risk of learning many subjects broadly but lacking disciplinary depth. Despite the growing perception of interdisciplinarity as the future of meaning making and working, the acquisition of disciplinary expertise was valued by a number of students. This indicates that interdisciplinarity does not necessarily replace disciplinary training for expertise in a well-defined field. Students are not afraid to acknowledge the challenges of interdisciplinary training and its inherent expectations. One student who completed his undergraduate work in Korea remarked, "The [boss] wants a Korean Steve Jobs who knows everything, but you can't know everything at the highest levels." Although brilliant individuals may provide exceptions to the norm, most students recognize that significant interdisciplinary accomplishments stem from collaboration and the addition of individual "layers of experience" or expertise to a particular problem or project. They recognize the value of attaining disciplinary knowledge, such as one student who observed the culture in her art and technology graduate program: "We're not a program that makes an artist into an engineer or vice versa. We're the place where people can work together, not change the disciplines. That is what real interdisciplinary work should be." Members of a graduate cohort said they consider themselves anti-disciplinary in the sense that they want to ignore the boundaries of the disciplines in which they work, but this approach tends to feel "political." One student stated that employment of specific terminology didn't matter because "we're all trying to get to the same place."

Students' fluid and flexible relationship to disciplinarity contrasts with perceptions of faculty or administrators who tend to emphasize a primary disciplinary identity. Students believe in the value of acquiring disciplinary skills but not in adhering to a single discipline when a multifaceted approach would better serve their purposes. This may or may not be a generational shift, as students believe, but today's educators should understand their students' perspective in order to better plan for and deliver meaningful instruction.

COLLABORATION

In general, students link the desire to engage in interdisciplinary work with the desire to be open-minded collaborators: to listen to others' ideas, accept assistance, embrace multiple iterations in problem solving, and relinquish insistence on sole credit. One student remarked that this approach represents a "more humble way of problem solving. . . . The desire for a broader understanding of how we can work together is the most powerful." Open-mindedness, a regular feature of collaborative work, leads participants to consider others' points of view, but students provided additional aspects. One identified a connection between open-mindedness as a posture during group interactions and a shift toward valuing group meaning making, as opposed to insistence upon individual contribution or merit. Not only do interdisciplinary and collaborative environments shape processes and address a predetermined challenge or problem, but they also promote an environment in which "creativity and innovation begins," as one student remarked. Another student said, "Any fun project considers multiple perspectives. It never works unless there is more than one mind. I go to the music students about a project I am working on in computer science. Mostly I start complaining about something not working, but then they'll mention a brilliant idea that makes perfect sense and then it works."

Collaborative work benefits from the implicit and explicit value of multiple voices and approaches, but it can also lead to challenges. "The characteristics of a team can be an obstacle," observed one student. "For example, if all of the team members are passive or active, this can be problematic. A well-organized team is critical." Students were keenly aware of this dynamic, although they mentioned consistent communication and time as two ways to help address complications. A graduate student said, "I find time is very important. I would define collaboration success as cohesiveness. Without it, it's people putting things together at the very end and only one person's vision being executed. Time is a solution to this problem." Students confessed

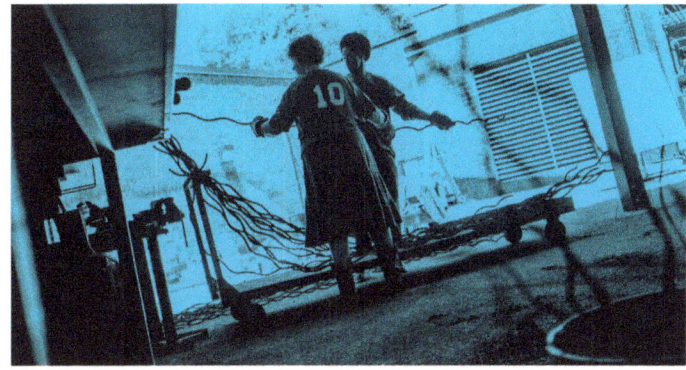

that they had to overcome personal biases against other disciplines or ways of collaborating that did not come naturally. A graduate student remarked, "I work in new media, at the intersection of art and science. Initially, I had preconceived notions that artists would circle around a problem and scientists work linearly, and that is not the case most of the time. With a lot of collaborations, [my views] have been impacted." Another student reflected on the difficulties of an ongoing collaborative course for design and engineering students at her school. "Art, design, and engineering students don't always understand each other," she said. "We initially had communication issues, and before the interdisciplinary work we did, a lot of people were very biased." She explained for the first year she "hated" the work she had to do in art and design, but eventually she changed her mind. As a previous student commented, adequate time seems to be an important consideration to fostering the attitudes required for successful collaborative work, shaping the actual outcomes, and helping to create an environment of mutual respect.

Students, like faculty and administrators, reported experiencing challenges with communication related to disciplinary vernaculars and habits of mind. Misunderstandings and disconnections arising from conflicting expectations or differences in disciplinary cultures affect students and faculty alike. Epistemological differences shape all stages of collaborative meaning making and practice, as do expectations of value: considerations such as deciding what activities or products qualify as research, how success will be measured, or determining an appropriate pacing for the project depend on such epistemological understandings and approaches.

Students indicated their eagerness for further opportunities to connect with like-minded collaborators. After the three-day Emerging Creatives conference brought together students and faculty from across the county, one student exclaimed, "I finally found my tribe!" Students value this kind of interaction, finding it eases some of the tensions arising from challenging interdisciplinary endeavors. A student remarked, "Personal interaction is important, and when we can't have it, it's very challenging. Each side has excuses about why they can't finish, etc., and so the social aspect helps and makes it more enjoyable." Traditional boundaries between schools, states, and regions seem to have little impact on the desire for or quality of collaboration. An enthusiastic graduate student discussed his involvement in a design and technology student conference in his home state, saying, "We cohosted it with our rival school, and that made it even better."

Exposure to collaborative, interdisciplinary, and arts-integrative learning transforms students' educational experience. They believe these experiences prepare them for future careers more effectively than traditional educational approaches and find that working together enhances their learning. Of course, collaborative instructional methods exist outside of arts integration, but the arts bring an aspect of creativity and innovation to projects not found in other settings, thereby enriching the student experience.

IMPACT

Students exhibited a strong desire to connect with the world outside of the university, whether to gain more experience or to fulfill an unmet need. Several students discussed gravitating toward professors and mentors who had one foot "in the real world" and joining outside organizations like Design for America in order to receive consistent and high-quality community-based support. They expressed a yearning for networks connecting them to others, with one working team at the conference drafting a proposal for an online platform connecting interdisciplinary projects and potential collaborators. Students not only want to be part of a community but also to serve their communities. One student remarked, "As an artist, I can take an individualistic approach to my work, but I am looking to make more holistic, community-engaged artworks. [It's] hard to be creative and impactful in a bubble."

Students often alluded to wanting to make an impact, using their talents to improve the world through involvement in local communities or shaping national or worldwide discussions as part of this generation's voice. They want to be part of something bigger than

themselves. A professor in architecture remarked:

Students want multidisciplinary work and courses because they want to make an impact, and they see the world not as part of boundaries but all as a mix of stuff that they pull in from a variety of different places to experiment. So we want to move all this up in undergraduate studies with the realization that may not be as deep as they could in other programs. Spring will be our first graduating class. But from other data I've had from a similar class, I've seen great results.

The professor's concession of a reduction of depth in subject matter implies challenges in achievement of the proverbial "T-shaped" student, with increased focus on interdisciplinarity sometimes necessitating reduction of depth in order to continue to meet expectations for program length. Students provided no conclusive evidence as to how they see this trade-off. A self-described conservative faculty member in music cautioned against trading depth for breadth:

Universities are very big on interdisciplinary work. (I'm a part of [interdisciplinary work] here, so I get it.) But on the other hand, the fact of students learning to be a part of a kind of way of thinking – a discipline – is crucial absolutely. So I don't think that interdisciplinary is any sort of substitute for embracing a subject and its way of approaching the world.

Another faculty member in the sciences said he feels "passionate about connecting to the students. Students respond to that. They want to impact the world, not just learn stuff, create something bigger than themselves. Then we've really done our job, not just force-fed them facts."

Perhaps the clearest student statement about the importance of impact, came from a student who discussed his reasons for changing majors. He said, "If I felt that being a voice major would have direct impact on solving problems in the world, I would keep my major." While this statement does not imply the arts have no impact, it highlights the challenge faced by departments in adapting their teaching to meet student needs. Without evidence that a given major promises to equip graduates to make a difference in the world, an academic area may face challenges in recruiting students.

Arts-integrative interdisciplinary learning becomes particularly impactful when linked to community engagement, as seen at **Otis College of Art and Design, Washington University in St. Louis**, and other sites visited.[23] Research universities might consider these exemplary programs when developing structured options for their own students, incorporating the arts with new or existing opportunities for community engagement.

CRITIQUES AND CHALLENGES

Although students expressed positive opinions regarding their involvement in arts integration, they offered substantive critiques of current efforts and explained challenges they faced. Some of these, such as navigating the territory between self-discovery and career preparation or experiencing financial pressures, generally apply to students across the spectrum of higher education. Others relate more directly to arts integration, such as the perceived absence of institutional support for interdisciplinary opportunities, difficulties in dealing with disciplinary vernaculars during collaborative experiences, or the perceived lack of community for like-minded students. Further, students cited university requirements in their majors as being problematic in their pursuit of arts-integrative engagement, and they expressed awareness of insufficient funding and space as impacting the types of arts-integrative educational experiences they preferred.

SELF-DISCOVERY VS. CAREER PREPARATION

Students find it difficult to pursue self-discovery and experimentation through the arts or through arts-integrative interdisciplinary courses during their academic careers because they face significant pressure to begin building their careers. An MFA student, when asked about recommended changes to her degree program, noted:

One thing is that people get here – this is the student culture – on a gerbil wheel of getting shows. This keeps them from accessing what this degree could be as far as taking classes in and outside their field – in other words, expanding knowledge. People are already trying to work on their careers in their art program, and it makes sense, but there is a loss. Then the three years are over, and all you can do is work on your career 24/7 without access to these great resources here.

Another student who had been a professional actor returned to school to major in theater only to switch majors to education. She found she already had the skills offered by the acting program and wanted something more. She said, "I already had a job in theater and didn't see value in paying for a degree when I already had a job in that field." The departmental focus on career preparation was a problem since it didn't allow her to pursue the areas in which she hoped to study.

Interestingly, an art curator outside of the university system remarked, "Unfortunately, universities used to set you up to be ready for a career. Now it's about what you've done outside the university that gets you a career. You have to hustle a little bit, build your brand." At first, this seems to contradict the previous characterization of departments as too career-focused. However, the quote implies equal value of knowledge and experience beyond acquired skill, seeing career preparatory activities as lacking in universities and found now instead in external internships and other such experiences. The director of an interdisciplinary entrepreneurship institute alluded to the conflict between career preparation and identity formation, remarking on the disproportionately low number of arts students participating in the program. She said, "[Only] 10% of our community is artists. I feel the reason is that art students don't claim that title [of entrepreneur]. To them, entrepreneurship means selling their stuff, and maybe [they] don't want this. Or [they] don't define entrepreneurship as broadly as I do." She continued,

Artists don't understand the [entrepreneurial] role they're playing, why they are necessary parts of the team. The challenge for us is articulating the value of very different thinking. An artist plays a very important role. It's a work in progress. They haven't been resistant (although some have). For example, dancers train to dance but then consider whether they will be dancers in careers or use it as way to open conversation differently. I'm not sure if they've thought of this yet. And I don't think it's their fault; I just think we need to hang out more. It's not fine art school's fault, any more than other schools – we see the same thing in engineering. We are going to design things but not focus on where they go or who needs them or who cares.

The director suggests that understanding and developing the individual receive inadequate attention in comparison to emphasis on teaching job-related skills. This leads to students without the resources to adapt or creatively meld their skills with the demands of the outside world. One student in the arts remarked, "I wish I could be taught more business and science, to be well rounded and have more resources to draw on." A director of an interdisciplinary research institute said, "We as academia have done a great job of siloing students. We've brought them in and asked them what they are going to major in, what their major will be, but we haven't had conversation about what impact they are going to make."

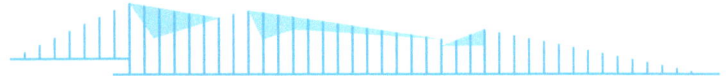

Another research director commented:

> Industry is telling us they want students who are entrepreneurial problem solvers – people thinking outside of the box and adding value. We don't look at the workforce the same way as we did 10 to 20 years ago. [It's] much more freelance and independent, [oriented toward the] small business owner, not a traditional career path working up the [corporate] ladder as much. Academia hasn't changed this, but students have figured it out. We need to get out of the way and give them opportunities to try stuff while they are students. They need to make stuff and try stuff and see that no one out in the world likes it or loves it.

The pressure for career preparation can also involve negative peer interactions and competition; these may not be conducive to learning. For example, the acting student who switched majors to education also noted that "the [other students] I worked with weren't good to work with, as they ridiculed me for wanting to teach. It wasn't 'real theater,' they said." A student in an interdisciplinary field, when asked about changes to her program, lamented, "We've gotten resistance from advisors letting their students take the cartooning class, given the conservative academic environment. Advisors worried that they will lose the students."

Despite an emphasis on skill building, students reported receiving little or no specific career advice or job preparation. For example, another student who changed majors said, "I used to study theater but changed to education because I couldn't get a job in theater.... I received no advice and training on how to make a living in the theater department." Yet another student remarked, "I'm switching from vocal performance to business. I'm a two [on a scale of five, with five being the highest] in terms of how well prepared I am for a job after graduation."

FINANCIAL PRESSURES AND UNIVERSITY REQUIREMENTS

Almost all students interviewed cited the financial burden of higher education as a significant barrier not only to initial entry but also after enrolling, thus affecting a student's choice of degree. For example, a professor of architecture discussed financial difficulties for students:

> We require these students to go buy and make stuff. We lose a whole percentage of the population when we require them to buy materials. Some don't have $50 or $1,000! I've seen some projects cost $1,000. And this causes problems in assessment – how to compare a $1,000-prototype vs. a cardboard one that someone couldn't afford. So this is an exclusive club; this is a real problem. It doesn't affect retention but affects engagement in the first place. I've seen students walk in and then leave when seeing what they have to buy. Then we look around and say, 'Oh, our diversity isn't there. How do we become more inclusive?' Well, that cost is a big issue.

Student interview participants indicated that they face challenges in accessing and accomplishing meaningful arts-integrative work. Suspicion of "inauthentic" manifestations of interdisciplinarity drives students to seek sincere and committed efforts at their educational institutions. Access to facilities and space proved very important to most students, who also mentioned their awareness that fiscal and structural limitations, such as curricular requirements, create major barriers to their interdisciplinary pursuits. Graduate students, in particular, cited the risks faculty who are engaged in arts-integrative work face in their quest for promotion and tenure, yet they did not indicate feelings of anxiety about the pursuit of interdisciplinarity in their own future work.

Student responses indicate that traditional university structures and underinvestment in authentic arts-integrative opportunities fail to meet their needs, characteristic of larger institutional norms within contemporary university culture. While these students enter the university poised to continue their interdisciplinary and collaborative engagement, U.S. higher education has been comparatively slow to meet these expectations. Students also identified lack of depth as a key challenge. Student responses range from observations that "the institution doesn't care, so [arts integration] doesn't happen enough," to "[the university has an] old, non-changing mindset," to specific requests for increased specialization on campus, calls for fewer festivals and shows, and a push for meaningful structural investment in specific training or institutes. Students also noted that even leading research universities with robust arts integration initiatives place too much emphasis on the public promotion of interdisciplinarity, as if the university continuously rediscovers interdisciplinarity's novelty and value.

Departmental motivations, such as a goal to raise enrollment or to rise in program rankings, may conflict with students' needs. A faculty member in music described why he believes his department discouraged him from pursuing a successful interdisciplinary lecture series, which arguably would provide a positive opportunity for students to explore and expand their interests. He said, "One of the reasons is that the department is looking to recruit students. [They think] I'm not going to recruit students because I had a biologist give a lecture; [they think] I will recruit because they heard my CD or want to study with me through my master class."

When asked about how they entered into arts-integrative activities at their home institutions, students provided a range of responses. In some cases, universities offered well-defined trajectories and options to students, including full majors or programs specifically designed for arts-integrative interdisciplinarity. In other instances, students reported seeking interdisciplinary areas due to fatigue caused by their previous major's or program's emphasis on strict disciplinarity. Most students, however, found their involvement to be a function of happenstance or serendipitous discovery, reporting that they had "stumbled" across arts-integrative interdisciplinarity while engaged in something else. Rather than embracing a set of disciplines or prior expectations clearly laid out by the university, students discover a path they choose to pursue despite the lack of precedent. They report that their accidental involvement in arts-integrative interdisciplinarity and its "hidden" status posed challenges to their access to this type of course or program. This perpetuates students' perception of insufficient institutional commitment to addressing their needs and to promoting student awareness of the future of industrial and cultural influence on society and the economy.

Existing curricular structures often create barriers to meaningful engagement. As one student observed, "We aren't encouraged to work interdisciplinarily; we have no structural incentives." Chief among these limitations, students mentioned a lack of flexibility within majors and programs, characterizing the program of study for their majors as "too strict," citing pre-requisites and tightly defined curricular trajectories. In some cases, for example, students must fill elective slots in their schedule with such things as recommended upper-level mathematics courses or additional studio credit hours in their home disciplines, rendering so-called electives as cloaked degree requirements. Students also identified a lack of time as an ongoing challenge. Furthermore, curricular and semester-based norms and structural divisions of time in university culture

lack the necessary flexibility for the iterative, creative nature of arts-integrative engagement. Some projects may require much less time than a full semester, while other projects may need a year or more, depending on the nature of the inquiry. In addressing this concern, a dean of a college of arts and sciences explained that the reason for strict disciplinary programming lies in accreditation:

As a best example, the strict curriculum in engineering is the result of ABET [Accreditation Board for Engineering and Technology] accreditation standards. Thus, there is little room in the curriculum for anything else. Disciplinary requirements in science and engineering are typically high. The choice of degree is thus important. You can't have it all ways, unless you are willing to take extra years to degrees. If a student is truly committed to interdisciplinarity, most universities offer self-defined majors or independent study degrees, where the major is constructed by the student with administrative approvals. However, students typically want the credentials that a standard degree offers, and they are not willing to sacrifice the perceived credibility of standard degrees for such a self-declared option.

SEEKING COMMUNITY

Students' perceptions of themselves as native to interdisciplinarity run counter to their experience in universities, which may fail to provide authentic support or opportunities for genuine engagement. Furthermore, physical layouts of campuses can place geographic barriers between the arts, sciences, or technological fields, and entrenched curricular and organizational compartmentalization can also create barriers to the high-quality interdisciplinary and arts-integrative learning experiences valued by students.[24] This lack of coherence and scarcity of opportunities for deep engagement lead to a lack of community, the absence of which caused some respondents to feel caught between disciplines in a negative sense.

Students yearn for communities demonstrating trust and relationship building across disciplines, but universities may or may not foster these possibilities. The same is true for creating measures of validation for students' interdisciplinary work. A student who said he approaches his work with "a foot in the art world and a foot in the science world" said colleagues in both areas judge him harshly because the institutional culture of his university has no established interdisciplinary community. Another student commented, "When artists and scientists work together, it is difficult to find a way to have success that is meaningful in both worlds,"

---

24   See Davidson and Goldberg for further research into the impact of physical campus layouts on student learning.

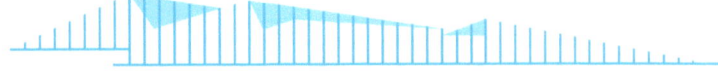

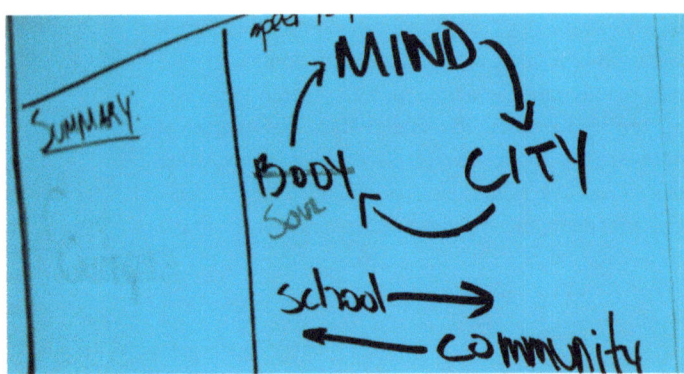

remarking on a "flashy" interdisciplinary project where, at the end, artists were not given an exhibition and biologists did not publish a paper. He said everyone enjoyed the experience, but "clear outcomes weren't established." Universities must work to establish validation measures for students and faculty engaged in interdisciplinary efforts in order to substantiate their declarations of support for such work, finding novel platforms for ascribing value and celebrating success.

STUDENT RECOMMENDATIONS

Limitations and challenges arising from existing curricular and structural norms dovetail with issues of authenticity and depth of engagement. A student mentioned that his university should establish a design school, not only because this was not in place but also because it could provide a home for interdisciplinary and collaborative scholarly and creative production. Students' suggested remedies included placing greater emphasis on providing opportunities for student-led and flipped classroom models. Another student recommended that the university require cross-disciplinary capstone courses, saying, "I wish we had more class projects that require different majors to complete them." Still others mentioned that universities should provide more opportunities to take courses outside of their home discipline, while others objected to having to pursue these courses as independent study. Of course, certain institutions do offer curricular arts opportunities for non-majors, but even in these cases, challenges exist. For example, courses potentially categorized as "arts-integrative" most often occurred within colleges of design, according to student respondents. Faculty tended to provide arts "exposure" rather than authentic "training" for non-majors. Students further mentioned a general lack of specific instruction in interdisciplinarity itself, saying that when faculty do engage in arts integration, it does not go deep enough into the dynamics of

interdisciplinary collaboration. This can also happen in co-taught courses, where students observe faculty tending to remain in their "silos." A student remarked, "Engineering professors think of students as engineering students, and art professors see them as artists," but they fail to create connections between the two fields even when co-teaching. This student suggested that universities provide opportunities to fill this gap, such as holding workshops on collaboration or requiring that direct student instruction in collaboration become a standard feature of such courses.

Respondents mentioned the lack of sufficient facilities or physical space for formal and informal arts-integrative interdisciplinary engagement. As one student said, "We need a central place for interdisciplinary projects to emerge and be conducted." This statement implies that students would pursue collaborative projects unconnected to specific curricular requirements. They recommended establishing a "Flexlab/Studio" space for making or production, available outside of any particular college's jurisdiction and adhering neither to a studio or laboratory framework. Aside from this attractive, but possibly costly, idea, students primarily want their universities to provide community and depth for robust and authentic initiatives. They would also like to see well-publicized and accessible training in the use of facilities so they know how to use equipment properly and safely.

Graduate students reported greater awareness of departmental or disciplinary power dynamics or trends and currents within their chosen fields of study. Students of the arts and humanities were cognizant of funding asymmetries as compared to the sciences and other areas of knowledge production, discussing what these limitations may mean to their potential careers, their present educational opportunities, and their professors' careers. They recognize faculty reluctance to engage in interdisciplinary or arts-integrative courses or projects, just as they observe the inter- and intra-departmental politics preventing the arts-integrative and interdisciplinary educational experiences they value. Several students mentioned they turn outside of the university to seek interdisciplinary experiences through jobs or internships, knowing such opportunities may be unavailable in other ways.

Students expressed a vision in which collaborative and interdisciplinary skills not only become highly valued but are also seen as necessary and expected in all aspects of industry and cultural production. Even though participating students attend the institutions involved in the Mellon Research Project, all of which were selected for their involvement in arts integration, students placed greater emphasis on problems or challenges than on successes or positive aspects of their educational experiences. Comments about a desire for authentic engagement and establishment of lasting arts-integrative, interdisciplinary learning communities and the detrimental impact of underfunding were pervasive.

Although students identified arts integration and interdisciplinarity as a generational shift, the same issues mentioned by students were those cited by other interview participants in the Mellon Research Project. Considering the extended body of information, similar issues exist across all sectors of participants, from students to faculty to upper-level administrators. Students, perhaps, lack the perspective to recognize their observations and concerns as congruent with those expressed by their professors or administrators, with a high degree of similarity present across demographic groups. Students, of course, lack the perspective of faculty or administrators due to the finite duration of their time at the university and their lack of familiarity with its business model(s). Therefore, although students' statements regarding such things as underfunding of favorite programs or perceived lack of facilities or space express genuine concerns, it may not always be possible to provide solutions. Students remain unaware of administrative concerns such as revenue/expense balance, which may prohibit solutions given existing limitations with student interest or enrollment. A dean of a college of arts and sciences commented:

> *The sense of underfunding is not limited to this community; it is a pervasive sense across universities. Further, the main currency in higher education is credit hour production, tuition, and fees. The arts tend to have the lowest number of students; therefore, the distribution of resources based on revenue/expenditure models can be problematic given the small class sizes and typically lower enrollment numbers. In the end, someone will need to pay the bills. All this in a climate where everyone feels higher education is already too expensive.*

Nevertheless, notable exceptions exist. The **OpenGrounds** initiative at the University of Virginia provides students with an accessible space for interdisciplinary collaborations,[25] and faculty elsewhere exhibited remarkable resourcefulness in finding space.

For example, a professor who established a program combining dance and media studies located a vacant art gallery on campus and received permission for her program to "squat in the space." When she did not have a budget for the necessary video recording equipment, she established a partnership with the media studies department; this allowed her students access to what they needed. Although students may believe universities have virtually unlimited resources, addressing their needs sometimes requires applied creativity coupled with human ingenuity and determination.

Not limited to arts integration, student concerns about conflicting expectations in their degree programs and their desire for greater flexibility in choosing courses allowing for personal growth or exploration express an ongoing theme in higher education. The same applies to students' perception of conflicting demands to acquire career skills through a focus in a single area of study and the expectation of their college years as a time for self-discovery through exploration. However, creating a balanced instructional model leading to disciplinary expertise – including direct instruction in career preparation along with internships, opportunities for undergraduate research, and service learning (such as the newly revised program at the **Department of Art and Art History** at the University of Alabama at Birmingham) – represents a step in the right direction. Another solution – providing flexible majors or personalized courses of study, such as the **Individualized Major Program at Indiana University** – may be another avenue universities could choose to explore in order to better meet students' needs and expectations.

Students provided important critiques of the arts-integrative or interdisciplinary courses in which they had participated; these critiques left them wishing for continued, meaningful experiences featuring authentic engagement in creative practice. They also hoped for clear outcomes and expectations in arts-integrative or interdisciplinary courses and for direct instruction in collaboration and interdisciplinarity as part of their learning experiences. Addressing these criticisms during the curriculum planning stage, perhaps using the resources provided in appendix 5, may provide the greatest advantage.

Financial issues usually require individual solutions. Matters of financial aid, scholarships, or grants do not specifically pertain to arts integration, while the monetary demands of an individual arts-integrative course would be subject to the instructor's requirements. Setting a limit on student spending could help to level the playing field within a course, as could requirements to limit students' projects to certain materials or providing supplies directly. For courses involving industry-ready project creation, corporate partnerships – such as those found at Penn State's **Studio|Lab** or in MIT's **Media Lab** – could supply necessary funding.

Perhaps the most important desire expressed by students was for authentic engagement in a lasting arts-integrative community. Researchers discovered two particularly successful exemplars in this area. The Arts Institute at the University of Wisconsin-Madison established "**The Studio,**" a residential learning community for students interested in the arts (Arts Institute, "Programs"). Similarly, the University of Michigan (UM) offers **Living Arts**, a living-learning community on the university's North Campus; it provides students in engineering, arts, architecture, and other fields with the opportunity to "explore innovation and creativity across disciplines" (Living). Not only do students in Living Arts share housing in a designated UM residence hall, but they also take an interdisciplinary class and work together on collaborative projects. This arrangement opens up opportunities for mentorship and student-driven programs and events. Such residential living-learning communities could represent the "fastest route to goal," according to a dean. "Optimized use of the extracurricular space through such efforts avoids all the credit hour issues and those related to defined course requirements.... The strategy is the fastest route to achieving interdisciplinary goals, offering facilities, co-localization, informal settings, etc...."

CONCLUSIONS

In general, students expressed high expectations for their colleges and universities, regardless of whether these apply to arts integration or to other aspects of their educational careers. Sometimes these expectations can be contradictory, such as the desire to receive a comprehensive education allowing for disciplinary depth yet also for personal exploration, all while still graduating on schedule. Time and money being finite, such aspirations may not be achievable. More opportunity for exploration reduces available time for disciplinary study. Greater focus on career preparation results in lessened focus on self-discovery. Graduating on time means only a certain number of classes fit into the student's schedule. Part of the experience of becoming an adult includes realizing the existence of these trade-offs. However, students do have much to offer in alerting faculty and administrators to their wishes, hopes, and desires, thereby informing programmatic and curricular improvements. Most significantly, faculty should ensure that arts-integrative interdisciplinary courses provide the depth and authenticity students yearn for and include direct instruction in collaboration and interdisciplinarity. Faculty should also remain mindful of students' limited financial resources, their need for a space to meet, and their recognition that creating a community of learners can be a transformative aspect of their involvement in arts integration. The student participants in the Mellon Research Project can become, in part, our teachers in this regard, leading university decision makers to create or modify curricular and programmatic choices to address student needs and perceptions.

FINDINGS

- *Students described themselves as "native to interdisciplinarity," seeing a natural fit between their artistic and other academic pursuits and maintaining a fluid and flexible relationship to disciplinary identity.*
- *Students expressed a strong desire to be part of a community of like-minded people involved in arts integration.*
- *Students want to be part of something bigger than themselves and to make an impact on the world, using their artistic talents through involvement in local communities or shaping national or worldwide discussions as part of this generation's voice.*
- *Students reported becoming involved in arts integration by chance, discovering a new educational trajectory through happenstance rather than intention.*
- *Students desire authentic engagement and establishment of lasting arts-integrative, interdisciplinary learning communities.*

RECOMMENDATIONS

- *Increase opportunities for students to enroll in courses that provide deep and authentic arts integration, including specific instruction in interdisciplinary skills and knowledge.*
- *Formulate policies and structures allowing greater flexibility in students' course selection to open opportunities for participation in arts-integrative courses.*
- *Increase publicity for programs or courses offering arts integration in order to attract students who might otherwise be unaware of these opportunities.*
- *Foster the establishment of arts-integrative interdisciplinary learning communities and provide open spaces in which students can pursue collaborative projects, including training for non-majors in the safe use of appropriate tools and equipment.*

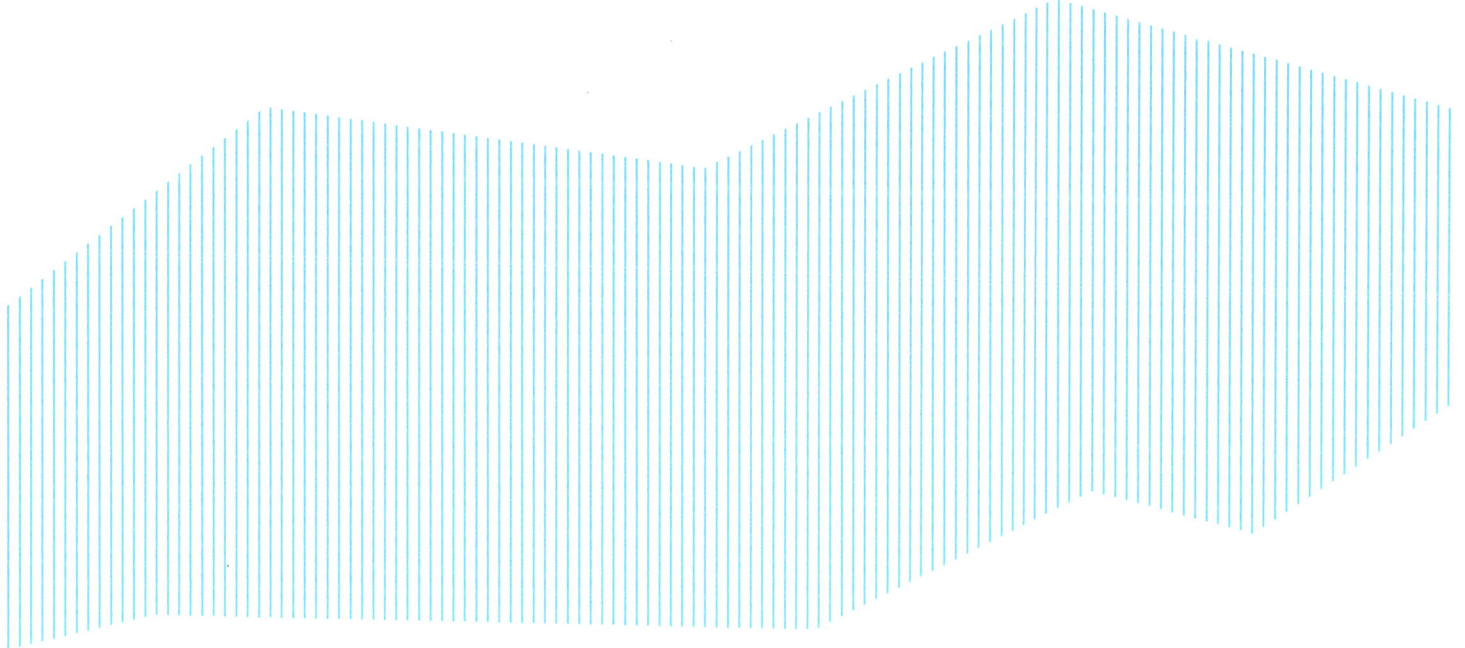

CHAPTER FOUR

CHALLENGES AND ADMINISTRATIVE CONCERNS

Each of the models of arts integration presented in chapter 2 has met with notable success at the universities participating in the Mellon Research Project. Notwithstanding these accomplishments, each faces challenges. Promotion and tenure present a central concern for faculty offering their arts-integrative work for committee consideration. Funding of arts-integrative work originates from multiple sources, sometimes accompanied by the perception of enhanced status for departments or individuals receiving large grants and diminished status for entities without similarly plentiful financial resources. Communication between partners from different disciplines was a concern for interview participants. Finally, institutional structures – such as policies regarding contact hours, credit hours, or systems for staffing and scheduling courses, physical resources including spaces for arts-integrative research or teaching, and methods of institutional recognition – proved troublesome as well.

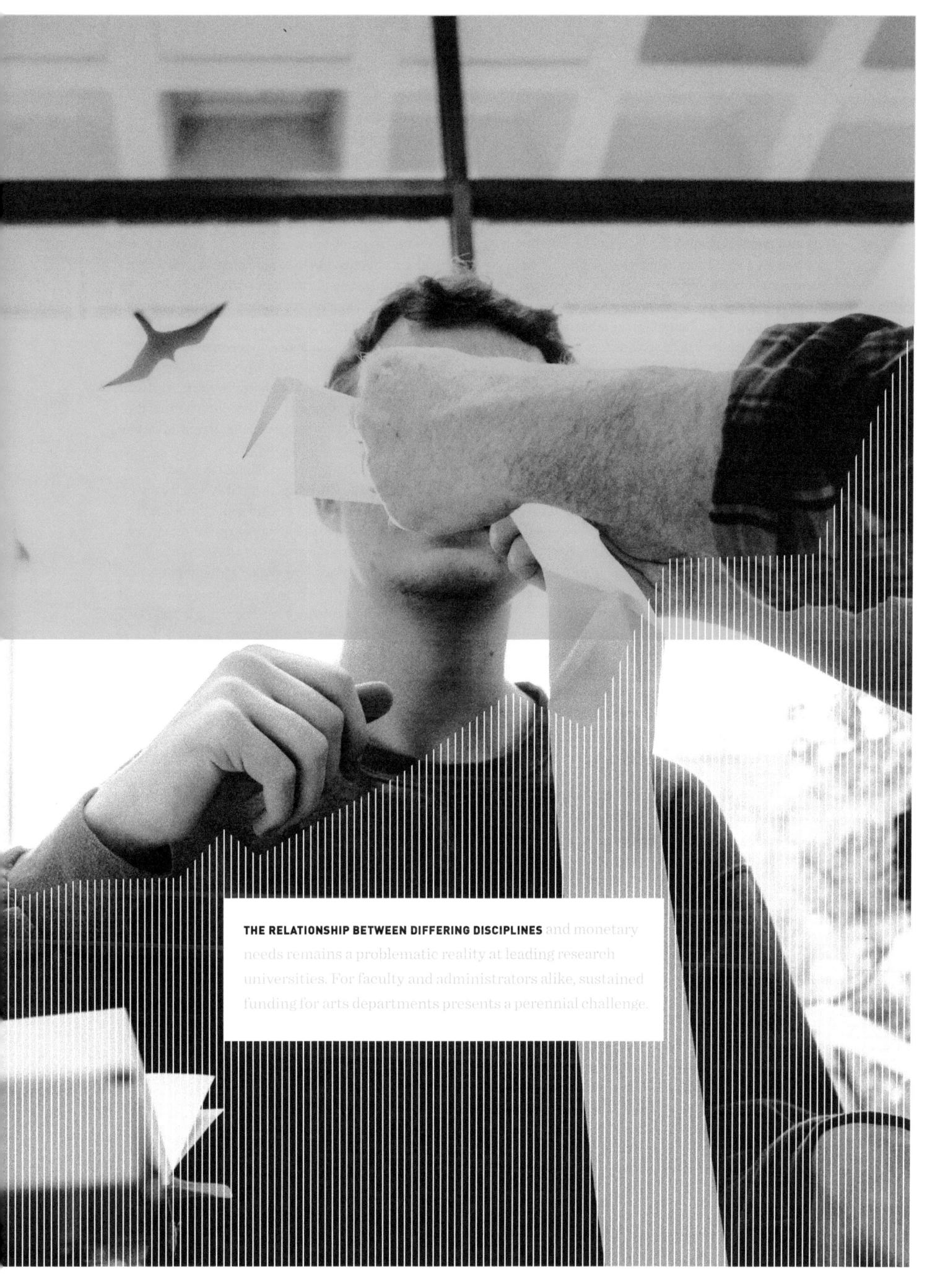

THE RELATIONSHIP BETWEEN DIFFERING DISCIPLINES and monetary needs remains a problematic reality at leading research universities. For faculty and administrators alike, sustained funding for arts departments presents a perennial challenge.

PROMOTION AND TENURE

Occupying a central position in academic life, institutional systems for faculty promotion and tenure offered one of the most significant impediments to arts integration articulated by the interview participants. A dean explained his understanding of promotion and tenure in higher education, saying that promotion provides recognition of what one's career has consisted of to date, looking back at one's accomplishments. Tenure, on the other hand, recognizes what one's career will be, looking forward to future contributions to the profession or academic unit. Perhaps not all administrators would agree with this explanation, but we might understand recognition of a faculty member's excellence as a key criterion in achieving both promotion in rank and tenure.

Independently from one another, two interview participants, each of whom has served his university for decades, explained the current system of promotion and tenure differentiating between research and creative activity. Following World War II, the GI Bill created a sharp increase in the number of university students, including those in the arts. At the same time, previous methods of art education through traditional conservatory systems shifted to a greater emphasis on university programs, leading the MFA to become the preferred credential for university arts faculty positions (Oakes). Established understandings of the term "research," such as those common to the sciences, did not fit the work of university arts faculty, leading to institutional policies accommodating creative practice as an equivalent means of achieving professional recognition towards promotion or tenure (Singerman).[26] According to both of the faculty members who related this history, the policy change initially benefited arts faculty and was intended to support and validate creative practitioners in higher education. However, each of the interviewees recognized that the situation has changed today. Differentiating research from creative activity has resulted in emphasizing the differences between the arts and other academic areas, not to mention reinforcing the stereotype of creative practitioners as "makers" rather than "thinkers." Instead of affirming creative practice as a legitimate scholarly activity, establishing two distinct evaluative categories has separated the arts from other academic disciplines. Those who promote arts integration hope to amend these conditions, which complicate the pursuit of promotion and tenure for those whose work does not fit neatly into creative works or traditional research publications.

Traditional categories of research or creative practice, teaching, and service may not recognize or reward work occurring outside of expected disciplinary norms. Faculty members engaged in collaborative or extra-disciplinary pursuits, such as a professor of art pursuing scientific research or a professor of engineering making works of art, must navigate rigid promotional structures. As one professor and director of graduate studies noted, the 20th-century research university model sometimes fails to recognize these professional activities: "We get 'credit,' but it's not built into the structures in a meaningful way. Tenure and promotion is everything, and it's all up in the air. I like buckets that make decisions easier as an administrator, but that doesn't mean the buckets that exist are correct or effective in doing that."

Given deans' or chairs' responsibility to quantify departmental productivity, an institutional lag seems to exist between present practices and the needed recognition of interdisciplinary or transdisciplinary work. Considering the evaluative triad of research, teaching, and service, how should a promotion or tenure committee assess a faculty member's work in a collaborative setting? Securing letters of recommendation from multiple experts can help assuage doubts a science panel may have about the quality of arts research or artists' concerns about a faculty member's involvement in the scientific community. Promotion and review committees must also pass judgment on how interdisciplinary teaching contributes to a faculty member's teaching portfolio. How does one evaluate a course with a 10:1 teaching ratio? How should the committee credit a member of the engineering faculty for a course taught entirely in the art department? How should the committee evaluate a studio artist for teaching occurring in a biology lecture hall? Evaluating the quality of arts-integrative research presents challenges if promotion and tenure committees have little disciplinary breadth.

Some institutions are remarkably progressive in their promotion and tenure policies, representing a shift from typical approaches. A professor of linguistics and developmental psychology working with human-computer interaction said:

Interdisciplinarity is part of [this university's] DNA. . . . In many places, people up for tenure have to pick who in their field will lead their review. This presupposes the linearity of fields like that. Also, chairs often say, "But what has she done on her own? How do we know which aspects of this research are hers?" These are

---

26   For a more comprehensive discussion of the history of the visual arts in higher education, see Singerman.

ways of discounting interdisciplinarity when the rubber really hits the road. But here, in a conversation about a pre-tenure candidate just the other day, one of the letters said she does a lot of collaborating, and it's therefore not entirely clear that it's a good path or what her individual contributions are. This really pissed off the committee, which is great. We would never tell her to stop doing what she's doing.

Such anecdotes indicate the potential for flexibility, openness, and willingness to engage deeply in a scholar's area of study in order to assess her overall contributions.

Most participants tended to indicate their universities took a more traditional approach to promotion and tenure. A professor of industrial and systems engineering who creates artworks in photography, origami, and collage as part of his scholarly engagement said the evaluators in his department did not know how to assess his creative output. He spoke of exhibiting his artworks in galleries and local venues such as coffee shops and of commercial success in selling his works. But he was unsure if this would count toward his tenure review, noting he may have to bring in people from the art department in order to determine whether his artistic work had value. We might observe this professor as being somewhat unaware of standards involved in assessing creative production, where local galleries, coffee shops, and even commercial success generally do not provide the type of validation necessary for professional advancement. Scholars in the arts usually must demonstrate artistic production meriting national or international attention. The professor's inexperience in his secondary discipline may not be applicable to other individuals choosing to venture beyond disciplinary borders, but it demonstrates a need for relevant knowledge of applicable promotion and tenure procedures even among participants themselves.

Other interviewees related similar stories of needing to take extraordinary measures to educate the members of tenure committees about their extra-disciplinary work's importance to their primary field of academic engagement. Letters of recommendation or the participation of outside evaluators might facilitate understanding in some instances. Participating administrators explained that faculty members' success in achieving promotion or tenure based on work outside of a given discipline would depend on the department to which the faculty member presented the work and whether evaluators perceived

it to have value to the department. The rank of the faculty member also factors into these deliberations. A professor of arts management (primarily in theater), who also serves as a dean of a college of fine arts, said:

The challenge is this: are they junior or senior faculty? There's a lot of talk about us needing to do interdisciplinary work, but the challenge comes when junior faculty are to be evaluated. The interdisciplinarity itself is not always appreciated in that tenure process despite the fact that it may be in the day to day. When I see [interdisciplinarity] happen, I am for it. But when a young faculty member is putting together a tenure portfolio, we don't want them to do something they weren't hired to do in a way that pulls away from what they were hired to do.

A professor of new media also addressed this distinction.

My collaborations did count toward my tenure. It's something we do fairly well here, but not systematically. It's more through liberal application of policies. . . . I'm going to look for the most traditional part of what you do, then I'm going to see how a collaboration either supports, serves, or diverges. As long as you're covering the traditional bases, having collaborations or reach-out, transdisciplinarity can really help beyond just frosting on the cake; it can show that you're a vital member of this community instead of being hyper-disciplinary. . . . Make sure that someone can have some nods toward traditional paths, and two, make sure that the collaborative work has products in mind. . . . Save the open-ended stuff for after tenure.

According to this faculty member, one can be more or less strategic upon entering the tenure process with an interdisciplinary portfolio. Seeking a campus mentor who has succeeded in presenting interdisciplinary portfolios to promotion and tenure committees may help avoid pitfalls or assist in preparing the strongest possible interdisciplinary portfolio for review.

Uneven implementation of promotion and tenure policies persists despite vocalized support for integrative courses or creation of faculty lines explicitly for collaborative and transdisciplinary work. An assistant professor in the arts stated that existing promotion and tenure procedures generally lack the capacity to support interdisciplinary work for which new faculty were hired. In these instances, junior faculty members face challenges when constructing tenure packets based on their interdisciplinary characteristics, finding their evaluations based on traditional criteria established prior to their employment. In such cases, young scholars would do well to evaluate promotion and tenure policies during their interview or hiring process, in order to be able to negotiate a more secure positioning within their initial contracts. At the very least, incoming faculty and rising graduate students should be aware of the paradoxes inherent within a department's aspirations to be collaborative and the reality of less progressive promotion requirements.

Knowing promotion and tenure decisions still occur within traditional frameworks, senior faculty members sometimes conducted limited co-teaching, perhaps developing some nontraditional curricula prior to earning tenure yet remaining cautious about pushing the boundaries too far even within explicitly transdisciplinary and collaborative contexts. As a professor of sculpture and digital media said, "I was a brand-new full-time faculty member when I created Art and Technology. This meant I couldn't do anything too wild, and consequently, I had to play it safe and couldn't develop it as fully as I wanted to at first. If I had been tenured or something it might have been a different story." Even junior faculty expressing confidence in their tenure dossiers worried about uneven application of new promotion and tenure standards recognizing collaborative work and partnerships with other disciplines. A junior faculty member in engineering planning to apply for tenure in the near future noted, "They'll see I didn't have my head in the lab the whole time. . . . I'm the only engineer [in my department] that's going to have an entry in the 'Exhibitions' part of my dossier. Not equivalent to a journal article but also not seen as a waste of time."

Promotion and tenure historically rest on individual accomplishment. Collaborative work can be a significant impediment for faculty members who primarily engage in connecting disciplines. The director of an institute dedicated to the arts on campus explained:

I know that universities all over are grappling with to what extent collaborative work can be evaluated as part of an individual's tenure portfolio. . . . Collaboration and the ability to do so in different ways – teaching and research – is part of an individual's profile. But I still think the gold standard in the humanities is the individual research project. It's difficult to imagine someone getting tenure solely on the basis of collaborative projects; these things are neither sufficient nor necessary for tenure, but you can imagine a particular case where the collaborative aspects of the profile are useful.

Often, young faculty need guidance about their careers, however their careers unfold. While the promotion and tenure process provides guidance and incentive to an academic career, effectively steering young faculty, the process can also have the opposite effect, as it limits productive investigation and new knowledge acquisition through the artificial construction of conceptual development.

Some institutions visited for the present study are working to revise their promotion and tenure procedures to accommodate collaborative and transdisciplinary curriculum and research. However, traditional practices continue to influence decisions even at the more progressive institutions, as committees generally expect faculty members in the arts to engage in creative practice while faculty in other areas must provide evidence of research meeting specific disciplinary standards. In one of the most striking examples, a faculty member in visual art described her productive partnership with health sciences, participating in groundbreaking research into the relationship between the arts and health. However, when she sought tenure, both her departmental colleagues and the dean of the college of the arts reminded her that she was hired to make visual art, not to conduct research in the health sciences. Fortunately, her professional arts practice, exhibition record, service, teaching, and external evaluations were sufficient for her to earn tenure, even though the dossier parameters permitted only half a page of text describing her work with the health sciences. In her present pursuit of promotion to full professor, she again approached the dean to see if her research with the health sciences would count, only to receive another negative response.

Similarly, a sculpture professor described his research collaboration in material science, producing works of great interest to scientific researchers from around the world. His live events draw national and international scientific researchers to witness his unique processes, and his accomplishments have been the subject of several articles in scientific journals. When this sculptor sought tenure, however, he encountered significant difficulties. Although his departmental colleagues, the university, and its administration fully support his efforts, at this institution a committee of traditional practicing artists from the college of visual and performing arts determines promotion. The faculty committee vote for his promotion split because he had not sufficiently distinguished himself along traditional lines. Institutional procedures dictate that the dean determines tenure but faculty committees determine promotion, with a split vote meaning the sculptor earned tenure but not promotion. He remains "stranded" as an assistant professor, unable to advance in rank even though his scientific research literally garners worldwide acclaim. This interviewee said 12 other professors also remain stalled in their promotion attempts, all of whom work for a university that values collaboration but is hobbled by an academic unit where influential faculty members value traditional accomplishment.

Procedures vary between the institutions, depending on definitions of research or creative activity. If certain activities provide departmentally acceptable criteria for career advancement and others do not, faculty members have less incentive to engage in partnerships outside of their primary disciplines. However, some of the universities studied lead the way in blurring the lines between research and creative activity in order to facilitate cross-disciplinary work. As a senior vice president and provost explained, "We want to be as inclusive as possible and have everyone understand that included in the term research, we have all kinds of approaches. It's research with a little 'r,' and by its very nature we consider it to be broad."

Despite efforts to change institutional policies to be more conducive to extra-disciplinary investigations, promotion and tenure policies continue to present obstacles, especially if faculty members fear interdisciplinary collaborations will detract from the promotion process. Promotion and tenure remain powerful tools by which to recognize faculty members and demonstrate institutional support for the value of curricular and research collaborations between the arts and other academic areas. Best practices may lie more in the application or interpretation of such policies than in the actual verbiage of the policies themselves.

FUNDING AND STATUS

A global concern for higher education today, funding was a matter of great importance to interviewees, especially as funding considerations intersect with perceptions of status connected to the allocation of financial resources. Lack of uniformity across the locations studied prevents identification of any one model as being the most successful in terms of designing a funding schema for arts-integrative programs. Indeed, further study could assist in examining how to increase capacity for research support for arts-integrated activities. Interview participants did not provide concrete data about their

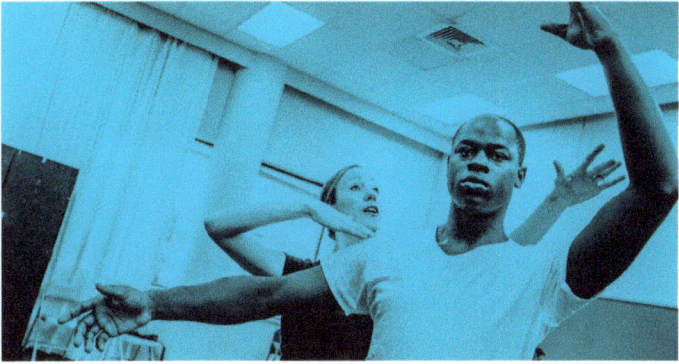

financial resources or budgets. Since funding for curriculum typically occurs through standard university operations budgets, arts integration funding models are not publicly available. Research funding, on the other hand, may similarly come from within the university or may be provided through grants or partnerships with private, corporate, or government entities. Participants mentioned funding from government entities such as the National Endowment for the Arts (**NEA**), the National Science Foundation (**NSF**), or the National Institutes of Health (**NIH**) most frequently, but they seldom spoke of private or philanthropic sources, although these also factor into arts-integrative activities. Funding for co-curricular arts programming is more complex and often comes from multiple sources. Yearly student activity fees pay for some programs, while students pay directly for such things as non-credit classes, field trips, or tickets to events outside the university (although some institutions offer these items to students free of charge or at a reduced cost). Some programs receive additional funding through grants from philanthropic organizations or charitable gifts, and student fund raising activities generate necessary operational revenue as well.

Most faculty and administrators reported challenges with funding and finances, which influence both faculty and facilities. An associate dean for educational technologies said,

> *[There are] too many good ideas and not enough funding to support them all. . . . We have a long-standing tradition of not saying no but never quite fully funding ideas. Everything is under-resourced. We find ourselves pulling 110%. Another challenge is helping to understand what the key priorities are and trying to support those and to make sure the infrastructure is in place to grow into areas we want to grow in. For me, space is a challenge. We are a couple years from a renovation project. Until then, we are really space-constrained. I would be surprised if*

there's any dean here that would say that funding isn't a problem. The state has cut our budget this year, so we've had to give 5% back, 7% next year. Those cuts we will work it out so it won't affect core mission. We can't [afford to] send faculty to a conference, but we won't have to cut any lines. Hopefully, we can replace lines that were open that were existing. We're not expecting any new positions any time soon, which is a challenge because enrollment is growing.

Of course, such concerns exist across the university, where funding seldom exceeds participants' needs in any program, department, or unit. Private universities commonly note reduced giving by donors or diminished funding by philanthropic organizations, and public universities face ongoing reductions in state and federal funding. Despite the universality of financial challenges, arts-integrative programs encounter some specific challenges.

Research projects in the sciences often receive a greater number of opportunities to acquire grants, although federal investment in science has declined in recent years (Porter). Nevertheless, as reported by the 2013 American Academy of Arts and Sciences' **"Humanities Report Card,"** the arts and humanities combined receive less than $0.48 for every $100.00 of funding awarded to STEM disciplines (American). Federal support for arts and culture tends to support exhibition, engagement, and activities, rather than investment in arts research or interdisciplinary experimentation. Most federal arts and culture granting programs specifically exclude support for educational aspects of higher education, thus diminishing opportunities to develop curricular and co-curricular experiments. At the same time, the arts may have more access to private philanthropic dollars related to community engagement and exhibition. Either way, the last decade has seen an increase in active efforts to collaborate between federal agencies, perhaps mirroring the arts integration trends on campus. As an executive director for research in a school for the arts explained, the NEA and NSF have partnered to extend dialogue on arts-science collaborations, the NIH has recognized the potential role of arts in healthcare, and **Americans for the Arts** has launched a National Initiative for Arts and Health in the Military, with support from the Corporation for National and Community Service (a federal entity).

Colleagues in the sciences, however, recognize the challenges faced by grant-seeking arts faculty. As a clinical neuroscientist commented, "For us in the College of Medicine, you have to be grant-funded before you even begin to make time for your research, and I realized that these folks [in the arts] have very few mechanisms for such funding." To that extent, motivations for focusing on arts research or creative products tend to emerge from the artist/designer, and in exchange for less targeted funding, arts researchers have more freedom to pursue lines of inquiry directly relevant to their conceptual trajectories, rather than pursuits dictated by federal or philanthropic research interests. In some sense, this freedom might contribute to igniting collaborations in fields dictated by external demands.

A dean of a college of liberal arts explained:
The major measure of research universities' success is federal funding dollars. This model doesn't really fit the humanities and the arts. Even if you get the Guggenheim, it's a fixed amount of money; it doesn't grow with prestige. So people like me, with missions that stretch across the humanities and fine arts, need to keep it clear that there are nonquantifiable measures for other forms of inquiry.

Growth of funding serves as a measure of success in research universities, with yearly statistics ranking institutions in order of federal funding for research and development.[27] Disciplines such as the arts and humanities seldom partake of such funding, which as the dean in the previous quote explained, requires them to find other methods of proving their worth.

Departments and programs at research universities gain enhanced reputations through funding success. Likewise, lack of external funding endangers an academic unit's status. Several interview participants addressed this problem. A director of architecture stated, "[The university where I work is] a major awardee of public research funding, and the arts are such a small part of that that I'm not sure we're taken seriously." A director of a social sciences institute also addressed this concern: "There's a hierarchy of support for institutes, with life sciences having the most financial support, [social sciences] at the bottom, and arts and humanities below that." More research could examine management strategies for such disparities and support mechanisms for arts programs to develop research or external funding capacity. For example, engineering and health units support research staff whose job is aggressively seeking external funding to support laboratories and the purchase of expensive scientific

---

27   A 2013 study conducted by the NSF ranked universities in order of federal dollars received for research and development, showing that the top ten institutions received 20% of available funds, out of 896 schools receiving federal money ("10"). Five of the top ten institutions participated in the Mellon Research Project.

equipment. Some comparable arts units have succeeded at developing this capacity, able to raise millions of dollars in support over the years, such as the **University Musical Society** at the University of Michigan or the **Stanford Arts Program**. However, these particular arts units remain outliers within university arts investments, thereby detracting from the material contributions the arts might make to arts-integrative projects.

The perception of inequitable funding can be quite demoralizing for those who aspire to collaborative research projects. A professor of humanities and women's studies who holds an MFA in drawing said:

One of the hardest things for the arts is that all of the granting and funding out there is structured for scientists and engineers, and we from the arts have very little choice but to come into them as instrumental actors. . . . It's a real problem in the university. We feel lucky if we get $3,000, whereas that'd be an insult in the sciences. The valuation creates a hierarchy, and the university values that valuation structure. Artists can't initiate an NSF grant or be integrated at the cellular level, really; instead, [we're] instrumental.

As this faculty member notes, most artistic collaboration on NSF grants provides supplements to core scientific development and must still meet the broader scientific criteria of the agency. When encountering this challenge, faculty truly confront the fact that federal agencies are themselves founded upon traditional disciplinary expectations and funded by Congress accordingly. Too much integration between agencies' goals would likely call into question the core mission of that particular agency to fulfill its original Congressional mandate, thereby endangering the agencies' funding.

Perhaps the most telling example came from a professor of music theory working with neuroscientists in a music cognition lab. He explained that the university had been unwilling or unable to provide what he needed in terms of space or material resources. Although he had been able to piece together funding, space to work, and other resources, his struggle to do this detracted from his ability to focus on his research, all of which negatively affected his project. He said, "Behavior experiments require that we control variables, including the space and what's around us. We don't have an adequate space to do that, however. . . . When a psychology professor gets a funded project like mine, they get a lab, course releases for a year, a lab manager, a post doc – a serious start-up package. But not in the arts." Such

comments reflect evidence that our universities have extraordinary potential to develop new knowledge, hosting a range of novel ideas, yet cannot actualize this new knowledge due to resource constraints.

The relationship between differing disciplines and monetary needs remains a problematic reality at leading research universities. For faculty and administrators alike, sustained funding for arts departments presents a perennial challenge. Such disparities between arts departments and others like chemistry, engineering, or even English lend some weight to the perceived disciplinary hierarchy in research universities. Those in the sciences, and to a lesser extent design and other fields, possess the ability to garner large sums of money through industry partnerships or through external awards with bodies like the NSF or NIH. In some cases, courses in those fields were possible solely because an industry partner funded a new computer laboratory, for example. We should also recognize disparities in program costs. The department of philosophy does not require a molecular imaging machine or electron microscope, for example. Arts programs have a long-standing reputation as being costly, but their total requirements pale in comparison to some in the STEM disciplines, providing justification for increased funding in those areas.

In the arts, funding agencies serve a broader clientele. Less reliant on the specialized research only possible within research universities, cultural agencies fund nonprofit arts organizations, local arts agencies, and general cultural organizations as well as universities. Funds offered by the NEA and the **Institute of Museum and Library Services**, for example, annually support projects, presentations, university art museums or galleries, and university libraries. When universities apply to the NEA, they can submit one project per year for a maximum award of $100,000. While a project might span two years, most applicants reapply each year, which can be labor-intensive. Comparatively, grants from science agencies can extend from three to five years, often providing $250,000 to $500,000 per year, allowing successful researchers a period of respite before the funding search begins again.

Yet these agencies are also subject to a culture that provides limited investment in the arts and culture. For example, the NEA's budget has remained flat over the last decade, with a 2015 budget of $146 million supporting over 16 arts disciplines nationwide (National Endowment). Compare this to the 2015 budget of $5.93 billion for the NSF (Mervis), and we can see the discrepancy faculty experience on a daily basis. Essentially, this quick comparison shows arts in general receive 2.5% of the investment of the sciences. Finally, these boundaries can be somewhat fluid, as the NSF has supported multiple arts-rich projects, including studies within its **Science of Learning Centers**, which examine how art forms contribute to cognitive development. Furthermore, a faculty member who also serves as an administrator reported that her department has to be very careful which grants it seeks so as to respect community arts organizations with which the university continually cultivates relationships. Her department expressed concern about competing directly with its own community and constituents. While this can be a weakness, universities can also work with partners to seek funding support on occasions where the university alone would not be eligible or would not be considered a strong applicant. For example, partnerships with municipalities allow universities to participate in funding submissions for which they would not be eligible as the primary applicant.

Curricular developments face the greatest challenge from external funders, as philanthropists and agencies assume student tuition payments will subsidize curricular innovation. At the same time, when arts departments struggle to fund even standard programs and curriculum, finding internal funds for new courses and approaches can be highly opaque, if not overtly discouraged. Worthwhile new ideas and approaches to curriculum remain unexplored because of this lack of support, and faculty members turn their attentions to the courses already occupying their teaching loads. A professor of theater said, "I think this kind of starvation [makes it] much harder to bring forward an initiative, especially an initiative that is outside the box." To address this challenge, universities might consider reserving funds targeted for curricular innovation in order to provide faculty with incentive for ambitious curricular development.

Funding models within institutions also present barriers to collaborative and transdisciplinary work. One dean in the arts noted that revenue-centered management practices skew the questions he has to ask of proposals for co-taught course offerings. He first asks, "Can I work with that dean?" If not, the proposal may not progress any further. His second question concerns the integrity of the partnership and awareness of implicit inter-university hierarchies based on discipline: "Are we equal partners, or are the arts being instrumentalized?" His third and final question aims toward himself and his department: "Do I believe in the faculty member

or not?" Consequently, this dean finds himself discouraging co-teaching and collaborative curricular development on a regular basis. Such vetting results in supporting only the highest quality proposals and partnerships, creating the types of courses students have vocally reported to him as transformative.

When only smaller portions of funding are accessible to artists, grants awarded by entities such as the NSF or similar organizations endorse the primary authority of the scientific partner in an arts-integrated research or curricular collaboration. More specifically, the non-arts partner remains the "primary investigator" responsible for the grant award. In these conditions, the arts appear supplementary to primary research rather than a full research partner with tremendous epistemological potential to develop new knowledge. As one interviewee explained:

Let me bottom line it for you: what makes us a great university? Is it our research or our concerts? Is it our grants and our citation index or our public art and exhibitions? Those are just pleasant fictions. The arts don't contribute to our Carnegie Classification. They're lucky they're here at all.

Or as the director of a school of business bluntly said, "What is the value of the arts at a Research I university? Is there any? I suppose they give us pretty things to look at and pleasant things to hear when it's not too strange. You know, normal art." As we develop arts-integrated efforts, whether in research or curriculum development, research universities must entertain these realities in order to understand possibilities for maneuverability and development within this environment.

Co-curricular programs in the arts[28] encounter somewhat different funding mechanisms than programs featuring arts integration in research partnerships or curricular collaborations. Researchers observed uneven funding for co-curricular programs even among organizations at the same university. Some programs enjoy generous financial resources and use these to full advantage. A student participant in the **MIT Arts Scholars** program reported that the organization was "funded by the Council for the Arts, which is a board of . . . alums who really like the arts and really generously fund us so we can go to art events and have fun. Sometimes people from the board will come to the events with us because they're involved in the arts in their own personal lives." At the same time, universities involved in this study range from private

---

28 This study concerns the ways co-curricular arts programs integrate the arts into students' overall academic lives. Unlike research or curricular programs that integrate the arts with other disciplines, co-curricular arts programs typically take a monodisciplinary approach. Such programs may include music performance groups, theatrical productions, or visual arts clubs.

to public, thereby possessing very different capacities for supporting student co-curricular opportunities.

Substantial funding through the Provost's Office sustains the **Visions and Voices** initiative at the University of Southern California (USC), allowing it to function as a high-profile, high-priority cultural arts program attracting outstanding headliners, large audiences, and enthusiastic participation by faculty and administrators. However, student organizations must usually piece together funding from several sources, often conducting their own fundraisers. Universities typically provide some form of grant monies for student groups, projects, or performances. A representative response addressing the multipronged funding structure of co-curricular arts programs comes from a program director:

There's funding available through student government, and that's a large portion of what students use to do their functions. Organizations that sell tickets use revenue from that; some organizations do developmental programming to raise money. Students put in their own money. Students go out to the specific granting organizations that are set up on campus. There are grants for multicultural programs. There are grants for arts programs. But they are specific to different kinds of things. And they can pool resources with other student organizations or through other departments. It really is a multifaceted, multilevel, lots-of-places sort of process to get your student organization funded. And I think that's true everywhere.

Co-curricular arts groups face perpetual challenges in funding their programs. Even faculty-led arts organizations like a marching band supplement their budgets with fundraisers such as selling cupcakes and brownies in the residence halls. Investigators found a particularly enterprising group at a university outside the Mellon Research Project; this group held a video game competition in the winter and a skateboard contest in the spring, raising funds by way of the participants' entry fees. Student-led organizations, particularly those with policies and procedures designed to prevent misuse of student activity funds, add a prohibitive level of difficulty for students seeking to establish a new club or group. One university's student activities office, for instance, requires new student organizations to register as a group and document their activities over a given timeframe. They must then submit this record of accomplishment and student participation before consideration for official status, which qualifies their group to receive student activity funds. This

process can take between two and three years, by which time the organizing members may have graduated or simply left the group. With hundreds of student-led organizations on most campuses, institutional requirements understandably exist, but meeting such stringent expectations can pose problems for groups seeking both recognition and funding.

Even after having achieved official standing, students report continuing needs for fundraising. A student leader of an a cappella singing group with official status described his group's experience with this situation:

We have two concerts throughout the semester.... Tickets are sold for $10 to $15 depending on the year, and usually we get about 1,000 people or so.... The second [concert] is in winter semester [when] we have a show that's called "Charity Fest," where all those proceeds go to charity. So we're also a charitable organization in that sense. We just put out a CD. We got grants from our campus organization – basically anywhere that we could get anything from. We're also sometimes paid for the performances that we do outside of campus.... So it's really multiple sources and anywhere that we can get the funds.

Students must be motivated to take on the skills necessary for supporting their co-curricular groups. Moreover, engaging in traditional fundraising or starting a crowdfunding campaign provides students with skills and experiences that can help them after graduation. Co-curricular groups appear to be a quiet source of entrepreneurship training. At the same time, this climate can present direct challenges for the new arts-integrative co-curricular activities to thrive, as start-up and sustainability require multiple investments from multiple actors on campus.

Funding presents perennial challenges no matter which aspect of university life comes under consideration and no matter the size or status of the institution. As a common concern, interview participants' statements regarding their experience with funding come as little surprise, nor do strategies for meeting these challenges represent groundbreaking research findings. However, recognizing the discrete conditions of funding in each of these areas enables us to build proactive strategies as we address the fragility and instability of the environments we inhabit. Everyone is subject to scarcity, from seemingly monolithic government entities to small student-run arts clubs.

Particularly for research and curricular arts integration efforts, funding remains tied to status and disciplinary identities, with STEM disciplines receiving a larger share of wealth and prestige than the arts. Arts-integrative partnerships drawing upon this association tend to reap the greatest benefits, although not universally so. Status and perceptions of hierarchy do not seem to plague co-curricular programs in the same way, but co-curricular efforts face their own sets of monetary difficulties.

Universities may still possess comparatively more fiscal capacity than other nonprofits struggling for survival in the arts, despite diminishing state funding. University development offices and the broad capital campaigns they conduct possess generative potential, as do private donors, who frequently fund programs, centers, and institutes through endowments or generous gifts. Although interview participants did not cite such efforts, these nevertheless present promising avenues for exploration, potentially yielding strategies to address funding concerns endemic to any academic endeavor adapted to arts-integrative activities.

COMMUNICATION: DISCIPLINARY VERNACULARS, DEPARTMENTAL CULTURES

Interview participants identified differences in communication, departmental cultures, or disciplinary languages as challenges to their involvement in arts integration. The director of a social science research institute commented, "It's not easy getting a psychologist and sociologist to talk to each other [because they have] different cultures, languages, publication outlets, and so on." Or as a faculty member in education said, "Terms used in one discipline are considered something completely different in another discipline. 'Context analysis,' for example, is specific and different from education to [computer science]." As a result, interviews revealed disciplinary vernaculars to be powerful tools but also structures demanding time and attention so that collaborators might create new languages or continue to function fully within their own distinct symbolic systems while at the same time bridging conceptual frameworks.

The norms, methodologies, literatures, and histories of academic disciplines comprise the foundation from which new knowledge arises, giving rise to highly specialized modes of thinking and speaking known as disciplinary vernaculars. Misunderstandings bred by conflicting variants of these specialized communication styles create ramifications more often than might be immediately apparent. Disciplinary vernaculars create barriers to access and, in some cases, may even cause individuals who adhere strictly to disciplinarity to question the value of working across disciplines. They can also raise doubts about the competence of colleagues who fail to utilize the same disciplinary jargon, and they may represent larger epistemological concerns. According to one professor of computational music, those in the arts and humanities might be perceived as having "poor ground truths" compared to scholars in fields like biology or computer science. Artists, scientists, and humanists alike may fall prey to oversimplifying another field or becoming the target of disrespect based on lack of familiarity with another's field of study. Arts integration builds bridges across these misunderstandings through productive research and curricular collaborations.

Differences in definitions become most apparent in answers to the interview question, "How do you define research?" This question prompted notably divergent responses. At one end of the spectrum, a professor of clinical neuroscience limited the definition of research to only those investigations utilizing the scientific method. At the other end, a dean of liberal arts and sciences said research is "anything we employ a faculty member to do."

Overall, interviews generated understanding of research as seeking "new knowledge about ourselves and the world we live in" (as stated by a vice president for research and dean of a graduate school) and "pushing the boundaries of knowledge" (as offered by a professor of theater, dance, and performance studies). A professor of art history explained: "Research means working at the edge of your own self-defined problem, searching for others [who] have thought about the problem from a million different angles, bridging seemingly unconnected aspects of seemingly unrelated things and then coming up with a brilliant and (provisionally) true result." One of the significant purposes of the university draws together various research methods to pioneer existing or new fields. While traditional research methods continue to be valuable, university scholars must also continuously interrogate methodologies. As a result, research techniques and types can change rapidly, as new discoveries change and shift the core practice of a faculty member. This might include incorporating new technology or producing discoveries that undermine past assumptions. Simply keeping up with pioneering alterations to a field remains a primary faculty responsibility. Communicating such alterations to collaborators can be time-intensive and demanding but may also productively lead to unexpected emergences.

Participants addressed problems in communication in different ways. Some felt their interdisciplinary activities actually facilitated communication rather than hindering it, while others' involvement in collaborative projects allowed them to realize their personal understanding of specific terms did not necessarily apply to all scholars, thus generating transformative insights. The professor of neuroscience who narrowly defined research according to the scientific method found that her collaboration with scholars in dance expanded her understanding: "I came to realize that these artists use the term 'research' to mean project knowledge-seeking or discovery, not to mean the scientific method per se." Participants cited the ability to learn each other's languages as important to successful collaboration.

Some interviewees drew from previous experience to facilitate communication with partners outside of their primary academic disciplines. For example, a professor of theater who also serves as the director of a school of performing arts explained that theater professionals must communicate frequently with scene designers about the math and science of how to make staging work or with psychologists about creating complex characters. This experience taught her how to communicate with research partners who have different perspectives. She emphasized: "From the start, it's always important that we make sure our goals and hopes are clearly articulated. It's an ongoing conversation when working outside of disciplinary boundaries." Similarly, a professor of psychology advised: "Successful collaborations are those in which people immediately ask for clarification. When people just barrel ahead and don't do this anticipatory and clarifying work in the moment, it's setting up a train wreck." Universities pursuing a rigorous arts integration mission might consider developing workshops to increase faculty skills in cross-disciplinary communication. Panel discussions provided for faculty might allow experienced transdisciplinary researchers to share recommendations, case studies, and benefits of embarking on extra-disciplinary collaborations.

Much scholarship explores distinctions between knowledge practices by examining the epistemological foundations within specific disciplines and across disciplines. This scholarship begins with the early Greeks and then moves to Edmund Husserl's *Crisis of European Sciences and Transcendental Phenomenology* (1936), Richard Rorty's *Philosophy and the Mirror of Nature* (1979), and Bruno Latour's *Pandora's Hope: Essays on the Reality of Science*

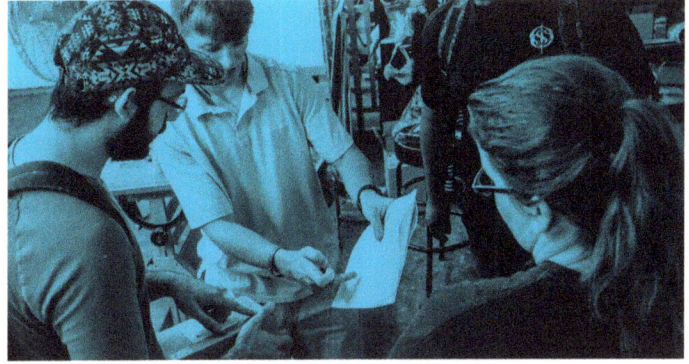

Studies (1999). Today, scholars critically evaluate knowledge vernaculars in terms of potential geographic, religious, political, or gender-based blind spots. Such critical evaluation results from scientific discoveries exploring how the act of observation can alter the object of study. While the absolute aesthetic values have eluded the arts, these 20th-century scientific discoveries actually imply that multiple observational viewpoints will yield richer documentation of particular phenomena within all disciplines.

Collaborators must negotiate various considerations as they work together, all of which require discussion across long-standing expectations and habits of mind. As a professor of quantitative psychology working with computer science and visual arts explained, expectations of which activities qualify as research, what could constitute learning outcomes, how to evaluate products or indicators of success, or determining an appropriate pace for instruction all depend on such epistemological compromise without sacrificing scholarly rigor. In one example, a professor of dance invited a professor of engineering to co-teach a course and potentially collaborate on a research project. The engineering professor expected the professor of dance would have planned all course elements and research goals prior to even the suggestion of collaboration. Her prior experiences of collaborative work within her discipline were, in her words, "plug and play." The norms and practices of dance research dictated another approach, as the professor of dance began at the level of ideation, not implementation. The professor of engineering learned that this misunderstanding had its roots in differing epistemological and disciplinary norms; this realization led to her to adapt how she approaches interdisciplinarity and her own teaching. In this case, rather than becoming a source of strife, the communications challenge served as a productive friction.

Collaborative work benefits from productive frictions. An art historian co-teaching with a neurologist described collaborative, transdisciplinary work as requiring participants to "understand disciplinary assumptions as productive problems." She went on to say, "It's an attitudinal adjustment that needs to occur, and it's also an opportunity to question your own assumptions. One must find the 'best frictions.'"

Finding these best frictions requires willingness to step out of one's comfort zone (area of expertise) to embrace ambiguity. This work requires self-reflective clarity regarding one's intellectual limitations and a willingness to seek more information to interact with these blind spots. Generally, such scholars exhibit traits of humility insofar as they experience a heightened awareness of their own discipline's boundaries, an awareness or curiosity that drives them to seek other sources of knowledge. According to a researcher in interaction design, such work also involves being approachable and allowing others to feel unthreatened when they seek one's expertise. A professor of media arts observed changes in disciplinary attitude experienced by himself and a computer science colleague throughout their long-term collaboration: "It used to be my side vs. your side, but over time it became the arts side and the computer science side, and [now] both sides are our sides. It's a negotiation of making things owned together rather than separately." Perhaps more case studies of how collaborative faculty achieve this "owning together" might assist promotion committees in understanding the singular skills and rigorous research sensitivities required to establish such common goals.

In curricular collaborations, the process of formulating a syllabus, for example, can act as a catalyst for cooperation in the early stages of course planning, becoming the basis for mutual respect and understanding. Faculty constructing these courses confront disciplinary vernaculars and disconnects throughout the courses. Simply standing in front of a captive student audience requires collaborating faculty to have developed their framework for points of overlap and disjunction within a semester. In some sense, faculty would already have developed an epistemological model for their collaboration, and this model would be embedded in the syllabus, readings, and course assignments. Courses involving students in interdisciplinary teams necessitate communication across the disciplinary norms in the context of real projects. The director of a game lab observed, "When

those involved in the collaboration speak regularly about what success will look like, they can map out ideas of how to accomplish this goal." Partners from music and engineering used Google Docs to develop a legend, translating their different term usages, tracking conversations, and demonstrating the increased fluency in their communications. Finding common ground across academic disciplines serves as a key to facilitating communication, while also creating productive frictions. An art historian, and the neurologist with whom she co-taught, saw their role as educators as a shared ground from which to unpack disciplinary vernaculars, frame expectations, negotiate epistemological differences, and create learning objectives. In a partnership between international politics and theater faculty, shared interest in the Frankfurt School and the works of a favorite author allowed participating faculty members to align disciplinary goals.

Shifting attitudes toward disciplinary identity influence most arts-integrative development. Those who identify as post- or anti-disciplinary tend to focus on practice, seeing the most productive scholarship as uncoupled from disciplines. One scholar suggested that higher education should restructure from a discipline-based model to a problem-based model over the next 50 years and that it should organize itself around grand problems, with a department of water, a department of poverty, and so forth. Under this model, disciplinary adherence would transform into a tool wielded in seeking solutions to these persistent challenges.

Within specific disciplines and fields, changing attitudes and methodologies create ebbs and flows of support for collaborative work, particularly in terms of perceptions of quality associated with these partnerships. A political science professor working in a research cluster encompassing film studies, English, economics, and agriculture remarked that his quantitatively focused peers see work in film studies as less rigorous, noting the quantitative turn in social sciences, which dominates his younger colleagues' graduate school training and continues to influence their research attitudes today. Similarly, a dean who established an arts college addressed this challenge by limiting technical and media partnerships – for fear of reduced quality. Insofar as this dean sought to build a world-class conservatory, excellence in the arts took precedence over interdisciplinarity.

Administrators grapple with these questions, as they must determine how arts integration participates in the vision and mission of their institutions. Should a department offer a yearlong artist residency to a distinguished artist at the top of her field – someone who is well respected in the arts community but focused single-mindedly on the aesthetic practice of the one discipline? Or should an artist with a clear history of excellence in partnering with medicine, life sciences, or another field receive this opportunity? Insofar as the word "university" derives from the Latin *universitatem*, the university represents the "whole or aggregate" of knowledges, as they come together within one institution through a community of scholars who must share, disseminate, preserve, and extend such knowledges. A dean of arts and sciences explained:

By concept, a university is the embodiment of diversity of thought present in many disciplines within one functional entity. The unification (uni) of diversity – university. Thus, the strain of diversity and dissent is contained within a single body aimed at furthering discovery and the dissemination of knowledge. The reason universities are so successful and have received support from society over the centuries is that they provide value, a result of the strain and intellectual exchange that occurs between the disciplines composed of divergent views and practices all housed within the university as a single entity. Managing this entity and optimizing the interactions between components while enhancing the opportunity for serendipity whereby seemingly disparate fields and points of view offer new opportunities and perspectives to each other and to the greater society is the challenge that all university participants must embrace. Depth of insight gained by disciplinary focus thus provides opportunity for serendipitous exchange through interdisciplinary exchange. New insights occur at the nexus of existing disciplines, thus spawning change, adjustment, new opportunities, and even the emergence of new disciplines all within the unified diversity of the university.

Within this study, institutions demonstrated a willingness to explore the "aggregate" of disciplines, engage in productive frictions, and better understand how single disciplines and collaborative efforts both contribute to robust intellectual communities.

Disciplinary vernaculars and departmental cultures complicate collaborations but should not prevent them. Participants found their professional experience enriched by collaborative experiences, which yielded productive frictions leading to enhanced understanding not only of their own particular fields of study but of the partnering disciplines. Individuals choosing to move beyond the borders of a given academic discipline become pioneers of collaboration and ambassadors of interdisciplinarity, promoting arts integration among their students and their peers.

STRUCTURAL CONSIDERATIONS

Multiple deans noted that their colleges and universities operate more like federations of semi-autonomous academic entities than as unified wholes, giving rise to both theoretical and pedestrian obstacles. Duplicative programmatic offerings emerge while programs fight for access to and control over space, facilities, and funding. Meanwhile, administrative procedures for launching, reporting on, and sustaining projects can vary from one department or college to the next. Such administrative variation becomes most noticeable when collaborating faculty find themselves mired in variant documentation, creating twice as much work in order to undertake interdisciplinary projects. As a result, faculty members pursuing such projects tend to be highly committed. They have established some leeway or flexibility with administrators who find ways to decrease administrative burdens, or simply ignore bureaucratic details in favor of forging ahead with promising experiments.

In the case of duplicate or overlapping programs, one faculty member noted that the decentralized structure at his university created a situation in which no fewer than eight programs in media arts were offered independently from one another. The university needed to limit the departmental agency to originate programming, allowing the existing media arts work to coalesce across the disciplines.

One participant – the director of an institute for multimedia literacy – reported that his research institute struggles to manage its position within the university structure. Over the last 15 years, this entity has created a well-respected PhD program, BA program, and an undergraduate minor. This successful teaching and research body continues to maintain its identity as a research institute, with no home academic unit. As a result, those who work within it have no access to tenure-track appointments. Further, the institute lacks the administrative support and positioning within the university that being part of an academic unit usually provides. While these conditions challenge all university centers and think tanks, further research could assess whether the arts-integrative institutes experience greater challenges than the typical research center. The nature of these challenges should be identified, and researchers might document savvy responses by directors who are able to sustain and develop their think tanks.

Crucial to universities, financial and administrative structures serve to expedite needs and goals of the university system. No administrative structure is perfect, nor can it serve all the needs of the entire community. Indeed, these structures are often works in progress, fluidly changing and evolving to serve their constituents. As a result, unintended consequences impeding the emergence of new fields and arts-integrative possibilities emerge. Some faculty members noted that they proceed regardless of support, in cases where funding is unavailable or administrative sign-off on a project launch remains unclear. Fully developed ideas ready for implementation generally receive administrative approval more quickly. Two faculty members from the same department referred to this as the "build the cart and then worry about the horse" model. A common practice organizes the collaboration in such a way that a single department under a single administrative body takes oversight of the project, paying for faculty time and handling other procedural considerations. This lends transparency to the process and eliminates a number of potential problems. Faculty members and deans from other institutions reported that their departments have a "let's try it" attitude, where faculty members pilot a course for a semester and then the department makes decisions on whether to offer the course in the future.

Curricular collaborations typically choose to cross-list courses, offering them to students in two departments. In such cases, departments need to determine how teaching faculty earn credit for co-teaching such courses. One professor of studio art co-taught a course in public art with a professor of American studies. Cross-listed in art and American studies, the course was reportedly "hugely popular." The first year, the art professor taught the course as an overload. In the second year, he received a course release from his home department. The art professor had to prove the value of the course before these activities could factor into his official duties. While this is perhaps a natural transition for any experimental activity, programs should more actively consider seeding such explorations, rather than accommodating them after the fact. Some interviewees

noted that pairing two curricular areas within the same college or school tends to be easier to accomplish than bridging organizational structures that exhibit greater diversity. Others observed that co-teaching opportunities remain more accessible for senior faculty who have earned tenure. Paradoxically, junior faculty seem to be most interested in co-teaching, while senior faculty prefer monodisciplinary teaching. To understand cross-generational approaches to pedagogy and arts integration more fully, undertaking specific studies could determine whether the observed trends in the Mellon interviews would apply more broadly. If so, universities optimizing for arts integration might tailor strategies to best serve various groups of faculty.

Teaching loads, regardless of rank or tenure, dictate faculty time and commitments. When two professors share the work, co-taught courses may count as half-credit. In such cases, the faculty member must teach another half-credit course to earn credit for a full teaching load. While such a credit structure seems very logical, co-teaching can often demand more time, including planning meetings unnecessary in individualized teaching models. Some institutions simplify the process for their faculty. A dean of arts and sciences explained:

We have enabled joint teaching. [Faculty members] don't need my permission – they just cross-list their classes. They might have to teach more than one class in order to make sure they are performing a full teaching load, but faculty co-teach all the time. It doesn't require anything special from me. We don't need to buy and sell their time as long as they are doing a full teaching load.

Several departments recognize a co-taught course as equivalent to a full course within a faculty member's teaching load. As a dean of a college of fine arts said, "Sometimes we just say, 'Okay, this is part of your load, and we'll call it good' without worrying about the money side of it." In justification of this practice, one professor of music noted, "It's expensive to have 20 students and 2 faculty, but there are few enough courses like it that it isn't a big deal. Everyone from the top down saw the benefit." Especially when community buy-in supports the project concept, deans and department administrators can often find inventive ways to negotiate the appropriate balance for collaborative faculty, equivalent to the professor's original contracted commitments. As these hybrid teaching models evolve, vacancies emerge in standard curricular offerings. Ideally, department chairs delegate the introductory level courses in the faculty portfolio, courses often taught by graduate students or adjuncts. An adjunct or lecturer could fill such vacancies, but this practice is not without pitfalls. One group of students benefits from instruction by two faculty members, while less experienced instructors, adjuncts, or lecturers instruct another group. The department also experiences an overall cost increase. A professor of political science and director of an East Asian studies center described impediments to his curricular collaborations:

Money is always an issue: who's paying for this? If I try to teach with someone outside the college of social science, it gets complicated. Who pays for my time: theater or cinema? There's a kind of academic extortion that takes place for displacement to hire someone to teach X course. So now we pretty much have to get someone from within the college. There are newer solutions for this now, too. This is a problem with revenue-centered management for the most part.

Several faculty members explained that co-teaching, even in situations where both partners teach in the same department, requires substantially greater effort than teaching individually, let alone across departments or even across colleges or schools. One dean of music remarked that co-teaching requires at least twice as much effort because, if nothing else, one loses the ability to make decisions unilaterally and quickly. Several faculty members and administrators reported feeling disheartened by such challenges. Some had to drop the collaboration during the planning or implementation phases, or if the course did become a reality, they found they had to donate their time beyond their normal teaching loads. The director of a school of performing arts observed that departments with few faculty lines and limited support find their already overburdened faculty members overextending themselves, leading to increased fatigue and unwillingness to reach out to colleagues in other disciplines and colleges.

Conflicting expectations regarding credit hours and contact hours can complicate collaborations in research and curricular development. Requirements for contact hours – the number of hours a student is "in contact" with an instructor – vary between the arts in other learning areas. In general, one contact hour in a lecture-based course equates with one hour of actual time spent in the classroom with students, although this may vary somewhat between institutions. Therefore, a three-hour class might meet for one hour, three times per week, 90 minutes, two times per week, or three

hours, once per week. A semester typically spans 16 weeks, with 15 weeks designated for instruction and one for final exams, bringing the total to 48 hours per course. (This also varies between institutions, which sometimes account for the final exam differently.)

Studio art classes adhere to different methods of calculating time, with studio hours counted at half the rate of classroom lecture hours. Thus, a three-credit-hour studio course might actually meet for six clock hours per week – or 96 hours each semester. Administrators must be meticulous about these policies: if an institution fails to meet contact hour requirements upon audit, it faces scrutiny, endangers accreditation, and possibly warrants corrective measures. Therefore, faculty must understand and adhere to these requirements as they plan for their co-teaching responsibilities.

Individuals seeking to work together from fields counting contact hours in the same way, such as professors from lecture-based disciplines like sociology and psychology, experience few problems with this issue. However, if the method of calculating contact hours differs between potential partners, such as studio art and philosophy, this can significantly influence the proposed course or project.

As a hypothetical illustration, Professor Smith, who teaches photography, and Professor Jones, who teaches anthropology, decide to develop a course in visual anthropology, in which students will create documentary photographs portraying different social groups. Presume each of these professors has a tenure-track appointment and is required to teach two three-hour courses per semester. For Professor Smith, each individual photography class involves six hours per week spent in the studio (12 hours when combined), only a small portion of which might include lecture, with the remainder spent supervising students as they work independently to create photographs. For Professor Jones, on the other hand, each individual anthropology class includes three hours per week spent in the classroom lecturing (or six hours for the two courses when totaled). While Professor Smith and his students must be in the photography classroom for twice as many clock hours as Professor Jones and his students in anthropology, the character of these engagements diverges. Smith's students must generate and critique new works, while Jones's students must critically interpret existing textual knowledge. Students experiencing both disciplines must develop critical

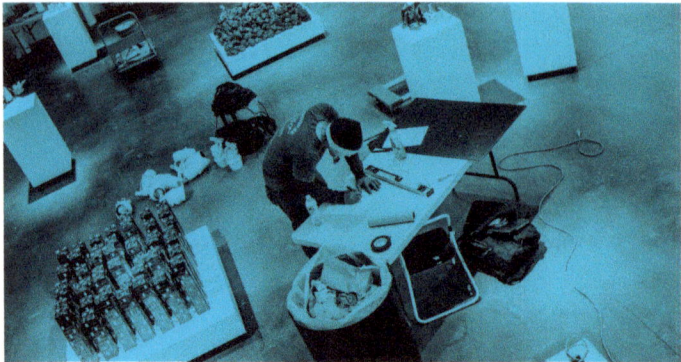

and independent lines of inquiry to succeed; therefore, the process to engage in each of these practices differs. Such courses interest students precisely because faculty embrace potential discord and deviation, perhaps in the hope that such discrepancies have the potential to reveal more to students about each area of study. Further research might examine whether or not collaborative courses provide direct access to understanding the paradigms of a single discipline, precisely because of the comparative practice at work. As such, some arts-integrative courses may actually foster faster progress in knowledge of a single discipline, heightening students' curiosity or engagement and driving them toward the other courses within the department in which they have developed a new interest.

Still, how should collaborative classes be scheduled? Should the departments split the difference between six studio hours and three classroom hours, meeting for four-and-a-half hours? Must both professors be present the entire time? Every pair of proposed partners might answer differently, depending on their administrators' views of the collaboration.

Contact hour requirements can also affect research collaborations. In another hypothetical example, suppose Professor Johnson of the chemistry department approaches Professor Williams of the graphic design department about working on a collaborative research project involving data visualization. Departmental contact hour requirements dictate that Professor Williams has 30% less available time to devote to the collaborative research project because his studio art classes meet for twice as many clock hours per week compared to Professor Johnson's chemistry classes. Unless the two partners agree to limit their time to an equivalent number of hours per week, this may either place Professor Williams at a disadvantage or require him to work overtime, often without

compensation. The project might impose a logistical problem for one partner or the other unless they work in the same location, requiring one person to spend time traveling to the other's lab, studio, or office in order to work together. Both partners would need to document their participation fully in order to receive consideration for promotion and tenure, so achieving an equitable distribution of work helps ensure the partnership will be mutually beneficial and will clearly contribute to their promotion package.

Structural requirements, such as inequitable contact hours and credit hours, might complicate collaborative teaching or research, but creative, determined faculty and administrators find ways and means of working within existing systems, achieving arts-integrative interdisciplinarity that meets university expectations while still achieving their own goals.

FACILITIES AND SPACE

The dominance of disciplinary vernaculars in broad university cultures also shapes funding and access to facilities. In proposals for classes or facilities, for example, administrators in the arts find themselves using the language of the sciences to make their needs intelligible to decision makers in higher levels of administration. One program director referred to theater studios as "labs." While competitive government funds and grants support many labs, studios appear to remain underfunded based on their own merits and needs. Consequently, when the artists and designers characterize their studios as "labs," decision makers sometimes assume external funds should sustain such facilities. However, no single external or national funding stream currently exists to support the construction, operation, and maintenance of higher education arts and design studio facilities. A dean of arts and sciences noted that his institution recently began collecting a lab fee to cover consumables and other needs for studio arts classes. He said, "For years, the sciences received lab fees covered as part of tuition and fees while the arts instructional needs were not considered under these processes. We obtained approvals without problem, but it was a revenue source that related programs were going without for years." While studio spaces can face budgetary challenges, universities do construct and maintain, often with the help of generous private donors, world-class theaters, performance halls, and museums. As artworks themselves, these spaces often provide service beyond the university community to citizens in surrounding towns, cities, and regions.

Arts departments face ongoing challenges regarding access to facilities and regular maintenance of their spaces. A significant "do-it-yourself" attitude exists among interviewees, many of whom remarked on their successes with finding space for their courses or projects, sometimes locating empty or unused rooms or converting storage areas to serve their purposes. Others, however, reported neglected routine maintenance of their teaching facilities even as new facilities for other purposes in the arts were under construction. In one case, no funding was available to repair or replace sagging floors in a school of dance, even though a state-of-the-art-facility for arts performance and for research integrating the arts, engineering, and other fields was in the final stages of construction. During a joint interview, a faculty member said, "The Center for the Arts is great, but we need our bread-and-butter spaces and facilities updated." A colleague added, "The bells and whistles [e.g., the Center for the Arts] are easier to fund via the state legislature than the more pedestrian but more needed spaces and facilities." Competition for limited resources can create resentments such as those expressed by these faculty members. When one's primary discipline seems to take second place to a new initiative, faculty naturally become defensive. Administrators must bear this in mind, ensuring that faculty understand the rationale behind budget items. For example, designated gifts or endowments prohibit monies from being diverted to even the most urgent, but routine, purposes, yet these philanthropic sources may fund impressive new facilities for arts-integrative interdisciplinarity. Sustaining faculty support for arts integration entails continuing administrative attention to meeting disciplinary needs.

As a limited resource, space remains in high demand, especially for purposes outside of everyday teaching. A professor of dance said, "There's not much space to meet other students.... All schools are in different colleges, so physically they're not in the same place." She wished they had "a community where it's okay to talk to each other and where we don't have to give something up to meet each other." Other participants cited the need for not only physical space for their collaborations to take place but also figurative space, that is, structures and systems allowing for their work in arts integration to grow and develop. Still others, such as a poet and director of an international creative writing program, yearned for "time and space to dream. You need to be able to do nothing, staring out the window and making oneself available." As an overall issue for

universities in general, concerns about lack of physical or figurative space may not apply only to arts-integrative efforts, but since arts integration most often occurs in addition to, or outside of, other routine facilities usage, lack of space presents particular problems.

Space creates problems for administrators, too. A vice provost explained:

Space is a prized commodity here. In pockets, yes, [the departments] are willing to provide space, but there is a larger culture that may not understand the value of these types of things. At the top – provost level, senior leadership – we get it. But it gets diluted as it trickles down to dean and faculty level. Faculty are a privileged group here, and we are the checks and balances to each other – no other group can challenge them – so things can get testy when people have nothing to lose. So we can draw lines in the sand on issues that are "less significant" or not as relevant. So we have a long way to go to where we [arts] get the same support as the sciences.

Ideally, faculty and administrators would work together to ensure equitable use of physical resources, including allocation of spaces for both routine and extraordinary purposes. Realistically, multiple factors affect such decisions, not all of which are under the administrators' control. University policy, overall budgets, scheduling, and human factors each play a role in most activities. And as with most situations, open-mindedness, effective leadership, and a willingness to work together can overcome the most challenging conditions.

Because availability of space for groups to meet engenders perennial concern on university campuses, co-curricular organizations unsurprisingly face challenges when seeking facilities to use. According to a program director:

The top resource that is in the shortest supply – and this is true of many places – is our facilities: rehearsal spaces, strong dance floors, practice spaces, art-making spaces – these are in very, very short supply, especially as it relates to co-curricular engagement. We have a number of theaters, a number of performance spaces, a number of classrooms, and various things, but it is not enough, and so also because there's not enough of it and because it has to support itself, they are expensive to use. You have students rehearsing in hallways and ... various places.... Space is a real issue on campus, for its scarcity and its expense.

High demand for these spaces creates several challenges for student groups. For instance, a student-led music ensemble wishing to hold a holiday concert in December might find the theater it planned to use booked two years in advance. Or the group may find the venue available but the fees too high to be offset by the number of tickets they expect to sell, due to university requirements for technical, custodial, and security staff to be on the premises when using the building. For new student groups, internal cultures and organizational structures increase the difficulty of securing venues. According to a program director:

> *It's kind of like vacation homes on some level – once you're in, you've got the opportunity to schedule that [a] year or two in advance, but if you haven't had that year or two, [it's not possible to choose the] date that you're only imagining in the future. There are some spaces that have [to be booked] two years ahead and also have a very prohibitive cancellation cost.... There are also these internal student organization hierarchies that exist.... It is hard to have the resources that you need.*

Every activity or purpose occurring on university campuses requires space, arts-integrative work no less than other areas. The more creativity and divergent thinking brought to the task of finding appropriate areas in which to work, the greater a project, course, or organization's chances to achieve a successful solution to this problem. A few potential means of addressing a recurrent problem include partnerships with nonprofit organizations, development of storefront spaces, pop-up events or galleries in off-campus properties or apartments, negotiated arrangements with community organizations, or the trading of labor for time using a space.

RECOGNITION AND RELATIONSHIPS

A university is more than a physical location. More than buildings or real estate, a university comprises all the students, staff, faculty members, and administrators who work and study there. Just like all human beings, university employees from the president to the groundskeeping staff crave recognition and valuation of their efforts. Some of this recognition takes place through formal channels such as promotion or tenure, some through awards or publicity, some through student or employee evaluations, and some though simple comments by a supervisor or administrator. Knowing one's efforts and hard work earned recognition, especially if someone took the time to express a positive message, can make a tremendous difference in employee motivation. Absence of this recognition leads to discouragement,

with incidents reported by several interviewees. Productive, positive relationships between faculty and administrators foster high-quality arts integration, but absence of such connections becomes an impediment.

Administrators certainly have many individuals in their charge and much to do in the course of their duties, but even inadvertently overlooking someone's achievements can negatively affect those on the receiving end of this oversight. Something as simple as attending a performance can mean a great deal to the organizing faculty member, while an administrator's absence seems conspicuous or even hurtful. The director of a center for the humanities, for example, expressed dissatisfaction with his provost, who had not attended any of the center's events, even though the president of the university had been present. His university also recently cut his program's funding, and when absence of recognition by the provost combined with the budgetary shortfall, he felt very discouraged.

For some interviewees, recognition seemed insincere. A staff member in a museum reported that her administration was "very interested." She continued, "They like a lot of aspects of what we do. They like the interdisciplinarity. It's very photogenic, what we do. But I do feel that we get trotted out as show-and-tell, but it doesn't really come back." She concluded, "Basically, everything we've brought in is through grants" rather than through funding from the department or the university. Verbal recognition without substantiation through reward, such as material resources or funding, seems hollow.

Administrative mobility contributes to difficulty with leadership structures in higher education. Deans, for example, tend to serve for limited terms before moving up to higher administrative positions or on to new institutions. Even looking at the original members of the Michigan Meetings that preceded ArtsEngine,[29] we can see movement among those administrators from their former institutions to their current places of employment. This can be beneficial in allowing visionary, creative leaders to share their knowledge and abilities with new faculties, but it can also create challenges for a faculty learning to adjust to new leadership. When asked about her university's support of her project, a director of a digital media center replied, "I'm so demoralized. There have been four deans since I've been here." She described the excellent leadership of one of these deans, who invited faculty to write white papers and develop faculty seminars about their ongoing work; this interviewee described this as "a wonderful, rich experience." She conducted a thorough analysis of her work for this project, showing

---

29   As detailed in chapter 1, a group of administrators and faculty interested in arts integration participated in two Michigan Meetings in 2011 and 2012, from which grew ArtsEngine, the Mellon Research Project, and a2ru.

similar activity at peer institutions, analyzing where her institution could better serve students, and formulating three future plans. The dean sent the study to the vice provost, the dean for student affairs, the head of the school of engineering, and others. However, after weeks of silence, the vice provost finally responded to a request for a meeting, at which she rejected two of the three plans, merely allowing this director to keep doing what she was doing with no growth. She said, "It gave me a bitter taste in my mouth," noting that she was not invited to participate with the school of arts and sciences as she'd been hoping. Changes in leadership have been problematic for her. "If there was someone whose job it was to gather a group together regularly, if all the people on your list got together yearly, I think it would be a huge improvement. But that's what we were doing five years ago. We're really not doing it now." Any initiative depends on consistent, positive leadership in order to succeed. High rates of administrative turnover can disrupt flow and momentum, introducing changed expectations. Such change can infuse an organization with new energy, but it can also dampen participants' enthusiasm or shut down otherwise promising programs.

Other interviewees reported feeling discouraged about the place of the arts within the university and an absence of administrative efforts to change this situation. If the larger university community fails to recognize the intrinsic value of the arts, inclusion of the arts in interdisciplinary efforts comes into question as well. The director of a dance department said she experienced "discouragement about the arts." She continued, "It's a constant fight and struggle for validation. . . . It's a paradigm that needs to be transformed. How much work on the ground can you do? You have to get it from above, not just on the ground. That's one of the reasons I've been disappointed because when I came here I was . . . working really hard to make a change and hit a limit, and that was it." A professor of dance at a different university echoed these views:

Too often dance can bring a lot to the process, but I get put off when art is seen as purely a means to teach something else – it becomes the ugly stepsister to the process. Art needs to be valued for what it can do, not how it can serve someone else, coming to a mutual respect before the work can be done. . . . That's one of the challenges within arts integration on campus. Arts are seen as frivolous or not real research or not having a place. I don't agree with that – the growing focus on STEM instead of STEAM.

Interviewees reported the damaging effects of attitudes trivializing the arts. The director of a center for the humanities said, "The idea of the arts as being a wonderful end in themselves without any applied necessity is disappearing." At this university, faculty noted a growing emphasis on active citizenship, with funds available for projects tied to applied sciences, improving the world, or benefiting society, but such goals seem to overlook "the idea that the entire improvement of the world has been based around the arts and culture. . . . The idea that Shakespeare made us [who we are] or dance can transform you as much as community service is being slowly retired." In this faculty member's opinion, the provost supports this changing emphasis and cuts programs in favor of cluster hires. This practice has notably embittered this interviewee's views. He said, "[These are] mostly just initiatives these administrators take to make it seem like they did something so they can be president somewhere else. They're all moving up and on."

Fortunately, not all interviewees exhibit this degree of cynicism, but leadership undeniably influences faculty perceptions of the challenges they face. A director of a digital media and learning center expressed this idea with great brevity. When asked what difficulties she had encountered, she responded, "Lack of leadership. High turnover rate. It's a large challenge." Like funding, leadership and turnover rates among administrators present areas for improvement across all of higher education and are not limited to arts-integrative efforts. However, newer initiatives, as is the case with those involving arts integration, tend to be less resilient than deeply rooted academic programs and more susceptible to problems caused by lack of administrative continuity. Interviewees by no means expressed universally negative reviews of their administrators; indeed, a majority of administrators involved in this study demonstrate exemplary leadership and are among the most influential individuals shaping arts integration efforts across the U.S.. However, individuals finding themselves in situations with inconsistent leadership unsurprisingly reported these experiences as troublesome.

The regard of one's peers or colleagues provides another source of either affirmation or conflict. A professor of theater expressed surprise about colleagues' reaction to her arts-integrative work:

In terms of faculty, I was expecting wide support from the project. But I'm encountering a surprising amount of resistance. One issue may be they don't understand my presentation well enough. Another problem is that art research is talked about being primary but is in practice viewed as a third part of the job. In most instances it's research, teaching, service, but here it's teaching, service, research.

Similarly, a professor of dance said, "Lack of respect comes from lack of understanding – I see this more as faculty to faculty. But some administrators who value the arts don't understand what it really means and to what extent, or the role it can play into the larger picture of life at university." Lack of understanding about the value the arts can bring to a campus or, conversely, the benefits interdisciplinary collaborations can provide *to* the arts, engenders a climate where arts integration may fail to thrive. Taking steps to inform the academic community about colleagues' work in arts integration may help, as could leveraging administrative support in order to nurture an environment that minimizes misunderstanding and promotes the benefit of collaboration.

Awards, grants, or other honorifics can help to provide motivation for faculty to engage in arts integration or to reward their efforts. As is often the case, however, interviewees seldom mentioned their achievements in this area: outside of one's CV or an application for employment, people tend to be rather modest when speaking of themselves, and the interview script neglected to ask specifically about awards or honors. Conversely, a professor of visual art foundations described his former service on a committee that awarded $5,000 grants for interdisciplinary research to faculty in the college of visual and performing arts. He said it was "surprisingly not used very much. We had a hard time giving away the money beyond the people on the committee. The program disappeared due to lack of interest. Interdisciplinary work is incentivized only by individuals now." This statement speaks to a need for broader efforts to promote arts integration among faculty; such efforts might not only minimize misunderstandings (as discussed in the previous paragraph) but could also foster greater interest in arts integration and improve collegiality.

A staff member who had worked tremendously hard on a research project, regularly logging 80-hour workweeks, spoke of being nominated for an annual departmental award given to outstanding staff. She expressed disappointment upon hearing that another staff member had won the award reportedly because she regularly brought treats for her colleagues and always had a friendly smile. Award nominees might not be privy to details regarding why someone actually receives an award, so rumor and resentment may well color this interviewee's perception. Nevertheless, this anecdote demonstrates the dark side of awards, which may bolster those who receive them but also create disappointment or resentment in those passed over. Again, such situations are not limited to arts integration, but when establishing an award program in the hopes of fostering arts integration, one must be careful to consider other unintended consequences as well.

Meaningful recognition takes diverse forms, just as individuals hope for different sorts of accolades or honors. To facilitate the process, an executive director recently suggested faculty should take a more proactive stance in bringing their efforts to their administrators' attention, especially by utilizing social media to publicize their arts-integrative work to their university communities. After all, individuals or organizations responsible for bestowing recognition, whether through formal awards or informal commendations, must first become aware of faculty efforts before those faculty can achieve eligibility for recognition. A certain degree of self-promotion facilitates this process, educating peers and academic community members about arts-integrative work and increasing awareness, possibly leading to greater recognition. Regarding buy-in by departmental colleagues, an associate dean for research suggested that increasing incentives in order to encourage participation becomes all the more important when a culture shift might be required.

CONCLUSIONS

Interview participants seldom described experiences with arts integration as trouble-free; virtually all had experienced challenges in some form or other. Matters of promotion and tenure, funding and status, communication across disciplinary boundaries, and considerations of institutional structures including physical space can either facilitate arts-integrative efforts or complicate them. Focusing on challenges may seem to have revealed a high degree of negativity among interview participants, but identifying these problems serves as a first step to addressing them. Some concerns, such as promotion and tenure, funding, lack of physical space, and difficulties with leadership or administrators, pervade higher education. Those engaging in arts integration presumably encounter such challenges with the same frequency as their monodisciplinary colleagues, but just because a situation may be common or typical does not mean it is inconsequential. We might see other concerns, such as communication across disciplinary vernaculars, as indigenous to interdisciplinarity. Interview participants across the institutions studied met each of these challenges differently, finding creative solutions serving as exemplars of best practice.

FINDINGS

- *Promotion and tenure emerged as primary concerns across faculty and administrative participants, who reported difficulties in obtaining or conferring consideration for aspects of teaching or research occurring outside of disciplinary norms.*

- *Considerations surrounding funding and associated perceptions of status pervade higher education. Participants reported beneficial partnerships between the arts and disciplines with greater access to financial resources, but they also spoke of difficulties encountered in perceived inequities with regard to resources or differentials in esteem between disciplinary areas.*

- *Communication between individuals in diverse learning areas can be complicated by disciplinary vernaculars or differing departmental cultures. However, such discrepancies can serve as productive frictions, enhancing participants' understanding of one another's perspectives and strengthening their partnerships.*

- *University structures may serve to complicate collaborations. Requirements for credit hours and contact hours, differing departmental policies or procedures, teaching loads, instructor displacement, or scheduling practices can affect efforts to co-teach across disciplinary areas or to engage in collaborative research.*

- *Like funding, facilities and space remain a problem at virtually every institution, not just those participating in the Mellon Research Project. Nevertheless, arts integration efforts may be particularly vulnerable to shortages in this regard because they exist in addition to standard programing rather than replacing it, which creates added burdens on available classroom, laboratory, or collaborative spaces. Furthermore, interdisciplinary collaborations with the arts may not fit comfortably within either of the partnering disciplines, presenting needs for space or facilities unavailable in a given curricular area.*

- *Recognition of one's professional efforts and positive relationships with one's peers and supervisors provide motivation for individuals to engage in innovative, forward-thinking activities such as arts integration. However, absence of recognition, insufficient administrative support, or collegial difficulties can create obstacles to arts integration.*

- *Identifying problems common to arts integration allows for formulation of workable solutions, increasing the likelihood of success in collaborative curricular or research efforts involving the arts and design.*

CHAPTER FIVE

BEST PRACTICES

The vision of arts integration manifests differently
at each of the institutions participating in the Mellon
Research Project, providing a broad spectrum
of successful strategies for implementation and
solutions for addressing challenges experienced
by interview participants. This chapter addresses
these strategies by highlighting institutions with
exemplary policies, practices, or programs in
curricular, research, programmatic, and co-curricular
categories. This selection of examples should not be

understood as an objective ranking; rather, they serve
as a representative selection of excellent instances as
observed throughout the data-gathering process.

CURRICULAR BEST PRACTICES

Models for best practices in curricular development
and implementation demonstrate a great degree
of variation between instances, taking approaches
spanning the continuum of fusion, infusion, and
diffusion. As noted in chapter 1, this study employs

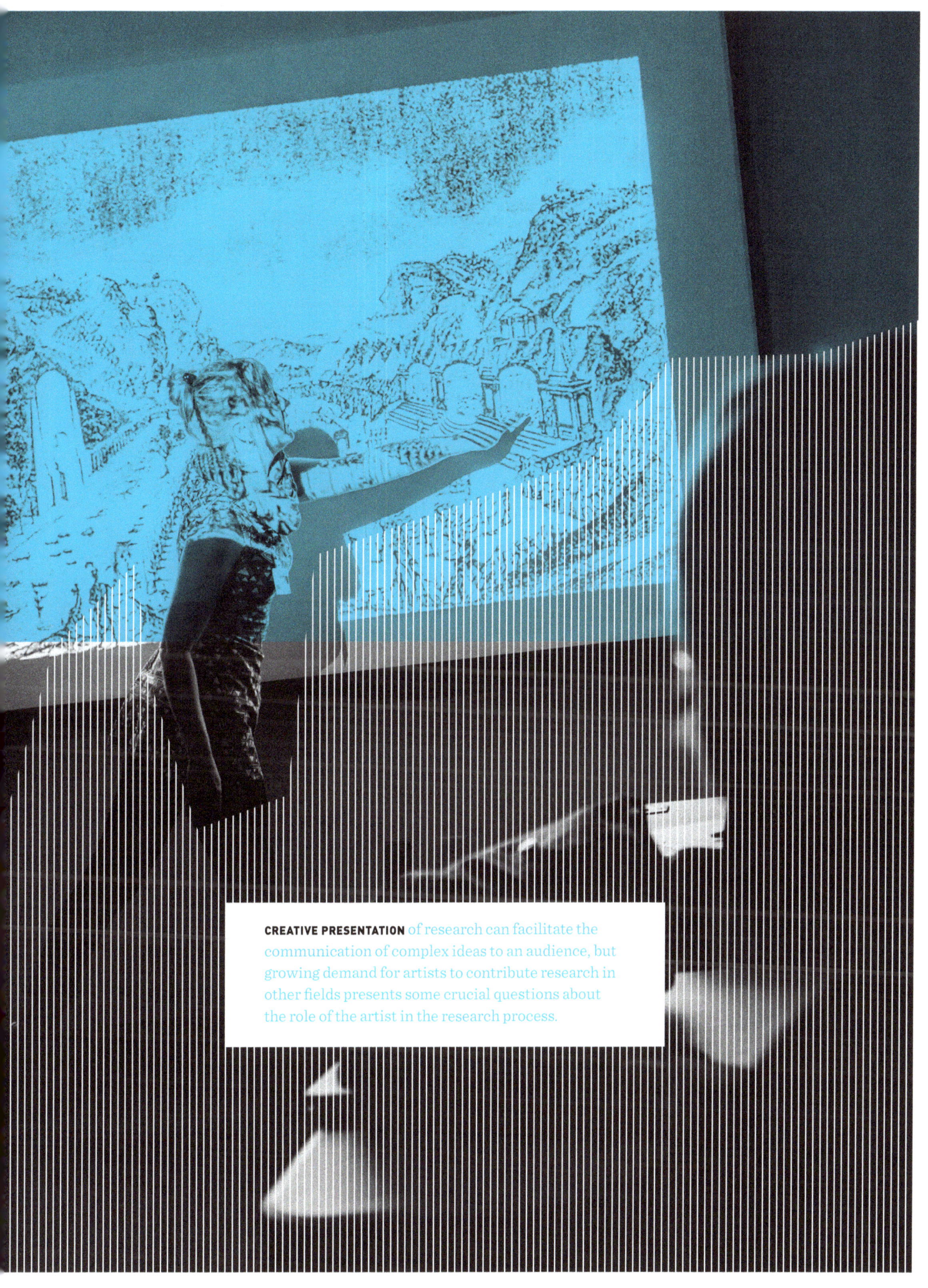

CREATIVE PRESENTATION of research can facilitate the communication of complex ideas to an audience, but growing demand for artists to contribute research in other fields presents some crucial questions about the role of the artist in the research process.

the term "interdisciplinary" to convey the idea of any partnership between one or more of the arts with one or more other academic areas. Such groupings may actually be transdisciplinary, cross-disciplinary, or anti-disciplinary rather than strictly interdisciplinary, and may involve varying manifestations of fusion, infusion, or diffusion in their approach to the combination of disciplinary perspectives. However, simply for the sake of textual brevity, the single designation of interdisciplinary must suffice. Moreover, arts integration is intrinsically interdisciplinary because it combines one or more areas of the arts with one or more partnering disciplines. Curricular arts integration occurred in varying forms at each of the institutions visited. The following examples provide an overview of the types of best practices observed.

First, the **Institute for Visual Studies** (IVS) at James Madison University (**JMU**) serves as an exemplar of best practice in the fusion approach to curricular integration; it fosters collaborations between two disciplines to create balanced, equitable, and synergistic partnerships made possible through visionary academic leadership. A high-ranking administrator emphasized his belief in the importance of the arts in higher education as one of the things bringing him to this university: "When I came to JMU, I was very impressed with the fact that the arts were treated very much as an equal partner and integrated with the rest of the university. We don't just put the arts off in a corner but work closely with other disciplines here." He explained that the university has a centralized budgeting system, unlike larger research universities where colleges and schools remain autonomous. He said, "We are a comprehensive university. . . . We try to act as one entity. Not a small liberal arts college, but we have a lot of characteristics that they do with how the disciplines interact." Facilitating interactions fosters an environment conducive to collaboration, as does promoting the view of the arts as equal partners, both of which support fusion approaches to interdisciplinary curriculum development.

IVS features scholarly, scientific, and creative inquiry into the nature of images, promoting discovery through the generation of artworks and products by multidisciplinary teams of students and faculty. IVS builds on the increasing prevalence of pictorial communication in society, from video gaming to online newspapers, addressing the need for data visualization, artistic appropriation of visual culture, and studies of visual rhetoric in politics. IVS seeks to help students learn how to be visually literate, drawing upon JMU's demonstrated leadership in imaging technologies through the Madison Digital Image Database and the Immersive Visualization System – a wall of 75 television monitors. IVS has become a centerpiece for the College of Visual and Performing Arts, helping to establish a multidisciplinary learning community and to explore connections between art, science, and technology, and thus providing an intensive, collaborative learning environment for students.

Professors who seek to establish a curricular partnership receive funding for their course development through IVS, allowing them to design syllabi, lessons, lectures, projects, and other necessary components. IVS buys the time of the professors in their home departments, providing monies for hiring adjunct faculty to cover the professors' regular teaching loads, compensating departments for what would otherwise be costly displacements. In return, the professors' home curricular units count the teaching of the collaborative courses towards the professors' credit loads.

Known as "Studio Seminars," these courses usually appear on a one-time basis, although some reoccur due to their popularity; one example is the "Math and Art: Beautiful Rigor" course, cross-listed as Art 492/Math 467 (Diop and Brown). The course syllabus describes the similarities between mathematics and art, stating that students will explore "four major themes that are common to art and mathematics: self-reference, closure, measurement, and completeness" by means of art media such as "digital imaging, relief printing, fabric transfers, crochet, video, and other processes." IVS Studio Seminars such as this "create conditions for innovation and . . . forge a committed learning community in which students and faculty from different disciplines work closely together on significant projects" (*Institute for Visual Studies*, "Courses"). An instructor of one of these seminars, "Writing and Illustrating Literature," said, "In the 12 years that I have been teaching at JMU, my IVS class was the most rewarding and inspiring classroom experience by far. The support of the IVS staff, combined with the enthusiasm and drive of the students and my partner instructor, made this the highlight of my career in higher ed" (qtd. in Edwards 26).

IVS's director explained that these courses "not only teach students to be critical consumers of visual culture but [also] help students build collaborative skills and critical thinking. The IVS studio seminars have changed the way people on campus think about what a course can be" (qtd. in Edwards 27). When interviewed for the Mellon Research Project, he described IVS as being rich in space, with a gallery, learning areas, and a workroom as well as other physical resources like a 3-D printer and large-format printers. IVS enjoys the goodwill of the campus community and an enviable level of autonomy, remaining free to collaborate with other colleges or departments because, as the director observed, the IVS staff "are savvy about aligning with initiatives that match what we do."

As a relatively new institute, IVS nevertheless grew to significance quickly within an institution placing increased emphasis on the arts; this emphasis begins with the president of JMU and extends through its faculty. IVS provides a stable structure within which faculty members from two disciplines can come together in a supportive environment, offers funding, facilities, and technological resources, and also addresses issues such as displacement and credit load. Although IVS operates on a comparatively small scale, open only to those courses incorporating visual imagery in some way, this model might be helpful to institutions interested in developing similar structures. JMU is a relatively small state university with limited resources, so this model exemplifies possibilities for groundbreaking arts integration fueled by administrative vision and creative problem solving.

Taking a different approach to fusion course development than JMU, **Ohio State University's College of Arts and Sciences** provides funding to sponsor collaboration between any two disciplines. These funds purchase time for two professors to develop a course and provide additional resources to support the course, including equipment, student travel, or other needs (Manderscheid). Ohio State University's commitment to interdisciplinary teaching is not limited to arts integration. Faculty may apply for $60,000 grants from the Battelle Engineering, Technology, and Human Affairs Endowment; these grants link science and technology with cultural and social issues and place primary emphasis on education or public service rather than pure research (Office). A professor of art said faculty in his department have received this funding almost every year, working with diverse departments such as agriculture or astronomy.

As an equal partnership, fusion represents best practice among the approaches to arts integration, avoiding placement of one discipline in the service of another. Infusion courses, on the other hand, utilize one discipline to support teaching in another learning area. Sometimes infusion of the arts occurs periodically throughout a course; other times it may occupy a single class period or arts experience. For instance, an MIT physics professor invited dancers to demonstrate how atoms and molecules move, and a professor of business at the University of Chicago invited the theater department to perform a one-act play to illustrate an economic principle. Such pairings might occur within the arts as well. A professor of sculpture could invite an engineer to explain the tensile strength of metals, or a ceramics professor may ask a geologist to speak about the properties of clay. In these instances of infusion, one discipline serves to enhance student learning in another field, but the instructional emphasis remains focused on the primary discipline.

Infusion takes a more informal approach than fusion because these pairings do not typically span the entire length of a course, sometimes occurring as an illustration or one-time experience for students rather than a truly integrated course. Students watching a play in a business course gain an enhanced understanding of the business principle the instructor wishes to convey rather than receiving instructional content in theater. Interested faculty usually operate on a case-by-case basis within known structures, seeking resources or approvals as needed. Therefore, best practices for infusion remain somewhat elusive.

Diffusion models engage students directly in arts practice, often through arts courses required for graduation. One professor within a single department usually teaches a diffusion course, introducing non-majors to academic content outside their major disciplines. Stanford University recently revised its undergraduate general education requirements to include "**Ways of Thinking/Ways of Doing**" courses. Students take two courses in Aesthetic and Interpretive Inquiry and at least one course in Creative Expression, thus incorporating the arts into the student's overall academic experience. Students have myriad options for fulfilling these requirements, which feature a wide range of courses in music, theater, dance, and visual art, among others. At **Texas Tech University** (TTU), students majoring in elementary or early childhood education can take courses in music and visual art designed to teach methods of making that teachers can utilize in their eventual classrooms. Students explore the basics of these artistic practices, discuss theories of their implementation, and develop their own creative and expressive potential in the hopes that they can bring these experiences to bear in their work as teachers of young children. Although this might sound similar to teacher education requirements elsewhere, these TTU courses immerse students in hands-on studio art experiences and in music performance, grounding theoretical explorations in the arts in personally transformative arts engagement.

Any course in which students from majors outside of the arts engage in creative practice or performance within the arts might qualify as diffusion, and fortunately, universities' general education requirements typically include such curricular experiences. Ideally, best practice in curricular arts integration presents students with multiple options, as with the Stanford University model, and provides opportunities to link such coursework to students' majors directly and overtly, as with the art and music courses for education majors at TTU. Students in any major field and at every level from undergraduate to doctoral study experience the benefits of hands-on participation in making, doing, creating, and performing, just as faculty members from across the university find that their personal participation in arts practice enhances their work in their major academic disciplines.

Student and faculty interviewees both stated a preference for classroom experiences featuring team-based interdisciplinary problem solving, a common component of arts-integrative courses; these interviewees expressed a belief in the value of such experiences to developing personal creativity. For example, when asked whether collaborative learning environments are more creative than those in which students work independently, a professor in education replied: "Absolutely, and they result in more creative outcomes. The world does not have jobs where individuals go into a room and be creative by themselves. The market doesn't work that way. We'd be doing a disservice if we only teach students to be creative by themselves." Similarly, a professor in engineering described his view:

It's important that we can convey [collaborative work practice] to our students; they are the ones that will carry it forward. They are the multiplier. That's why I build large teams and companies that can carry it forward. The most value is in conveying that approach, sharing and working together, understanding that it

takes a team. The era of the lone genius in the lab who solves the world problems is still there, but it becomes smaller. Most of it is something where you learn from other areas.

Another professor of engineering commented on the relation between art and engineering and the value of interdisciplinary teamwork:

[Art is] not just aesthetics; that's not why I seek it. There's value in the artistic space and thinking in its own right. If you get a bunch of mechanical engineers in the room, they converge on the same thing and nothing new happens. Successful design firms don't follow that model. Why should we do that here? I admit that 80% of my students will go off and only ever work with engineers. They'll bring value to a product and make really good widgets, but there's inherent value in talking to others outside of that realm. It simply seems like the right thing to do.

However, even climates trending toward collaboration continue to value and celebrate individual accomplishment. The system of K-12 public education emphasizes individual achievement, as does most of higher education, including traditional practices for faculty promotion and tenure. Participants in collaborative ventures must possess something of value to bring to the table, and in the case of students, this necessitates their acquisition of bodies of knowledge and skill, habits of mind, and expertise within particular academic disciplines. Students recognize the necessity of skill development and the continuing importance of individual accomplishment. Indeed, a student working on the Mellon Research Project annotated the engineering professor's quote above with the comment, "I disagree – some of the biggest breakthroughs in history were solitary. This is more a fad than truth."

Best practice suggests striking an advantageous, dynamic balance between these two poles of collaboration and individual accomplishment. If the pendulum swings too far in the direction of team-based learning, we risk losing the creativity arising from the deep concentration of solitary work. If the trend skews toward individual accomplishment, we may lose the benefits of team-based creativity. A dean in engineering said:

I think the students are better off to have a well-recognized discipline and have a broad education. It's not in their interest to graduate in some very narrow specialty because in the course of their career things could change a lot. And they will always be better off with a recogniz-

able degree. But we also need to continue to foster the evolution of knowledge into new areas.

Curricular programs featuring arts integration, regardless of the depth of the collaboration or combination of disciplines, add breadth to students' educational experience. They engage students in knowledge areas other than their major fields of study and add value to their overall academic experiences.

ADMINISTRATIVE CONSIDERATIONS

Arts integration naturally represents only one aspect of administrators' interests or duties, even for those whose primary responsibility is for an arts-integrated program or organization. Administrators participating in this study demonstrated exemplary leadership, allowing arts integration to thrive under their guidance by communicating a contagious vision, offering meaningful recognition, and empowering their faculty and staff. Issues of promotion and tenure remain a central concern for interview participants across the sites visited, and they are addressed here through the presentation of exemplary administrative practices.

LEADERSHIP

Across the 46 participating institutions, a given program's success depends on one or more key individuals who are able to maintain the contagious vision, wise decision making, and dual focus on "big-picture" issues and practical day-to-day concerns necessary to realizing faculty efforts. The Mellon Research Project prohibits mention of individuals by name, disallowing specific discussion of these exemplary leaders. However, best practices in academic leadership share common characteristics identifiable in those who guide flourishing academic enterprises. The following discussion presents a compilation of observations of the extraordinary individuals leading their organizations to new heights.

First among these characteristics, exemplary leaders possess the ability to communicate a contagious vision for excellence in arts integration. They provide a structure in which transformation or adaptation can occur by building and maintaining support systems that embolden the members of the organization to reach higher and go farther than before. A dean explained:

You want to foster the success of everyone in the organization. People tend to look to deans for vision, and though I have that, I am only one person. The best I can do is to be open to ideas that surprise me, and I

have some ability to put my limited resources behind initiatives. Deans think very hard about ideas that come before [them] and try to use resources to the greatest impact.... We have to encourage people to take risks and push out on the boundaries and praise them when they do well, make it known that such work is exciting and worthwhile. I can help foster and drive ideas.

As this dean indicated, a leader must also possess the ability to provide meaningful recognition to employees, maintaining their level of satisfaction in the workplace. Absence of positive acknowledgment undermines faculty and staff morale, whereas receiving positive administrative attention is empowering. Furthermore, the excellent leaders observed through the interviews place their employees in the forefront, facilitating professional growth while refraining from taking credit for the accomplishments of others. This inspires faculty and staff to engage more deeply in working towards the organization's success. A university president commented on this:

This leadership role is not just mine: it's a role that I share with other administrators and with the faculty. Many of the best ideas of a university aren't coming from the top. It is our job to identify them and escalate them and, where they can be made broad, to spread them across the university. Much of my leadership is actually creating an organization where that can happen.

Next, excellent leaders demonstrate the ability to apply improvisation, working within existing systems and with available personnel in order to address challenges through whatever approach best suits a given situation. Speaking on the idea of sustaining innovation within an organization, a professor of business said that excellent leaders possess an understanding of the "importance of allowing nondestructive messiness," which, he said, "is not rewarded in companies and classrooms." Knowing how to motivate employees, being able to step back and allow faculty to innovate, and creating a workplace environment in which employees feel empowered and secure create conditions conducive to arts integration.

The outstanding leaders discovered through the Mellon Research Project embody these characteristics, demonstrating foresight, creativity, and intelligence. They maintain awareness of the present state of their organizations while also keeping a clear vision for the future, looking both to today's demands and tomorrow's agenda and envisioning where they expect their organizations to be ten years down the road. They support and empower employees, demonstrating an attitude of respectful concern for individuals' personal well-being and professional interest in their work. The most remarkable organizations participating in the Mellon Research Project trace their success to outstanding leaders who provide high-quality direction for their programs, initiatives, centers, institutes, departments, colleges, schools, or entire universities. Researchers could pursue a great deal more study regarding leadership of academic arts organizations or arts integration efforts. For instance, artists who ascend to administrative roles may find it difficult to continue their arts practice, which places them at a disadvantage should they choose to return to arts practice in the future. The relationship of one's arts practice to one's leadership style might also provide an interesting avenue of study, as could further investigation of the creative measures arts leaders must employ to meet challenges inherent to academic units perceived as having lesser status and facing greater scarcity of funding and resources as compared to flagship programs in research universities. These topics, and more, would provide researchers with plentiful opportunities for additional study.

PROMOTION AND TENURE

As discussed in chapter 3, matters of promotion and tenure are of great significance to arts integration efforts, determining whether a faculty member's work will merit these crucial considerations. Some participants reported that their institutions were in the midst of reexamination of promotion and tenure policies in order to ensure that arts-integrative, interdisciplinary, or collaborative work will count toward an individual's pursuit of career advancement. In the next stage of this research, documents will be collected to compare and contrast existing policies and assess how they may have evaluated interdisciplinary projects within their purview.

Iowa State University proved the most outstanding exemplar of best practice in promotion and tenure policies. The university president and provost established an institution-wide understanding regarding faculty involvement in activities diverging from disciplinary norms. The actual language of the university's promotion and tenure policy remains unchanged, but the president and provost authored a document outlining the philosophy guiding promotion and tenure activities across the university. Evaluators consider activities and research in which expanded scholarship (between one or more fields) provides

quantitative and qualitative arguments in support of the faculty member's achievements. Hiring practices reflect this inclusive emphasis, with new faculty hires representing both monodisciplinary and multidisciplinary specializations. The provost's office holds classes to instruct new faculty in the expectations of their unique academic positions. This approach is effective, systemic, and achievable, requiring no extraordinary resources or changes.

Iowa State was the only participating university to implement a university-wide solution to one of the most troublesome impediments to arts-integrative and interdisciplinary faculty activity. Iowa State's approach ensures that the committee members and administrators engaged in evaluation for promotion and tenure will operate under this shared understanding, promoting consistency and fairness through wise application of administrative mandate in order to support nontraditional activities that allow arts integration to thrive. Based on Mellon interviews and data reviewed in this study, this represents a best practice for promotion and tenure due to its top-down, systemwide approach. Other universities take a similar approach by liberally interpreting policy on a case-by-case basis, achieving varying levels of success. Most institutions continue to wrestle with this problem, seeking appropriate policy language in order to achieve consistency between departments, colleges, and schools.

CENTERS AND INSTITUTES

Universities often establish centers or institutes that provide facilities, personnel, and resources necessary to foster the growth of knowledge and facilitate collaboration across departments and disciplines. These can serve multiple purposes, encompassing both curricular partnerships and research collaborations. Those involving the arts were of greatest interest to the Mellon Research Project. Examples in this section demonstrate the range of partnerships and possibilities discovered, emphasizing their distinctive features rather than striving to present a comparison or a comprehensive overview.

CENTER FOR ARTS IN MEDICINE, UNIVERSITY OF FLORIDA, GAINESVILLE, FLORIDA

One of the strongest exemplars identified is the **Center for the Arts in Medicine** at the University of Florida (UF). Under the oversight of the College of the Arts, "the Center provides a framework for interdisciplinary collaboration among University of Florida faculty and students, healthcare providers, clinical artists, and our local and global communities. The Center develops and effects interdisciplinary research studies and educational curricula on all levels and serves as a national model for the arts in medicine research, education and training" (Center for Arts in Medicine, "About"). The Center works in tandem with the UF Health Shands Arts in Medicine program, providing art therapies and an artist-in-residence program at the UF Health Shands Hospital and incorporating the arts into patient care, community outreach, and education.

In a **TEDx talk** given on March 21, 2015, the Center's Director, Jill Sonke, explained that the arts do not replace medicine, nor are artists healers. Rather, "the arts make medicine and the patients it serves more whole" (Sonke). She described a program created as a partnership with the UF Center for Movement Disorders and Neurorestoration:

In the spirit of a research university, we brought clinicians, neurologists and occupational therapists and physical therapists along with our dancers into our dance studio – our laboratory – and we created a dance class that we knew would be safe and fun, engaging, and help address both the challenges and goals of people with Parkinson's disease. . . . This is a real, full-on dance class where people with Parkinson's disease and dance majors dance together and they're challenged physically and artistically. (Sonke)

Projects such as this characterize the interactivity between the research, curricular, and service aspects of the Center, which successfully integrates the arts across the essential facets of a leading research university. According to interview participants, other partners include the Florida State Office of Rural Health, the Shands Department of Nursing, the College of Education, the Digital Worlds Institute, and many of the university's scientific and medical areas.

The Center has invested in cultural competency training to support international and rural work; this training has contributed to the Center's success in crossing cultures within the university itself. The Center has also conducted deliberate studies of partnership, with staff dedicating themselves to clear and open communication. An interviewee explained, "We in the arts are better [at communicating] than our partners . . . , which is something we have brought to our colleagues. We also have partner retreats where we

take a lot of time for planning, and we do this regularly, throughout our partnership, just to check in and make sure we're both still getting what we need out of it."[30]

The Center receives support from the dean at the college level and assistance from the business office, which handles administrative needs and helps to manage the Center's accounts. The Center's requirements for physical space are limited. An administrator explained, "We're a pretty easy program in that regard. . . . Our work is in existing sites: the hospital, in classrooms, [and] a tiny amount of office space." Funding has grown over time. One administrator[31] explained:

The dean decided we needed to start a center, but there was no funding for space or anything. We still did it, though, and it took a few years to be approved by the Board of Regents. We got some seed funding for a few projects to get the ball rolling. We've grown organically with external funding; we're a blend of revenue and grant-based funding. We used to be fully grant-funded, but in the last three or four years, we've changed our role to be a Responsibility-Centered Management program; and we've created opportunities for entrepreneurialism as an interdisciplinary research center. Under this model, the administration is even more enthusiastic about our work.

Because the Center offers a degree-granting program, tuition provides a portion of the Center's budget, allowing for a level of financial stability that is supplemented by grants. The administrator explained that the Center has received more than 90 grants over time, from the State of Florida, federal agencies such as the Department of Defense, Department of Commerce, and the National Institute on Aging, and private foundations, such as the Kresge Foundation, as well as support from individual donors.

The Center offers a variety of programs and degree options: an online MA and graduate certificate in Arts in Medicine, a graduate certificate in Arts in Public Health, an undergraduate certificate in the Arts in Healthcare, and an undergraduate certificate in Dance in Healthcare. The Center also offers study abroad programs, summer intensives, special training programs, professional development and internships, along with an AIM for Africa program that establishes initiatives creating "cultural bridges between the arts and healthcare in the U.S. and several African nations" (Center for Arts in Medicine, "AIM").

---

30 Due to the nature of this interviewee's work, the position title and discipline have been omitted in order to ensure anonymity.
31 Due to the nature of this interviewee's work, the position title and discipline have been omitted in order to ensure anonymity.

Study of the relationship between the arts and human health occurs not only at the University of Florida but also at other institutions participating in the Mellon Research Project. The University of Michigan, for example, maintains a **Gifts of Art** program, bringing works of visual art and musical or theatrical performances to the university's hospitals (Gifts of Art, "Programs"), a growing field of interest with great potential for further development. As an administrator in the Center for Arts in Medicine explained,

> *When we first started, people thought it was weird.... It was challenging, and many people thought performing in a hospital was flaky. But ... over the course of years, people went from uncomfortable to thinking it was nice that we were there into broadly establishing in the medical community why [the arts are] important and valuable. Clinicians want their patients to be engaging in the arts; they've seen its value for their patients now. There's a host of studies on what the arts can do for their patients.*

The University of Florida's Center for the Arts in Medicine merges practice, research, and teaching, bringing the arts into full partnership with healthcare sciences. Furthermore, its structural and financial model demonstrates sustainability, relying on income from tuition rather than grant funding alone.

MASSACHUSETTS INSTITUTE OF TECHNOLOGY (MIT), CAMBRIDGE, MASSACHUSETTS

In another example, MIT maintains a broad and systemic valuation of the arts, an especially remarkable feat given the absence of a college of the arts or specific program in traditional visual arts. However, MIT demonstrates an active engagement with the arts by using the "center" concept as the basis of systemic arts integration through the Media Lab, the Center for Arts, Science & Technology (CAST), Arts at MIT, and the program in Arts, Culture, and Technologies (ACT).

As both a research and curricular unit, the **Media Lab** at MIT promotes "a unique, antidisciplinary culture" and the "unconventional mixing and matching of seemingly disparate research areas" (MIT Media Lab, "The MIT"). The Lab encompasses a degree-granting program in Media Arts and Sciences and a research program supported by more than 70 members, including corporate sponsors, who provide most of the Lab's $50 million annual operating budget.

The Media Lab was founded by Nicholas Negroponte, a pioneer of human-computer interaction, and Jerome Wiesner, who sought to lead MIT to be "more than science and engineering ..., to make something like a home or salon for people who didn't necessarily fit in their traditional disciplines, who crossed lines," according to a member of the Media Lab faculty. The Lab offers a Master of Science and a PhD but no undergraduate degrees, although it also has a first-year undergraduate program emphasizing project-oriented work and an Undergraduate Research Opportunities Program in which students work with Lab researchers. A composer and cellist who has been with the Media Lab since its inception in 1985 described his research as "very highly related to creation," involving the creation of new instruments in order to portray his musical vision. The Media Lab, he said, "is unlike an engineering school" because projects "are about deep motivation to express a vision in some way: partly artistic, conceptual, and technical.... It's about making art in a more complete way or in other dimensions than are possible [otherwise].... The work we do here in the Media Lab is about new ways to connect with the public." The composer further explained:

> *Each professor at the Media Lab has a lab and pursues their projects with students, both undergraduate and grad students.... It's hard to peg if someone is a musician or a programmer or whatever because they're constantly pursuing new knowledge.... The hope was that scientists, technologists, and artists could share and grow the magic between them and we wouldn't run back to independent departments, but we'd be anti-disciplinary and make this lab our home intellectually and structurally.*

Part of the School of Architecture and Planning, the Media Lab maintains its independence from that school and from MIT as a whole in several aspects. First, it receives little in the way of financial resources from the university, remaining primarily self-supporting. Next, graduate students apply directly to the Media Lab rather than to the university admissions office, giving the Lab much greater flexibility in selection of students. The Lab also runs its own searches to fill faculty positions, although the Dean of Architecture and Planning must approve new hires. Matters of promotion and tenure also reflect this independence. A faculty member explained,

> *Tenure goes through the university-wide process. But here's the thing: nobody at the Media Lab has a traditional discipline or tenure package because of the nature of the Media Lab.... We're looking to hire people we*

think we can cultivate, and we want to give them tenure, generally. In the Media Lab, we want people [who] are changing the world, incredibly creative people [who] can be controversial.

An MIT dean further said, "Other institutions say 'research and creative practice,' but MIT has done away with that kind of language and evaluates based on the culture of the discipline and the modes of inquiry.... Each candidate and each dean does it differently." At MIT, a faculty member can earn promotion to associate professor without being tenured, which allows earlier promotion and greater time to build a case for tenure.

In another exemplary instance of arts integration, MIT's **Center for Art, Science & Technology** (CAST) "facilitates and creates opportunities for exchange and collaboration among artists, engineers, and scientists" (Arts at MIT, "About CAST"). A joint venture between the Office of the Provost, the School of Architecture and Planning, and the School of Humanities, Arts, and Social Sciences, CAST provides support for cross-disciplinary initiatives that integrate the arts into other curricular areas and promote the creation of new artistic work. CAST sponsors a Visiting Artists program and offers assistance with "presentation and curation of performing and visual arts or design relevant to the research of engineers, scientists, and the MIT community as a whole" (Arts at MIT, "About"). CAST also supports graduate and postdoctoral research. CAST was founded in 2012 on a grant from the The Andrew W. Mellon Foundation to bring together the many curricular and cross-disciplinary teaching and research efforts at MIT. The organization received a second $1.5 million grant from The Andrew W. Mellon Foundation in April 2015. CAST has provided funding for "more than 20 artist residencies and collaborative projects with MIT faculty and students, 12 cross-disciplinary courses and workshops, two concert series, and numerous multimedia projects, lectures and symposia" (Lacey).

Participants in a joint interview comprising CAST administrators including a dean, two directors, and an associate provost reported that they hoped CAST would seed cross-disciplinary courses at the general education level and throughout the curriculum. For instance, an affiliated research group, CSAIL (Computer Science and Artificial Intelligence Laboratory), employs "the inventor of computational origami; he's an engineer, mathematician, artist, and computer scientist. CSAIL also has a roboticist, who worked

with a dance troupe and robots." In this conversation, the executive director of arts initiatives said, "MIT is a place of constant experimentation, constant invention," and the director of CAST added, "We have a unique flavor of arts here. It has something to do with design, elegance, beauty, pragmatic making.... There's a distinctive approach here at MIT, whether one is writing music or writing code. That's why students have no problem going from one subject to another and are able to figure it all out and integrate it in their minds."

Also under the auspices of the School of Architecture and Planning, the MIT **Program in Art, Culture, and Technology** (ACT) provides "an academic program and research center which facilitates artist-thinkers' exploration of art's broad, complex, global history and conjunction with culture, science, technology, and design via rigorous critical artistic practice and practice-driven theory" (MIT Program). A comparatively small unit, ACT offers a Master of Science in Art, Culture and Technology as well as courses at both the graduate and undergraduate levels. However, ACT offers no undergraduate degrees, and in order to provide students with wider access to course offerings in visual arts, it established inter-institutional partnerships with the Massachusetts College of Art and Design and at the School of the Museum of Fine Arts Boston. Both graduates and undergraduates can also take courses at nearby Harvard University and Wellesley College.

MIT's emphasis on integrating the arts through the Media Lab, CAST, ACT, and through various Arts at MIT programs (Creative Arts Competition, Art Scholars, Grad Arts Forum, student performance groups, the Student Art Association, and more) belies the popular view that MIT exclusively focuses on STEM disciplines. Its level of arts integration through anti-disciplinarity and the establishment of organizations linking research and teaching and the institution-wide commitment to the arts' contribution to the motto Mens et Manus (Mind and Hand) combine to make MIT an institutional exemplar of best practice in arts integration (Arts at MIT, "Mission").

THE ARTS INSTITUTE, UNIVERSITY OF WISCONSIN-MADISON, MADISON, WISCONSIN

The **Arts Institute at the University of Wisconsin (UW)-Madison** provides a "collective voice and vision of the arts" at the university (Arts Institute, "The Institute"), seeking to advance the arts on campus and promote artistic expression and experience as a means toward engaging and understanding the world. The Arts Institute sponsors Art Awards for faculty and graduate students, an Interdisciplinary Arts Residency Program, a "Creative Arts and Design Learning Community" in a UW-Madison residence hall, development of cross-listed courses enabling artists-in-residence to teach classes, and sponsorship of the Wisconsin Film Festival, among other emphases. In 2014, the University established the Institute as an independent division, allowing it to offer its own curriculum, proving especially important in light of the fact that UW-Madison does not have a College of the Arts.

Among the Arts Institute's initiatives, a partnership with the Wisconsin School of Business and the Division of Continuing Studies provides business skills to artists and creative professionals, in part by means of a cross-listed course titled "Arts Enterprise: Art as Business as Art." Other initiatives include the Image Lab at the Wisconsin Institute for Discovery, an Office of Multicultural Arts Initiatives featuring events such as hip-hop dance competitions and open mic nights, and a website highlighting public art around the campus. Two new programs are also currently in development – one in Communicating Science, the other in Entertainment and Digital Technology.

The Institute works to develop new interdisciplinary arts curricula that integrate experiential and service learning, internships, performance and public presentation, training in teaching and learning, entrepreneurship training, and the application of arts skills to non-art fields. The Institute also sponsors research through art studies, producing reports for the university and the Madison community.

Partners of the Arts Institute include campus institutes, groups, and other departments such as the African Studies Program, the Division of Continuing Studies, and the International Institute, among others; community organizations such as the Forward Theater Company, the Madison Symphony Orchestra, and the Wisconsin Historical Society; media outlets such as the *Badger Herald* and Wisconsin Public Television; and individual sponsors. The Institute has 136 affiliated faculty from a variety of academic areas such as Afro-American studies, art, art history, business, communication arts, dance, design, education, film, media studies, music, theatre and drama, and others. The director reported that 16 faculty and students are currently working on a curriculum for presentation to the provost, outlining areas their academic partners hope to be developed. According to the director, Communicating Science,

the medical school, and the veterinary school "are champing at the bit" for this curriculum to be completed, while utilizing students to help develop and test new curricula helps to speed up the development process.

The Arts Institute predates similar efforts at other institutions, yet its recent resurgence and growth might serve as an exemplar for institutional peers. The Institute began as the Arts Consortium in 1975, for the purpose of sponsoring, arranging, and fostering structured collaborations between other disciplines and the arts. In 2014, the university administration established the Arts Institute as a curricular unit, allowing it to offer credit-based courses featuring all aspects of arts integration including fusion, infusion, and diffusion models.

Unlike other centers or institutes relying on grants or sponsored research for their funding, the Arts Institute partakes of tuition and university-level funding. The Institute presently works with 136 affiliated faculty, with the Arts Institute buying time from home departments. Courses occur as sustained efforts rather than one-time offerings, as is typical with collaborative arts-integrated courses elsewhere; a degree program and additional curricula are currently in development. The director described the organization as being "in the middle of several different programs that address arts integration," including digital technologies, the use of arts in addressing humanities and sciences, and efforts with the School of Business to bring art education to all business students.

One of the faculty affiliates (a visual artist working with biology, engineering, and chemistry) described his philosophy of arts integration, which is applicable to the Institute's overall emphasis: "Art finds its way into everything. People say the arts must be more integrated into [other areas], but art is already in everything, and everything is to understand the presence of the arts within it."

The Arts Institute has a significant presence on the UW-Madison campus. According to its website, more than 32,000 individuals participated in Arts Institute programs during the 2013-2014 academic year, and its Wisconsin Film Festival alone produced an economic impact of $1.17 million for the greater Madison area (Arts Institute, "Resources"), bringing the arts into greater prominence on campus and in the surrounding community. Even taking into account this emerging organization's status as still in the process of developing its degree programs and curricula, the Arts Institute at UW-Madison successfully traverses the difficult terrain of identity. It has become a fully funded curricular unit, and it has established feasible strategies that allow faculty members to teach sustainable arts-integrated courses, for which they receive due credit. The Arts Institute's successful organizational model eliminates several challenges and impediments identified by interview participants across institutions, providing strategies of potential usefulness to other institutions.

STUDIO|LAB, PENNSYLVANIA STATE UNIVERSITY, STATE COLLEGE, PENNSYLVANIA

Studio|Lab at Penn State, like MIT's Media Lab, engages in sponsored research. Founded on the premise of compatibility between art and science, it serves as "a 'studio' for scientists to refine the aesthetic dimensions of their work" and "a 'laboratory' for artists to test the performance and impact of their work," existing at the "powerful nexus of creativity and empirical inquiry from which innovation emerges" (*Studio/Lab*, "What").

Studio|Lab features collaborations with local and international researchers on diverse projects. These include data visualization, materialization, and sonification; video or photo documentation and communication; research study icons and branding; time-oriented design and data analysis; experimental interfaces and interactive stimuli; and website and document development. Strategic interdisciplinary relationships foster "the precision, fun, and beauty of art-sci" (*Studio/Lab*, "What"). The organization enjoys 2,000 square feet of studio and lab space, occupied by 16 scientists and artists (*Studio/Lab*). Partners include the PSU Social Science Research Institute; the PSU Institute for CyberScience; the College of Arts and Architecture; the College of Health and Human Development; the Survey Research Center at PSU; the Hamer Center for Community Design; the Bennett Pierce Prevention Research Center; the PSU Center for Healthy Aging; the Learning Factory at PSU; and SharkArm Studios, a student-founded, independent game design company (*Studio\Lab*, "Studio|Lab Partners"). The Social Science Research Institute funds Studio|Lab, with faculty holding appointments in various organizations such as the College of Arts and Architecture, the College of Health and Human Development, the Department of Computer Science and Engineering, and the Department of Psychology (*Studio/Lab*, "Studio|Lab People").

A research group, Studio|Lab offers competitive fellowships at the undergraduate and graduate levels, providing financial support and opportunities for participation in advanced research. Studio|Lab grants seed funding to students, researchers, and collaborative groups engaged in cross-disciplinary work demonstrating exceptional potential (*Studio/Lab*, "What"). By bridging diverse departments to integrate art and science in genuine research projects involving partners both within and outside of the university, Studio|Lab demonstrates excellence in research integration.

Penn State also supports the **Institute for the Arts & Humanities** (IAH), an organization dedicated to "fostering collaboration and dialogue between artists and humanists" through public events and symposia, performances, and exhibitions (Institute for the Arts). Faculty and graduate students work with scholars and artists nationally and internationally, providing a model for collaborative and interdisciplinary research and teaching. IAH provides funding for collaborative teaching, faculty grants, and graduate student summer residencies, and cosponsors resident scholars and artists, along with the College of the Liberal Arts, the College of Arts and Architecture, and the commonwealth campuses. IAH is one of Penn State's 12 interdisciplinary research institutes, including the **Social Science Research Institute**, the parent organization of Studio|Lab (Pennsylvania). With multiple opportunities for arts-integrative study and research, Penn State provides an exemplary model among its peer institutions.

THE INSTITUTE FOR CREATIVITY, ARTS, AND TECHNOLOGY (ICAT), VIRGINIA TECH, BLACKSBURG, VIRGINIA

ICAT offers another model of best practice in arts integration, self-identifying as a "transdisciplinary living lab" comprising five studios: Idea, Image, Impact, Implement, and Interact.[32] Each features a different aspect of the combination of art, science, and technology. "Idea" explores transdisciplinarity and creativity in STEM disciplines. "Image" seeks to reveal science through the arts, particularly through computation and interaction. "Impact" focuses on the continuum of the body, computation, and imagination. "Implement" features new materials, objects, and creative methods. Finally, "Interact" stimulates local innovation and cultural awareness (Institute for Creativity, Arts, and Technology, "General"). ICAT's facility features a space called "The Cube," a virtual reality space for "research and experimentation in big data exploration, immersive environments, intimate performances, audio and visual installations, and experiential investigations of all types" (Institute for Creativity, Arts, and Technology, "The Cube"). Unlike most virtual reality environments, The Cube allows for multiuser collaboration with data, featuring real-time interaction research, and a full-scale, multiperson walk-through of virtual environments. This installation occupies a four-story space in Virginia Tech's new Center for the Arts.

Primarily a research institute, ICAT also facilitates undergraduate courses and two graduate degree programs: an MFA in Creative Technologies through the School of Visual Arts and an interdisciplinary graduate education program in Human Centered Design, leading to a graduate certificate or an individualized PhD through Virginia Tech's Interdisciplinary Graduate Education Programs. ICAT also provides outreach programs to K-12 through MAKEr Camp, featuring robotics, engineering, and music; the GAMES Project, teaching pre-algebra to middle school students through gaming technologies; and workshops, contests, and Alternative Informal Learning Environments (Institute for Creativity, Arts, and Technology, "K-to-12").

Similar in concept to Penn State's Studio|Lab or MIT's Media Lab, ICAT brings the arts, STEM, and other academic disciplines together in collaborative research and curricular partnerships through organizational structures and operational philosophies, thereby establishing the arts as an equal partner in research endeavors. An ICAT professor with a background in civil engineering, mathematics education, and interaction design explained,

> *I'm sold on the transdisciplinarity because each of the distinct, diverse disciplines involved has an equal share – a seat at the table. When done right, there's a nice interaction and dialogue here. In transdisciplinarity, you can have individuals that straddle disciplines but are stronger in one or the other nonetheless, and in that environment they are challenged to play to their strengths because there's already someone at the table who can fill in the gap.*

ICAT's emphasis on transdisciplinarity fosters innovative research across its four focus areas, capitalizing on the physical resources in its state-of-the-art facility and the strong support of the Virginia Tech community.

THE ALLOSPHERE, UNIVERSITY OF CALIFORNIA, SANTA BARBARA, CALIFORNIA

At the University of California, Santa Barbara (UCSB), the AlloSphere provides one of the most impressive physical installations encountered through the site visits for the Mellon Research Project. The AlloSphere is a three-story-tall scientific instrument for "visualizing, hearing, and exploring complex multi-dimensional data" (*The AlloSphere Research Facility*). A composer leads this program, working at the intersection of music and computing sciences along with the California NanoSystems Institute. The AlloSphere moves beyond 3-D visualization and virtual reality systems, providing a completely anechoic (echo-free) chamber equipped with high-resolution projectors, an optically opaque yet acoustically transparent sphere, a real-time sound synthesis cluster of 140 individual speakers, and an array of computing and processing equipment allowing for unprecedented content and prototyping of scientific data. Program materials describe the AlloSphere as "an instrument similar to the telescope, in that it will enable scientists to see data in new ways that provoke insight. It is also like a violin or a symphony orchestra – an instrument to compose for and to play" (*The AlloSphere Research Facility*, "About"). Associated with other research laboratories at UCSB, the AlloSphere also works with external organizations on collaborative research projects. Present projects investigate concepts such as interactive visualization of atomic bondings; examination of the brain as an architectural space; creation of an interactive simulator for virtual experiments in the delivery of chemotherapy to cancerous tumors through nanoparticles; and a simulation and display of the quantum mechanical wave function of a single electron (*The AlloSphere Research Facility*, "Research").

The AlloSphere stands at the frontier of the intersection of music, visual art, electronic technologies, and a vast array of sciences, making it a prime exemplar of best practice in arts integration.

THE ADVANTAGES OF CENTERS AND INSTITUTES

Centers and institutes provide a physical and conceptual home for arts-integrative interdisciplinarity and sometimes also incorporate curricular offerings and degree programs. Some centers or institutes feature partnerships with other campus units, community organizations, or corporate sponsors. Within these organizational structures, the arts become empowered to serve as more than an embellishment to research in other disciplines, included as valued collaborators on high-level research projects. Beyond these identifying characteristics, centers and institutes establish environments where arts integration can thrive, imbuing faculty, staff, and students with identity as part of a vital community of like-minded scholars. This sense of community was evident during the research site visits, standing in marked contrast to interviewees who had taken a more pioneering stance for arts integration within otherwise monodisciplinary environments. Participants in joint interviews conducted at centers and institutes appeared very comfortable with one another and their interviews tended to take a more positive tone. Overall, specific correlations between centers and institutes were not identifiable beyond the inclusion of the arts. Factors of longevity, organizational structures, participating disciplinary areas, funding sources, and research design appear to be specific to each location rather than sharing common features. However, centers and institutes provide a structure that welcomes the arts as members of research teams, fostering an intangible sense of community not found elsewhere. Positivity emanating from these communities may account for their attractiveness to scholars and students, as well as energizing the collaborations occurring within these organizations.

RESEARCH BEST PRACTICES

Of course, research represents one of the areas of greatest interest examined by the Mellon Research Project, given that the study featured RU/VH universities. Some of this research takes place at centers and institutes, as featured in the preceding section. Other research occurs at the level of singular projects conducted by individuals whose work integrates the arts with an array of partnering disciplines.

INDIVIDUAL PROJECTS

At the level of individual projects, outstanding instances of best practice identified in this study were far too plentiful to cite in their entirety, so selected examples must suffice. These will not be identified by institution because doing so would compromise the interview participants' anonymity.

The first example comes from a professor of music theory who leads a research group investigating the role music plays in human cognition. This utilizes neuroscience and neuroimaging, employing functional MRIs to map the parts of the brain experiencing music. Research proceeds according to traditional scientific methods, establishing experimental paradigms, gathering behavioral data, and employing those data to inform neuroscience thereafter. The professor reported that colleagues in psychology were "wonderful, great collaborators." However, he reported significant obstacles in development due to his university's structures:

> *[This] is a technological institution that has become something much larger. The model for how it treats faculty, however, is still skewed toward its science traditions. If you have a grant from NSF, for example, you can buy yourself out of teaching for a semester or year. You can pay yourself over the summer, get students like crazy, whatever. And this is all competitive, external funding. As an arts person on a nine-year tenure track, we get a one-semester leave in our seventh year. This means that [we're] doing real, hard research in the arts with a big course load and no mechanism to buy one's self a leave – whereas colleagues in the sciences have a number of mechanisms. [It] puts me at a disadvantage. At the University of Chicago, the University of Michigan, or Yale, I would have a set of resources I don't at a place like this. It's [specific to this institution]: that the arts are "over here." The arts have strangely made the argument that they want to be left alone under the conservatory model. And that came with a cost: we're cut off from funding, drawing advanced students in, etc.*

This professor also addressed the scarcity of funding and resources, explaining that he had to struggle for space for his lab and make the best of inadequate facilities and that he felt envious of others engaged in scientific investigations who regularly received start-up packages. He must devote time he would prefer to use in his research to piecing the project together rather than actually doing the work. However, despite these challenges, his work has been productive and rewarding. He said, "I do what I do because when psychologists do work with music, they often deal with music in a very naïve way. We can bring a much deeper understanding of music to the field. Instead of a musical novice but a scientific expert doing this work, I'm a music expert and a scientific novice." Illustrative of his standing as an example of best practice, this professor also studies music as an essential human activity, recently publishing a book featuring the impact of technology on musical interactions, both on a personal and societal level, commoditization of musical activities, and their social meaning. His determination to pursue interdisciplinary arts-integrative research despite placement within an environment with significant obstacles

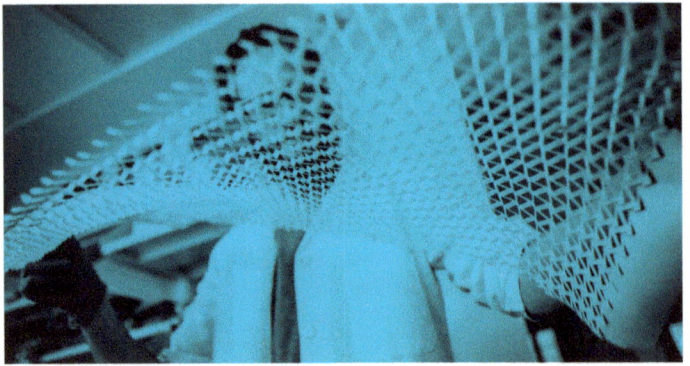

and challenges makes this professor an excellent exemplar of best practice in individual research.

A second example of best practice in arts-integrative research features a postdoctoral fellow in cognitive science, among a number of researchers working with a patient suffering from extreme amnesia due to viral encephalitis. The patient had been a professional illustrator and musician, and the researchers have used her connection to art and music to see which areas of her memory remain functional, studying parts of the brain utilized in learning. Because scientists have precisely identified the parts of her brain which no longer function (those previously thought to be necessary to learning) and because the patient nevertheless possesses the ability to learn (albeit on a limited basis), researchers have been able to make new discoveries not possible otherwise. The patient retains most of her artistic and musical abilities, so her artworks, her creative process, and her musical performances serve researchers as a window into her cognitive functioning.

Funding for this study comes from a brain science institute, which worked with the patient's family to create an art exhibit of her pre-illness and post-illness artworks. The researcher interviewed for the Mellon Research Project worked with artists from an art museum affiliated with the university. In one instance, an artist helped the researcher develop a test asking the patient about artistic technique. The researcher said, "In creating these questions and examining her I worked one-on-one with this [artist] because I don't have a background in art. In terms of the content, you have to rely on other artists. You have to have these collaborations – I wouldn't have been able to do it without them." This researcher engages in active collaboration with artists, utilizing art and music as research tools in order to conduct a scientific study in which the subject's artistic engagement provides

an essential component of the research process. The arts assist scientists in assessing a patient's artistic practice in order to draw scientific conclusions – a productive interweaving of these domains. Although this study utilizes the arts instrumentally rather than forming a full partnership across disciplines, the scientist not only works with artists and the art museum but also with researchers at multiple universities, demonstrating the characteristics of a high-level arts-integrative research partnership.

The third featured researcher works at the intersection of the visual arts and healthcare. One of her projects investigates the effect of creative expression on retention of caregivers' sense of self in the face of overwhelming stress and fatigue. Her project engages caregivers through art-making exercises, guided art discussions, and personal reflection. This research features curriculum that brings students and community members together in investigating issues of personal identity and the role of creativity in healthcare. In this setting, students in the school of art and design interact with participants in the university's geriatric center and memory loss programs, working collaboratively in order to create art and to learn from one another. Another of this professor's courses also partners with the same organization. The courses examine memory, aging, and expressive art, and blending lectures with poetry and story building, visual arts exercises and art projects, iPad apps for creative projects, dance, and musical compositions.

In addition to her research and teaching, this professor has served as a visiting artist in the university hospital, where she facilitated the creation of a large art installation featuring the contributions of hundreds of participants ranging from doctors to patients, from hospital maintenance workers to patients' families. Individuals wrote their hopes and wishes on fan-shaped papers, which were folded and then incorporated into a work of art subsequently installed in the hospital, fostering a sense of community as well as providing an aesthetic addition to the hospital environment.

The professor serves as an example because her work spans visual art and medical applications, as well as seamlessly incorporating research and community outreach within curricular and clinical settings. The skill and finesse with which she has blended her arts practice with research and teaching serves as a model of best practice.

ARTS AND HUMANITIES RESEARCH

The majority of research collaborations observed in the Mellon Research Project take place between the arts and STEM disciplines, but partnerships with humanities and social sciences exist as well. For example, the University of Illinois established the **Illinois Program for Research in the Humanities**, which sponsors research clusters of faculty and graduate students who investigate questions or subjects in the humanities and the arts. As an example, the "Youth in Creative Cities" research cluster explores the potential expansion of publicly engaged scholarship of the arts and humanities by reaching out to cities and micro-urban communities, involving public arts and humanities in the Imagining America program (Illinois).

A collaboration between public arts, humanities, and digital arts, directed by a professor of intermedia, takes place at another institution (not identified to protect the anonymity of the interviewee). The director described his program as a "digital studio for public arts and humanities," a studio which encourages public digital arts practice among student and faculty researchers. He reported, "At any given time, the studio is working on 40 projects at various forms of engagement." The director has taught a course called "Intermedia, Artists, and Community," which placed students in semester-long residencies in local nonprofits. He explained that their charge was "to listen, play the role of outside observer, and see how the arts can be integrated into the problems" encountered in these settings.

Additional examination of research partnerships and comparisons between fields collaborating with the arts could shed light on comparative participation between STEM, humanities, social sciences, or other fields. At present, however, our focus is to identify examples rather than quantify or categorize participation in arts-integrated research by various disciplines.

Certainly, extraordinary individuals beyond those highlighted in this section of this study participated in the Mellon Research Project. However, as publication limitations could not allow for a full catalog of participants' accomplishments, this must suffice as a representative sample of the remarkable work occurring across the 46 institutions visited.

BEST PRACTICES FOR COLLABORATIVE RESEARCH[33]

Best practices for collaborative research projects differ from those involving teaching or curriculum. Discrepancies in contact hours and workloads still present a potential problem in terms of finding time to work together, but presuming the partners reach an agreement regarding a work schedule, research credit and recognition can be problematic. In the sciences, physics in particular, publications list multiple people as members of a research team, a crucial factor in considerations of promotion and tenure for each of those named individuals. The humanities place greater emphasis on individual accomplishment, although research collaborations or partnerships occur as well. Arts faculty earn recognition for their individual creative practice. Although artists and designers engage in academic research activities during the creation of their artistic works or performances, outside cultural observers or hosting cultural institutions produce documentation and publication of their works. In other words, successful visual and performing arts faculty become the subject of study in museum catalogs or monographs, critical reviews, video documentaries, and blog posts, while art historians publish in traditional academic journals. Arts research refers to a variety of studio, rehearsal, and recursive practices, which provide the foundation for artists and designers to produced finished concepts, products, or performances. These processes, however, very often remain in the background, leading artistic works to appear to have emerged into the world in a completed state. The creative process remains invisible to the audience, whereas extensive documentation typically supports the products of formal research.

Creative presentation of research can facilitate the communication of complex ideas to an audience, but growing demand for artists to contribute research in other fields presents some crucial questions about the role of the artist in the research process. As mentioned in chapter 3, systems of recognition and reward may fail to validate the accomplishments of individuals who work outside of disciplinary boundaries, especially if their efforts intertwine with those of their partners. Nevertheless, partners and collaborators should seek cross-disciplinary recognition for their work in an effort to press the boundaries outward and effect change from within, especially those artists who work with non-arts researchers in conducting data visualization, sonification, or other artistic presentations and embodiments.

Identified best practice in collaborative research between investigators from arts and non-arts disciplines recommends artists' inclusion on a

33 Portions of this section were taken from Mackh, *Achieving*.

research team from the inception of a project. Even if they do not claim expert knowledge of the research subject, artists possess the capacity to ideate and conceptualize complex concepts expressively and tangibly. Artists can contribute to group discussions by sharing divergent perspectives, and they may be especially skilled in finding and identifying problems, taking unexpected multivariable approaches to emerging challenges, and finding novel solutions to perplexing research dilemmas. Furthermore, artists gain a more comprehensive understanding of the research subject if they become part of the team from the start, making the task of visualizing, sonifying, or embodying the data more likely to succeed.

Researchers may not realize they could benefit from artists' participation in their project until later on in the process, however. When artists join near the end of the project, they might not receive credit for being part of the research team but rather may be credited as illustrators (or similar role). This has little benefit for the artists and may sometimes be perceived as demeaning or exploitative. Becoming so-called "visualization monkeys" does not offer artists substantive consideration toward career advancement in their own department in the same way an exhibition or performance usually would, even if considerable amounts of time and energy have been poured into the project. Therefore, inclusion as members of the research team represents an important accomplishment for arts faculty, broadening the scope of their professional profiles and enhancing their reputation within the community of scholars.

Each collaboration encompasses a unique set of circumstances, involves participants with different perspectives, and encounters different institutional expectations. To avoid potential pitfalls, both the researchers initiating the project and the artists invited to participate must be very clear about their roles and expectations, perhaps employing tools found in appendix 5. These planning questionnaires incorporate ideas gleaned from the interview process, in an attempt to facilitate research by addressing multiple aspects potential partners should address. Advance planning may seem to be tedious or even uninspiring, and the length of these questionnaires can be daunting. However, working through the considerations involved in a partnership before beginning the actual project can prevent problems reported by the interview participants, making these tools useful for achieving best practice.

CO-CURRICULAR BEST PRACTICES

Unlike the research or curricular models presented in this chapter, co-curricular programs incorporate arts experience into students' overall educational experience rather than taking an interdisciplinary or integrative approach. As introduced in chapter 3, for the purposes of this study, researchers grouped co-curricular programs into five general categories: on-campus cultural events; student-led clubs, groups, and arts organizations; faculty-led clubs, groups, and arts organizations; non-curricular arts instruction; and off-campus excursions and cultural events.

ON-CAMPUS CULTURAL EVENTS

Most universities sponsor performances by professional musicians, host theatrical performances, bring in guest artists or lecturers, or provide similar cultural arts opportunities. As an illustration, the University of Southern California (USC) provides an exemplary co-curricular arts and lecture series titled **Visions and Voices**:

Visions and Voices is a university-wide arts and humanities initiative that is unparalleled in higher education. . . . [It] fulfills the goals set forth in USC's strategic plan; communicates USC's core values to students; and affirms the human spirit. Highlighting USC's excellence in the arts and humanities, the initiative provides an inspiring and provocative experience for all USC students, regardless of their major or class level, and challenges them to expand their perspectives and become world-class citizens who will eagerly make a positive impact throughout the world.

Emphasizing the university's commitment to interdisciplinary approaches, the initiative features a spectacular array of events conceived and organized by faculty and schools throughout the university. With presentations by critically acclaimed artists and distinguished speakers, the series features theatrical productions, music and dance performances, film screenings, lectures and workshops. In addition to the events held on the . . . campuses, students are also offered a variety of opportunities to experience Los Angeles's dynamic cultural landscape at events throughout the city. (Visions)

Students receive free admission to these events, sometimes including food or giveaways such as T-shirts or tote bags to encourage student attendance. The most notable difference between this program and on-campus cultural events elsewhere lies not in the number of events (although they are more numerous than at other universities) nor in the diversity of offerings (although USC provides an especially rich mixture of opportunities). Instead, the key difference is in what happens after the performance or lecture. Discussions following the performances or presentations turn each event from an evening's entertainment into an interactive learning experience. According to the Visions and Voices website,

Every ... program invites students to dialogue and engage with artists, writers, professors and special guests. These interactions provide a dynamic experience of the arts and humanities and encourage active exploration of USC's core values, including freedom of inquiry, respect for diversity, commitment to service, entrepreneurial spirit, informed risk-taking, ethical conduct and the search for truth. This approach to the arts and humanities can make every future scientist a better scientist, every future lawyer a better lawyer, every future business professional a better business professional and every future artist a better artist, contributing to a better society as a whole. (Visions)

An initiative of the USC provost, Visions and Voices now spans a diverse array of university departments. An administrator in the university library credited this program with raising the library's profile across the university, explaining how it began by bringing in scholars to discuss the intersection between science and art, growing from a single event into a yearlong project, and finally becoming a vital part of the university's culture. Interviewees at this institution cited this program as being instrumental in starting conversations about arts integration across the campus and in generating interest in the arts among the student body and campus community.

A program director explained that faculty members propose the events, which are reviewed by a committee of approximately 30 faculty members. The arts deans also propose and sponsor yearly programs from their individual colleges. Each event's facilitator shapes a reflective component to follow signature events, working with the performer or presenter to tie the presentation to the values of the university. Early years of the program placed a greater emphasis on this reflective component than on the performances themselves, but as they achieved a more balanced approach, the program achieved greater success. According to a dean, "It's really truly infused the campus with the arts in a meaningful way, not just an entertainment-oriented way."

USC's Visions and Voices program enjoys an advantageous proximity to the artistic, cultural, historical, and technological wealth of Los Angeles, which serves as a ready source of presenters and performers. The program also benefits from unusually enthusiastic support by the provost's office and the goodwill of the university community. These resources allow the program to thrive, serving as an exemplar of cultural arts programming.

STUDENT-LED CLUBS, GROUPS, AND ARTS ORGANIZATIONS

The universities studied feature hundreds of arts-related clubs or student-led organizations such as:

* *A cappella singing groups and traditional vocal ensembles ranging from chapel choirs to swing choirs*
* *Broadcast media, such as radio and television*
* *Creative writing, poetry, and literary arts*
* *Design and engineering*
* *Ethnic/multicultural and traditional dance troupes, such as ballet, jazz, tap, hip hop, salsa, and tango*
* *Fashion and fashion design*
* *Instrumental ensembles, bands, and orchestras*
* *Music composition, experimental and non-traditional instruments, electronic music, and other musical innovations*
* *Publications, such as arts magazines, newsletters, and genre-specific arts publications*
* *Societies for arts appreciation*
* *Student arts advisory boards or councils*
* *Theatrical performance ensembles or troupes and those related to film/cinema appreciation or production*
* *Visual arts clubs featuring painting, ceramics, anime, sculpture, digital art, photography, and more*

Some participating universities welcome incoming students with an event introducing them to the plethora of arts organizations available; these events are often organized by students interested in sharing their love of the arts with those new to campus. For example, the University of Michigan **Student Arts HUB** sponsors such an event each fall, encouraging incoming students to join its more than 150 diverse co-curricular arts groups in yearly operation across the campus. According to an administrator, more students participate in the arts through these organizations than in the arts departments' curricular programs.

Students actively seek these opportunities when they arrive on campus. The program director explained, "Today's students expect to be involved with groups of like-minded people – they crave that interaction.... One of the things about college is that it's supposed to start opening you up and give you all of these opportunities to try something new."

This program director held focus groups with the leaders of student organizations, seeking to determine the value of co-curricular participation in the arts. Some students' responses did not come as a surprise, such as appreciation for continuing to participate in the arts as they'd done in high school or the pleasure of being "part of a troupe, part of a band, or part of a team creating the arts." Students cited opportunities to develop their leadership skills, self-confidence, and similar attributes. Perhaps more surprisingly, even students majoring in the arts reported that co-curricular participation was essential to their career success since opportunities to be part of the most important performances or shows remain prohibitively exclusive. By design, student-led co-curricular programs accommodate a wide range of students and can allow more individuals to build their artistic portfolios, repertoires, or résumés for applications to graduate school or future employment.

FACULTY-LED CLUBS, GROUPS, AND ARTS ORGANIZATIONS

Students seeking to incorporate arts experiences in their academic lives frequently turn to faculty-led arts opportunities, which typically welcome students regardless of declared major. However, in some cases, students majoring in the specific discipline of such a club or organization might have mandatory participation in such groups as part of their curricular requirements. For example, a student majoring in vocal performance might be required to join a faculty-led choir or ensemble unconnected to a particular course or participation grade.

Involvement in these groups provides valuable opportunities outside of the students' degree programs, and these opportunities are often seen as a highlight of students' educational experience. An associate dean reported 65% of the members of the university's marching band came from the university's College of Engineering, explaining, "Many students want to go back and forth between the arts and sciences as a part of their education, but hard science degree programs aren't structured to allow for that." The marching band provides an important chance for non-music majors to continue their engagement in music performance without detracting from their studies.

Typically, music and theater offer more faculty-led co-curricular opportunities than the visual arts, but marching bands, pep bands, symphony orchestras, choirs, choruses, vocal ensembles, and other varieties of musical performance groups exist on a majority of college campuses, as do co-curricular theater programs and opportunities for engagement in the visual arts. The universities involved in the Mellon Research Project similarly foster strong music and other arts groups on their campuses, distinguished by their recognition of student engagement in the arts as part of a campuswide strategy for arts integration.

Some of the sites visited place an especially high value on co-curricular programming. As a program director explained, "Very few of our programs are explicitly curricular. . . . Going beyond the bounds of the classroom is assumed." Administrators recognize that integrating curricular and co-curricular opportunities can lead to increased student involvement. According to a dean:

Students have so much on their plates already, and they will generally do what's good for their grades first, their careers second, and then things that they enjoy like the arts. There's a lot of competition for their attentions in [our] area, which is different than, say, [a] town [that] has little going on. So we have the challenge of doing what's good for their interests, their career, and their classes. That's why we try to tightly integrate the curricular and co-curricular, offering leadership opportunities, and so on, working with professors to get them to see that we're doing work that dovetails with their curricular or resume work.

The dean indicates that students feel pressure to achieve high grades, but by integrating curricular and co-curricular options supported by faculty, the university facilitates student learning across both modalities.

NON-CURRICULAR ARTS INSTRUCTION

Overall, students can find diverse opportunities for lessons, classes, and additional non-credit learning opportunities in the arts. Among a multitude of choices, students learn how to play the harmonica, tap dance, or throw a vase on a potter's wheel; they learn how to participate in improvisational comedy, sing in a barbershop quartet, or draw anime characters. Seemingly, whatever the student's interest in the arts, one of the universities in this study might provide a non-credit class, lesson, or workshop to match. Students constantly request new clubs or co-curricular activities, so these options tend to change from one academic year to the next.

The Massachusetts Institute of Technology (MIT) represents one of the best exemplars of co-curricular arts instruction. In its **Student Art Association**, students can engage in studio art experiences through non-curricular classes offered through a student art

association in continuous operation for 40 years, established in response to student demand for a creative outlet within an intensive STEM environment that formerly offered few curricular arts options. The organization currently employs five art instructors who teach beginning and intermediate classes in photography, ceramics, drawing, painting, printmaking, and sculpture. Designed mainly for students, it allows university affiliates to participate as space permits, spanning different majors and levels of educational attainment. Participants register for the classes with the association and pay a fee for participation.

MIT also sponsors an **Arts Scholars** program, which "brings together students who are passionate about exploring the diverse array of arts available at MIT and in the Boston area and interacting with fellow students, faculty artists and other experts in the art world. The program [features] monthly excursions or workshops, with an expert in the relevant field of art in attendance" (Arts at MIT, "Members"). Selective membership procedures require an application accompanied by a recommendation from a professor or staff member; the application is then followed by an interview. Membership includes sponsored outings to local shows, exhibits, and lectures; up to $1,000 in self-governed seed money for member art projects; priority admission to graduate arts forums; discounted classes in the Student Art Association; funds for tickets to exhibitions for off-site student research; one guest pass for a current scholar to host an art scholar candidate at an exhibition or event; and a lasting community that acts as a touchstone for graduates (Arts at MIT, "About Arts").

The Arts Scholars students come from across the university and pursue a wide variety of interests. Excerpts from their published biographical sketches reveal this diversity:[34]

I am an undergraduate student studying Chemical Engineering. . . . I rowed crew all of high school and continue to do so. . . . I have a long history of creating visual art and a deep abiding love of oil paints. . . . I also play violin and viola.

I am double majoring in Electrical Engineering and Music. . . . At various times, I have been involved in MIT's Symphony Orchestra, Muses, Musical Theater Guild, Concert Choir, Chamber Music Society, Chamber Chorus and Gilbert and Sullivan Players, and when not in rehearsals I enjoy listening (and singing along) to music by artists from Palestrina to Rihanna, reading and speaking French, baking, writing music, knitting

and crocheting, watching Disney movies and giving tours of MIT.

I'm a graduate student in the nuclear engineering department and I love to be creative! I play piano and flute, compose tonal music and figure skate. I also like to paint in watercolor, build furniture, sew clothes and cook. I believe that constructive fun and creativity is necessary to balance out the stress and seriousness of my nuclear engineering studies.

These students' biographical sketches demonstrate their passion for the arts, diverse involvements, and dedication to their primary areas of study. Their arts involvement serves to enhance and support their studies, providing a creative outlet and source of beneficial recreation.

Boston University, like MIT, offers a similar program led, in part, by a student advisory council and featuring an **"Arts Insiders"** program, created to ensure "students develop an active and participatory role in the arts as a meaningful element" of their student experience and their personal, academic, and social development. Unlike MIT's Arts Scholars program, Arts Insiders welcomes all interested students rather than being selective. Students enroll using an online form and receive notices about the group's events, such as on-campus performances by departmental, faculty-led, or student-led groups, off-campus events, or similar activities.

Student involvement in these organizations provides a focused, structured experience not possible by attending cultural arts events alone, nurturing a community of students with similar interests and facilitating the students' enjoyment of and engagement with the arts.

OFF-CAMPUS EXCURSIONS AND CULTURAL EVENTS

Universities may facilitate opportunities for students to experience cultural resources located off campus. Options at participating higher educational institutions depend somewhat on the geographic location of the college or university. Clearly, students attending an institution located near a large city could take advantage of a greater variety of cultural resources than those at an institution far from such amenities. Depending on the institution, destinations can include:

- Professional musical, theatrical, or dance performances
- Museums of art or culture
- Artists' studios or workshops
- Gallery walks
- Festivals or cultural events
- Poetry readings or spoken word performances

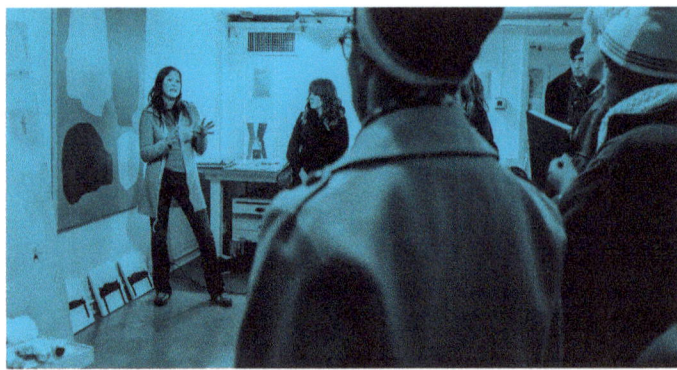

As with other co-curricular experiences made available to students, the distinctiveness of off-campus excursions offered by the universities studied lies in the recognition of the value of engaging students in the arts as an important component of their educational experience. According to a provost, "Artistic engagement brings immeasurable value to our social and academic development, impacting not only the way we perceive the world but how we approach so many disciplines, from the sciences to the humanities. . . . [T]he arts are fundamental to the . . . student experience inside and outside of the classroom" (qtd. in BU).

By facilitating students' attendance at cultural arts events, universities serve an important function in developing audiences. Students learn to discern high-quality performances and artistic products, become familiar with the norms of appropriate audience behavior, and may develop a lifelong interest in the arts through this exposure. Given a generation of reduced emphasis on the arts in K-12 education since the passage of No Child Left Behind in 2002, today's college students face adulthood with sometimes vastly reduced exposure to once commonplace activities such as attending a performance by a symphony orchestra or seeing a live theatrical production. Co-curricular excursions to such events may provide a student's first opportunity to experience a live performance, view works of visual art firsthand, or interact with artists during a studio visit. Even for students used to such experiences, co-curricular excursions allow for continuing engagement with the arts as well as fostering positive interactions with peers holding similar interests. Therefore, these types of co-curricular programs offer valuable experiences integrating the arts with students' campus life and laying a foundation for continuing arts appreciation later in life.

DEDICATED LEADERSHIP OF CO-CURRICULAR ARTS PROGRAMMING

The most notable best practice for co-curricular arts programs features establishment of a staff or faculty position dedicated to facilitating arts programming for students, a role taking several forms depending on the university under consideration. Boston University employs a Managing Director of the **BU Arts Initiative**, within the Office of the Provost. At Johns Hopkins University, a full-time director and several other staff members, housed in the department of Student Life, lead the **Homewood Arts Programs**. An assistant director and program coordinator in the Office of New Student Programs at the University of Michigan oversees the **Arts at Michigan** and Student Arts HUB. At USC, the Office of the Provost, specifically the Associate Provost in the division of Academic Affairs, leads **Visions and Voices**. At the University of Florida, a professor of environmental engineering sciences heads a committee overseeing the **SEA Change** program. Except for the director of Homewood Arts at Johns Hopkins, most of these administrators have additional responsibilities beyond overseeing co-curricular arts programming, but simply by maintaining a position of this type, these universities tangibly demonstrate valuation of the arts by ensuring thriving arts organizations on campus. At some institutions where students can choose from literally thousands of co-curricular options, establishing a new student organization can be a bewildering prospect. A staff member dedicated to facilitating arts organizations can make all the difference between the success or failure of a new organization.

Excellent co-curricular programming depends on outstanding leadership. The aforementioned individuals exemplify this characteristic, as do numerous other faculty, staff, and administrators who include co-curricular program oversight among their normal duties. The Dean of Religious Life at USC, for example, oversees a "**Spirituality and the Arts**" initiative and supports programming in ethnomusicology, student art exhibitions, theatrical performance, and architectural installations including an inflatable chapel. He explained that his office works closely with over 600 student clubs and over 100 student religious organizations, many of which include the arts.

Co-curricular programs experience constant flux, with new groups forming and other groups ending each semester. Administrative oversight improves a group's chances of survival, whereas groups entirely led by students necessarily experience frequent turnover in their leaders due to graduation or attrition. The complexity and fluidity of co-curricular programs require someone who exhibits the best practices in leadership described earlier in this chapter, especially the ability to be a big-picture thinker while maintaining a firm grasp of minutia such as policy and scheduling.

RECOGNITION SYSTEMS FOR CO-CURRICULAR INVOLVEMENT

Beyond establishment of dedicated positions for administration or oversight of arts programming in a co-curricular context, best practice includes broad institutional recognition of the value of these opportunities in students' overall academic lives. Best practice also involves providing students with a means of validation of their involvement in co-curricular activities. Students receive an academic transcript upon graduation, providing evidence of the courses they undertook and credits they earned, but generally speaking, no documentation proves their academic careers were richer, broader, and deeper as the direct result of their participation in co-curricular arts programming.

Some institutions have begun to implement a "digital badge" system as a means to capture and recognize co-curricular student accomplishment. Based on the concept of merit badges in youth organizations and bolstered by students' familiarity with digital gaming, a digital badge system recognizes student accomplishment with a digital logo or icon suitable for display on the student's webpage, résumé, social media profile, or professional documents. The MacArthur Foundation and Mozilla Foundation have partnered to create the **Open Badge Infrastructure**, designed to allow institutions to implement badging and to provide a means for students to curate and manage their digital identities (Ash). Universities might implement such systems to allow students to track their achievements outside of the classroom, giving them a resource for sharing this information with potential employers.

E-portfolios collect and curate accomplishments both in and out of the classroom through digital documentation. Teacher training programs utilize portfolios, also required in some arts disciplines, as a helpful tool for aspiring educators' job searches. Developing portfolios allows students to integrate their curricular and co-curricular engagements with an eye toward providing evidence to potential employers. The **Association**

for Authentic, Experiential and Evidence-Based Learning (AAEEBL), known for promoting the use of e-portfolios in higher education, emphasizes the value of e-portfolios in student learning. Eleven of the institutions participating in the Mellon Research Project are also members of AAEEBL.[35] Such tools allow students to reflect on their own educational process, promoting insights as students synthesize diverse learning experiences (The Association for Authentic, Experiential and Evidence-Based Learning, "About").

The use of e-portfolios is not standardized: students can collect evidence on a website, or the institution may host students' e-portfolios, sometimes through an external hosting service. E-portoflios are not limited to students: such collections prove useful for corporate professional development documentation and replace traditional paper-binder methods of evidence collection for promotion and tenure processes. Hosting services include:

DIGICATION: a platform provided through educational institutions (used by Boston University, for example) (Digication)

FOLIOTEK: a portfolio service contracted by the educational institution or by individual users, with applicability to accreditation, collection of strategic data, or provision of e-portfolio services to students (Foliotek)

PASS-PORT: a company providing e-portfolio services to institutions not only for student use but for institutional assessment and faculty promotion and tenure (Pass-Port)

Co-curricular transcripts serve a similar function for students. One of the institutions in the Mellon Research Project has begun to offer such documentation, and a database search revealed universities outside of the Mellon Research Project participants that are offering co-curricular transcripts. For example, the Student Activities Office website at Purdue University Calumet states:

> A **Co-curricular Transcript** ("CcT") . . . will help you get the competitive edge for securing employment, internship opportunities, graduate school admission and scholarships. A CcT is a document that complements your academic transcript by verifying your co-curricular involvement. It will be a valuable asset for students when trying to get ahead. (Purdue)

35 These institutions are Boston University, Dartmouth College, Harvard University, Indiana University, MIT, Pennsylvania State University, Stanford University, University of Kansas, University of Michigan., University of Virginia, and Tufts University (The Association for Authentic, Experiential and Evidence-Based Learning, "Academic").

Students at universities such as Kean University (New Jersey), the University of Tampa (Florida), and the University of Dayton (Ohio) have access to similar documentation. At each of these institutions, students self-report some of these data into a designated university website. For example, the **University of Dayton** suggests students include the following items:

- *Leadership Development – organization, activity, conference or program*
- *Educational and Skill Development – participation in any co-curricular learning experiences – i.e. workshops, training programs, or volunteer experiences – related to personal or professional development*
- *Awards and Honors – any type of formal recognition bestowed upon an individual or as a part of a group*
- *Student Organizations and Activities Participation – membership in any organization, club, activity, or program that requires sustained participation*
- *Community Service – must take place during enrollment as a student at University of Dayton*
- *Athletics – membership in any intercollegiate competitive sport or intramural team during enrollment at University of Dayton (Student)*

Co-curricular transcripts, e-portfolios, and digital badges provide valuable career documents for students. Moreover, they add a layer of institutional validation to co-curricular activities by creating an objective record. Official recognition via these recordkeeping systems moves co-curricular activities from sources of recreation or entertainment to a higher level of valuation, lending increased institutional importance to students' activities outside of the classroom or lab.

RECOMMENDATIONS FOR CO-CURRICULAR PROGRAMMING FROM INTERVIEW PARTICIPANTS

Several interview participants offered advice to those considering expansion or improvement of arts-related co-curricular programming; this advice addresses student recruitment, involvement, and alternative funding:

- The idea of letting students do and own their own projects – instead of just outreach for us – is really effective and is a good continuing commitment to students. Having a student on the board, too, is a good thing; having a student voice in decision making is key. . . . [Offering] student memberships, too, treating individual students as members is a really good way of building individual interest and involvement. Integrating the museum into their daily lives. (director of engagement, campus museum)
- Having an event open to all new students, early on,

is good: offer food, get them in the doors, and embed content in that social experience. (director of education, campus museum)
- [Our programs are] successful because they are nimble; summer series try to do things that are really attractive to the larger public, for example. Having a ton of programs and being nimble in that regard is really useful. (academic liaison, campus museum)
- I think [funding for co-curricular programs] should be endowment driven. Why not? We could do distinguished programming series at relatively small amounts of money, much less than a center or institute or a chair. We can do it in a way that's creative, endowed, active, and affordable. You can do a lot of "firsts" this way, which can shine a serious light on the co-curricular, and then it can become something curricular or whatever else. It can be really good for the curricular side and for many other programmatic forms. By proving the worth and excitement in this format, it can snowball as a development opportunity for an endowed chair or whatever. It's a marriage, not a competition. [We're] not serving different masters. (dean)

Educational institutions, in general, hold events to engage students in co-curricular programs early in their academic careers, especially at the beginning of each new school year. Observed best practice for co-curricular programming overall includes conducting specific outreach for arts-related programs and establishment of a position designated to provide oversight and support for such programs. Instituting systems of formal recognition through digital badges, e-portfolios, or co-curricular transcripts also represents best practice in this area.

OTHER BEST PRACTICES

A number of best practices observed during this study did not fit precisely into predetermined categories of curricular, research, programmatic, or co-curricular aspects of higher education. Presented categorically, the following examples consider aspects of extra-institutional partnership, community outreach, flexible degrees, and supporting and sustaining practice.

EXTRA-INSTITUTIONAL PARTNERSHIPS

Partnerships between universities or pairings of higher educational institutions with corporations, community groups, or other organizations exist across the landscape of higher education. Considering these relationships from the perspective of the arts, the School of the Art

Institute of Chicago (SAIC) engages in research and collaboration uncommon among stand-alone schools of art, providing a model of best practice outside of a research university setting. First, it established the **Shapiro Center for Research and Collaboration.** This organization supports classes sponsored by corporate partners Crate and Barrel and Motorola; in these classes, students design items offered for sale in CB2 stores[36] and work in sponsored collaborations with organizations such as a Chicago public elementary school to design a new cafeteria layout encouraging students to make healthier choices. The Shapiro Center also collaborates in a project with the University of Chicago's Urban Center for Computation and Data and Argonne National Laboratory in a project placing environmental sensors around the city and developing experimental data infrastructures to improve human life. Another partnership involves the Foundation for Homan Square; this partnership established a community center for art and design education programs in the former Sears catalog production facility located in the North Lawndale neighborhood of Chicago.[37]

Beyond the Shapiro Center's initiatives, SAIC established a partnership with the University of Chicago (UC) through the **UC Arts, Science & Culture Initiative.** The 2014-2015 Graduate Collaboration grants included 13 graduate students from UC and 5 from SAIC, forming 7 collaborative teams engaged in independent transdisciplinary research projects. In another partnership, students and faculty from SAIC and Northwestern University worked on a joint project "combining big data with collaborative research, studio arts, and visual communication design" to develop a summer course entitled "**Data Viz Collaborative,**" which resulted in an exhibition at SAIC's Leroy Neiman Center in August 2013 (School of the Art Institute of Chicago, "Big"). Experimental projects from three research groups were exhibited: "Big Data and School Choice" (in the Chicago area), "Mapping Genealogy and Ancestry," and "Eye-tracking: tracing the gaze in an image." The course also featured faculty research presentations, computer programming workshops, and field trips. "In today's increasingly data-driven world, artists and designers have much to contribute to innovation alongside scientists and engineers," according to SAIC President Walter E. Massey, himself a physicist (School of the Art Institute of Chicago, "Big"). SAIC also teamed with Northwestern's Segal Design Institute and the McCormick School of Engineering

in a 2015 course titled "**Data as Art.**" "This class truly shows what so many at Segal and McCormick teach about whole-brained engineering," according to a Northwestern student, "in that engineers can think creatively and artists analytically, and when they all do it together, the outcomes are even better" (qtd. in Segal).

SAIC utilizes STEM-integration with the arts rather than arts integration with STEM, including a **scientist-in-residence** program, lectures about such topics as "Colliding Art and Science: Particle Physics and Architecture at Fermilab and Common Research Methods in Art Practice,"[38] and an institutional prioritization of connections between students of the arts and corporate, academic, and cultural entities outside of the school. This reverses the typical idea of taking the arts in to other disciplines and instead brings other disciplines to the arts. SAIC provides students with an exceptionally high-quality visual art education while radically departing from traditional delineations between artistic disciplines, thus pursuing unprecedented connections with STEM through extra-institutional relationships.

COMMUNITY OUTREACH

Several of the participating institutions do an exemplary job of reaching out to their surrounding communities through the arts, including Otis College of Art and Design, the University of Michigan, Washington University in St. Louis, and the University of Virginia.

At Otis College of Art and Design, community engagement represents part of the core student experience alongside foundations courses and liberal arts and sciences requirements. The **Creative Action** program "offers project-based courses that match multidisciplinary teams of students with local and international community partners" (Otis), introducing students to environmental and social issues through institutional partnerships with public agencies and nonprofit organizations. Students develop creativity by focusing on genuine problems, thus gaining essential skills for future careers in art and design. Although educational institutions typically offer options for community engagement, Otis exemplifies best practice by placing such activities among students' core requirements, not just as an elective but as a mandated component of the educational experience.

---

36 CB2 is a division of Crate and Barrel.

37 For more information, see School of the Art Institute of Chicago, "Shapiro Center for Research and Collaboration: Sponsored Classes," and School of the Art Institute of Chicago, "Shapiro Center for Research and Collaboration: Research Partnerships."

38 For more information see, School of the Art Institute of Chicago, "SAIC," and School of the Art Institute of Chicago, "Art."

In a partnership between Michigan State University, Eastern Michigan University, Wayne State University, and faculty from the University of Michigan's School of Social Work, School of Art and Design, and School of Music, Theatre & Dance, **"The Boulevard House"** takes a settlement house approach to project-based learning at an off-campus location in south Detroit. The Boulevard House "incorporat[es] five dimensions of social change needed to create lasting impact in social, political, and economic spheres within which distressed neighborhoods operate: comprehensiveness, synchrony, integration, long-term perspective, and inclusiveness" (Gant 1). Community partners, such as El Museo del Norte and the People's Community Services of Metropolitan Detroit, work in concert with faculty and students from the university to provide services to the community while also engaging in curricular and research activities on site. Projects feature historical and museum exhibitions at the site; weekly "Kaffe Politik" sessions gathering community members to enjoy coffee while reading and discussing the Sunday newspapers; monthly "Social Cinema" film screenings accompanied by discussions; and "Salon Saturdays" featuring the work of local artists, musicians, spoken word, and facilitated discussions (El Museo). The Boulevard House exists as a work-in-progress, modeling best practice in arts integration through the linkage of social work and the arts in conjunction with community partners and establishment of cross-institutional partnerships.

At Washington University in St. Louis (WUSTL), the **Sam Fox School of Design & Visual Arts** houses several ongoing socially engaged collaborations between the university and community. Among these programs, CityStudioSTL, in partnership with WUSTL's Skandalaris Center for Interdisciplinary Innovation and Entrepreneurship, offers faculty and students the opportunity to work with local community groups and residents to ideate, plan, and build public projects. Past projects include construction of an outdoor classroom for an elementary school, "design/build" courses for community members, and a digital fabrication studio in which students created an avian observatory for a migratory bird sanctuary, in conjunction with the Audubon Center at Riverlands and the Army Corps of Engineers (Sam Fox School, "CityStudioSTL").

Two programs reach out to public school students. The WashUCity Design Partnership involves high school students in learning the principles of communication design through a graphics class at University City High School. Led by WUSTL communication design majors,

students in this class develop their creative strengths and explore career opportunities (Sam Fox School, "WashUCity"). The Alberti Program-Architecture for Young People offers a studio workshop for fourth through ninth graders that features hands-on experience in sustainable design and introduces students to 2-D and 3-D architectural problems (Sam Fox School, "Alberti").

Last, the University City Sculpture Series has explored public art since 1986, involving "more than 200 students, 17 professors, 4 deans, 2 chancellors, 60 commission members, and 2 mayors" (Sam Fox School, "University City Sculpture"). Participants collaborate to propose temporary works of public art, working through details such as location selection, estimates of project costs, and design models. They present their proposals to the city, which funds creation and installation of winning projects. Not all projects include outdoor installations: winning projects for 2015 encompass an exhibition of tintype photographs of St. Louis community members, an installation of large concrete hands holding semitransparent historical photographs of activist moments, an outdoor living room space, and a monument in the form of a transparent plexiglass stockade (Sam Fox School, "University City Sculpture"). A University City Gallery Series joined the Sculpture Series in 2013, displaying gallery-based works in painting, drawing, printmaking, and photography (Sam Fox School, "University City Gallery").

Similar partnerships between arts and design and community organizations exist at schools both in and out of the Mellon Research Project; however, WUSTL demonstrates best practice not only through its programs' value to both the Sam Fox School and the St. Louis community but also through these partnerships' long-term stability. Attainment of this level of institutionalization safeguards against the danger of investing large amounts of time, energy, and resources only to see a program fade away; instead, these partnerships are firmly established as valued parts of the Sam Fox School's culture.

In another instance of outreach within the university and to the surrounding community, **OpenGrounds** at the University of Virginia, both a civic partnership and intra-campus effort, "builds creative, collaborative partnerships between individuals and institutions to generate innovative solutions for critical societal needs" (OpenGrounds). Under the leadership of the Office of the Vice President for Research, OpenGrounds began in the School of Architecture as a flexible space designed to encourage collaboration, according to its founding director. Intrigued by the idea of enhancing the studio environment as a place for informal student interaction, the Vice President for Research suggested the university needed more such spaces and formed a student design group in collaboration with the director and a noted architect then serving as a visiting professor. Two of the graduate student members of this group, said the founding director of OpenGrounds, "had the idea of not doing a building but doing a network of places around the university that we could enhance and turn into spaces for gathering shared ideas and building off of existing infrastructure. We realized that we could get started without having to raise so much money."

OpenGrounds utilizes a space called the OpenGrounds Corner Studio, which holds "open hours" each day. Students, faculty, and staff can use the space to work together, seek feedback or input in working out ideas, or discuss projects, all while using its interactive technologies and the whiteboards lining the studio walls. The Corner Studio provides a large, continuously transformable room designed for performance, exhibition, and meetings. Drama and music faculty participated in its design, allowing for high-end theatrical and musical performance with capability for projection. The space accommodates small group interaction rather than large gatherings. The founding director explained:

If you are actually going to get a group together from different schools to have a conversation, this is the place to do it: you are on no one's home turf. We're trying to accelerate a culture of creativity and curiosity. We put this at the high level where new ideas would be sparked, [where] people [are] opening up new territories of research. It's not about managing long-term collaborative projects. It's not strictly about innovation and entrepreneurship. Some of them are leading to interaction between faculty that never would have happened. The goal is to be the spark, a catalyst on a very high level.

Funding for OpenGrounds comes from a mixture of sources, including grants, corporate partnerships, and the Vice President for Research. The founding director reported: "one of the big benefits of what we're doing is [that] we've been able to engage alumni [who] haven't traditionally been engaged with their own schools, but they saw something new, they got excited, and we ended up connecting them with the deans."

According to the founding director, OpenGrounds demonstrates excellence by utilizing existing resources

and works to build "lateral networks across the university . . . , curiosity-driven, question-driven research that engages all of the disciplines as a means to spark different directions for the university." In a move away from the 19th-century hierarchical structures of the research university, it seeks a reorientation toward founder Thomas Jefferson's original vision for the institution. The founding director said: "How do you transform an institution? You can start with trying to change the structure: reorganize disciplines, move pieces around, change incentives. The other is you start doing projects, prototyping ideas, working on questions and collaborations that require people to come together from different fields and build a stronger team of diversity."

OpenGrounds also models best practice through the strong support of the university president and the vice president for research. The founding director said, "There was a willingness to take risk. We are seen in some ways, by the low financial commitment, as low risk. Potentially high risk on the intellectual side, but the key is to find the faculty to get it started who are willing and interested in moving this way." Intentionally eschewing the structure of a center or an institute and initially requiring little in the way of physical or monetary resources, OpenGrounds addresses a need articulated by interviewees by providing an environment in which collaborations and partnerships integrating the arts can take place organically.

Otis College of Art and Design, the University of Michigan, Washington University in St. Louis, and the University of Virginia serve as models for practices other institutions might adopt. Educational institutions usually express support for community engagement or service, but these four institutions achieve remarkable results by integrating the arts with their goal for community involvement.

FLEXIBLE DEGREES

At **Goldsmiths, University of London**, students can pursue an individualized course of study at an institution known for its interdisciplinary approach to education. Graduate students create their own programs of research-intensive study featuring collaborative, innovative, and creative connections to academic and non-academic organizations. Although not specifically an art school, the arts factor into the university's primary identity and rich history. Goldsmiths alumni have been exceptionally successful in their careers as artists, including Turner Prize winners, Oscar recipients, Mercury Music prizes, Ivor Novello Award winners, and BAFTAs, attesting to the success of its preparation of graduates.

Granted, the system of higher education in the UK differs from that of the U.S., but the flexibility of the degree programs at Goldsmiths, the level of individual attention students receive, and the university's philosophy of active interdisciplinarity all combine to make Goldsmiths a model U.S. institutions would do well to study at greater length. The Goldsmiths program departs significantly from the traditional conservatory approach present at U.S. educational institutions, where a much more rigid approach to training in the arts remains prevalent. The high quality of the university's graduates testifies to the program's effectiveness, presenting intriguing possibilities for additional study.

SUPPORTING AND IMPROVING PRACTICE

A final model of best practice exists at the **University of Alabama at Birmingham** (UAB), which underwent a major revision of its studio art program during the past year. The program completely rewrote its curricula in alignment with **National Association of Schools of Art and Design** (NASAD) competencies and also incorporated university emphases on writing across the curriculum, undergraduate research, service learning, team-based learning, and community engagement.[39] The new curricula create a clear progression of learning within each artistic discipline; furthermore, the chair implemented a syllabus build tool to be utilized by all faculty, providing direct instruction in its use along with training in writing high-quality outcomes and objectives for all courses offered in the department. Faculty were provided with prototype syllabi and instructional materials for use at their discretion in the newly redesigned courses. After just the first year of these programmatic changes, the department's enrollment rose 6.5%, according to the chair, who reported increased faculty enthusiasm about the changes and energy for improving their teaching practice and increasing their students' knowledge and skill as artists.

Not all higher educational institutions would choose to undertake as extensive a curricular and programmatic revision as has UAB's Department of Art and Art History. However, this exemplary effort supports and improves pedagogical and administrative practice, leading to enhanced teaching and learning and benefitting all stakeholders.

OPPORTUNITIES FOR FURTHER STUDY

The Mellon Research Project's findings reveal valuable insights while also uncovering areas where additional acquisition of knowledge would be beneficial, such as exploring connections between arts integration and curriculum development, the impact of personal arts integration on one's professional pursuits, and the recognition of the value of failure and risk-taking inherent in the arts.

CURRICULUM DEVELOPMENT, EDUCATIONAL THEORY, AND FACULTY DEVELOPMENT

In curricular development involving arts integration, the Mellon Research Project could not fully address the educational theory and philosophy undergirding these efforts. Much could be explored though examination of the relationship of instruction in the arts in comparison to other fields. Researchers might also study these teaching practices in terms of differences between pedagogy (teacher-directed instruction, transforming into student-centered instruction), andragogy (teacher-facilitated instruction, which has transformed into learner-centered instruction), heutagogy (self-directed learning), and approaches such as academagogy or omnigogy (fluid, flexible movement between instructional methods) and digigogy (distance learning or online learning) (Winter, McAuliffe, Hargreaves, and Chadwick).

Engaged learning, which has been a topic of much interest in academia for at least the past decade, provides another means of understanding arts integration. The arts provide intrinsically engaging content, allowing students to connect with course topics on a more emotional or visceral level than through lectures, textbooks, and research papers. Furthermore, making and doing activate different parts of the brain than reading and listening, providing an enhanced learning experience and greater student engagement. In the "Science and Engaged Learning" edition (Winter 2005) of the Association of American Colleges and Universities' *Peer Review* journal, senior fellow Stephen Bowen provides an explanation of student engagement as occurring in a hierarchical progression. First, student engagement with the learning process indicates basic attention and academic effort on the part of the student. At the next level, students engage with the object of study, a common practice in both the arts and sciences in which students directly examine, characterize, analyze, or evaluate something in order to build new knowledge. The third level of student engagement involves the contexts

---

39 Bruce Mackh, the Mellon Research Project Director, served as an independent consultant on this project.

of the subject of study, in which the student considers the breadth of knowledge surrounding a given subject. Bowen suggests interdisciplinary study's suitability to this level because students look beyond the object of study to its cultural, ethical, or environmental placement. The final level of student engagement deals with the human condition. Particularly prevalent in the social sciences and humanities, this level of engagement rests on the belief in all knowledge as socially constructed and dependent on sociocultural contexts (Bowen).

To combine Bowen's comparison of these levels of engagement with other higher educational initiatives, **TABLE 7** might be helpful, including a column for common arts integration practices.

A great deal more exploration of the relationship between higher educational theory and arts integration remains, but the Mellon Research Project cannot presently address this important connection. Similarly, it cannot fully investigate the topic of arts-integrated research. For example, the study investigated participants' experience with the impact of disciplinary vernaculars and departmental cultures on their research and curricular collaborations, asking participants specific questions in these areas. However, factors outside of their specific experience in these collaborations remain unexplored, such as asking an artist whether she had

ever studied research methodologies or questioning a scientist about her background knowledge of educational theory or philosophy. Indeed, students of the arts generally do not receive direct instruction in research methodologies, and although they may well engage in research processes during the creation of their artistic works or performances, they might experience a prohibitively steep learning curve when collaborating with scientific researchers committed to a certain approach to investigation. Likewise, aside from members of the college of education, educators from virtually all academic disciplines traditionally receive very little training in instructional methodologies, making the task of curriculum design even more complex due to challenges accompanying partners' divergent disciplinary assumptions.

Those who seek to engage in arts integration must develop a cognitive map encompassing the systems, practices, methods, and methodologies with which they will work. They must be aware of funding, administrative concerns, assessment, means of valuation, and measures of success. They must be prepared to explain how the arts have made their program, course, or project better than it would otherwise have been – to justify why all this effort has been worthwhile if they hope to persuade others of the value and benefit of these programs, courses, or projects.

TABLE 7.
STUDENT ENGAGEMENT
AND ARTS INTEGRATION

LEVEL OF ENGAGEMENT	RELATED CONCEPT	TYPE OF ARTS INTEGRATION
Engagement with the learning process	Active learning	Infusion of the arts into another discipline
Engagement with the object of study	Experiential learning	Diffusion – hands-on making and doing
Engagement with contexts of the object of study	Multidisciplinary learning	Fusion – equal partnership between arts activities and content in a partnering discipline
Engagement with social and civic contexts	Service learning	Participation in arts-integrated community service or in arts-integrated sponsored research

In their new book, *Creative Schools: The Grassroots Revolution That's Transforming Education*, Ken Robinson and Lou Aronica argue for a new educational model, explaining the present situation in which higher education remains trapped between the 19th-century assembly-line educational model arising in the Industrial Age and the demands of the 21st-century employers students face upon graduation. K-12 education continues to train students for individual achievement on high-stakes tests, valuing conformity to instructional standards established by legislators, not educators. Present business and industry, on the other hand, seek employees skilled in critical thinking, creativity, and the ability to collaborate. Universities must somehow bridge this chasm, providing students with more than just a traditional monodisciplinary education. The 20th-century paradigm under which students go to college, study one thing, and find a job doing one thing for the rest of their lives no longer applies, underscoring arts integration's potential value to provide an infusion of the very characteristics suppressed during students' prior academic experiences. However, until university educators begin to understand why this situation exists, why the arts can provide a remedy, and why they should be willing to form curricular partnerships between the arts and other academic areas, the road ahead will continue to be difficult.

PERSONAL ARTS INTEGRATION

The idea of integrating arts participation into one's personal life rather than specifically into a course or project arose frequently during the Mellon Research Project's investigations, with countless students, faculty members, or researchers citing their personal creative practice apart from other scholarly pursuits. A doctoral student in nuclear physics wrote poetry and composed music while monitoring a nuclear reactor; a Nobel Laureate in physics painted with watercolors; and the MIT Arts Scholars reported active participation in an array of the arts. At an institutional level, the University of Michigan supports the **Life Sciences Orchestra**, comprising members of the U-M Health System, Department of Biomedical Engineering, the School of Dentistry, and related academic divisions. Open to faculty, staff, students, alumni, and volunteers in the life sciences, the organization provides a performance outlet for those with previous musical experience and builds a sense of community across the life sciences divisions on the University of Michigan's campus (Gifts of Art, Life). Personal engagement in arts practice offers promising possibilities for future research, but as it represents somewhat of a divergence from the original emphasis

of the Mellon Research Project, full pursuit of these intriguing ideas during this study proved infeasible.

RISK, FAILURE, AND 21ST-CENTURY CAREER COMPETENCIES

Another intriguing idea encountered during the research for this study concerns the concept of failure and willingness to take risks. A professor of genetics and director of an institute offered some insights into this area, illuminating much about the topic of arts integration. Although somewhat lengthy, his full remarks on this topic appear below:

How do you manage failure and reduce its risk and benefit from it? Oddly enough, the private sector is much more sophisticated on issues of failure and risk than academia; Academics are essentially individuals that are so fundamentally risk-averse that they've never left school and stay in the same institution all of their lives. Risk is getting in a boat and traveling over the ocean when you're told there is an edge you are going to fall over. Risk is articulating a vision that is likely to be very disquieting to a lot of people. This institute has a different objective than many departments on campus. A department on campus that has to teach has a very different set of objectives than one that is set on exploration and discovery.

As academics, we always turn failure into success. It's almost impossible to find an academic who will say I failed outright – they will always say they failed in a stated goal but learned something else more important. It's learning, but it's also dishonest. I want failure to be "It's a disaster and mistake and wrong path, and I'm starting over and doing it differently." That's what I have to protect. And [I have to] be honest and reassure them – that it's ok to be fundamentally wrong and misguided, and unless you are [wrong] enough times, I don't think you'll make a breakthrough. History attests to this – not to this other mode where we incrementally stagger along never really making mistakes and always finding some prophet in the path that you then retrospectively call risky. Risk is embarrassment and risk is pain. ... And this, again, is an area where disciplines of the scientists have an awful lot to learn from the artists. Artists often have made difficult decisions – [I have] many artists and novelist friends who go unpaid for years because they believe in what they are doing. That's risk – real risk.

The arts encourage risk-taking, experimentation, and exploration, but university students arrive on campus pre-trained in risk aversion, having grown up in an academic system rewarding them for achieving 100% on an exam, not for trying an exam multiple times until they "get it right." When students enter the workforce, they find no such situation exists in adulthood: life demands a high capacity for iteration, a willingness to try and try again, seeking new means of addressing challenges. Integrating the arts in the university helps to address this need, as students are involved in participatory investigations simulating likely conditions outside academia.

Of course, students should enter the university with competencies in reading, writing, and mathematics and with basic knowledge of science and history. However, the deficits identified in students' capacity for creative expression, critical thinking, problem solving, or ability to conduct collaborative work – the skills addressed through arts integration – indicate a serious problem in the U.S. system of P-20 education,[40] which has not kept pace with the changing nature of the careers and professions students must take up in adulthood. Such reform extends beyond the scope of the Mellon Research Project, yet university educators should become aware of this situation and should understand the reasons why their arts-integrative efforts have become crucial.

The primary rationale behind arts integration in the research university rests in the nature of 21st-century human civilization, which demands a greater capacity for creativity, innovation, collaboration, and communication than ever before. Shifting employer expectations place increasing value on effective communication, the ability to work in teams, decision making, critical thinking and analytical reasoning, and the ability to apply knowledge and skills to real-world settings (Hart). In a January 26, 2015, article for the Washington Post, Arizona State University faculty member Jeffrey J. Selingo asked, "Why are so many college students failing to gain job skills before graduation?" Selingo said employers find students to be "severely lacking in some basic skills, particularly problem solving, decision making, and the ability to prioritize tasks" (Selingo). He reported that employers find students who had pursued activities outside of their major and who had participated in internships during their undergraduate years were those more likely to succeed in the workplace. This makes a strong argument for the value of co-curricular programming, which features just such areas of engagement. Furthermore, the arts-integrative curricular and research options examined in the Mellon Research Project offer multiple pathways to develop problem solving, decision making,

and prioritization, representing standard features of students' involvement in arts-based investigations.

From medicine to teaching, from corporate administration to mechanical engineering, fields of human endeavor have become more collaborative, more inclusive, and less static than they were a generation ago. Moreover, technologies continue to accelerate change in virtually every aspect of life, increasing the demand for adaptability. Recognizing the presence of the arts within every field and developing the ability to engage with them successfully in these contexts may well become the hallmarks of a university education in the future. This suggests a two-pronged proposition. On the one side, artists should receive an education allowing them to merge into professional contexts as well as honing their skills toward individual artistic achievement. On the other, students pursuing majors outside of the arts should receive an education imparting awareness of the arts and fluency in the creativity and collaboration expected in the workplace. In no way should this suggest that attaining monodisciplinary expertise has become passé. But it is not enough. Best practice demands universities impart knowledge of and experience in the arts to all students because doing so equips students for the constant change they will encounter throughout their lives, allows them to recognize the arts surrounding them, and prepares them for active participation in making and doing to enrich their personal and professional lives.

CONCLUSIONS

Every institution and each individual participating in the Mellon Research Project offered an example of best practice in one form or another. Part of the work planned under the next Mellon-funded project at ArtsEngine and a2ru is to create a detailed catalog of these individual and institutional exemplars and to draw out further data suitable for deeper analyses. Based on the information presented in this chapter and considering the vast array of best practices discovered during the past three years of interviews, several themes emerged.

BEGIN EVEN IF THE OUTCOME IS UNCLEAR.

Success sometimes simply means taking the initiative to begin, even when participants cannot foresee the outcome. Whether called "build the cart and then worry about the horse" or "do what you can from where you are," projects succeed even without a substantial budget, significant administrative support, or changes to existing policy. Change sometimes begins on a very small scale, with one person who has a good idea and chooses to act upon it. Researchers identified such examples throughout the project, particularly among faculty members who pursued their collaborative, arts-integrative, and extra-disciplinary projects or courses despite daunting challenges and obstacles.

If such change spreads beyond its point of origin, a level of institutional acceptance becomes necessary. This may exist on a comparatively small scale, within a single department or division, or it may extend throughout the university. Individuals with a contagious vision initiated substantive change using only the resources and influence at hand. In other words, to begin one must sometimes simply begin.

This study offers aspirational examples for those considering the launch of a new arts-integrative effort, not a prescriptive manual or roadmap for how to do arts integration. Each example developed independently and organically within a particular environment, undoubtedly differing from existing conditions present at other locations. The point is not to replicate the example precisely but to find inspiration for scaling, adapting, and implementing these ideas elsewhere. While designation as a best practice depends on four factors (parity, sustainability, institutionalization, and replicability), new arts integration efforts could not meet all of these criteria from the start. One must consider the "thingness of the thing," as philosopher Martin Heidegger pondered in his essay, "The Origin of the Work of Art" (Heidegger). Thingness, to Heidegger, moves beyond material substance, referring to the fundamental being differentiating an object from other objects or ideas. When we look at an example of arts integration such as Visions and Voices at the University of Southern California, we could perceive its funding mechanisms, location, widespread institutional support, and even the facilities in which guest artists perform or present as being unattainable for most institutions aspiring to such programming. However, if we look for the thingness, or essence, of Visions and Voices, finding it in the informal post-performance interactions between artists and audience members, we can determine ways to work around our own institutional, geographic, financial, or material limitations to establish workable strategies for implementation of similar, yet adaptively scaled, efforts.

The four aspects of best practice – parity, sustainability, institutionalization, and replicability – may prove elusive. Collaborations may involve unequal partnerships, never achieving parity between participants. Projects, programs, or courses may occur just once, using the limited human and material resources at hand and falling short of institutional or departmental acceptance. Clearly, even among the institutions featured as models of best practice, substantial differences in resources and structures affect the programs offered. James Madison University's Institute for Visual Studies provides 3,000 square feet of space for arts-integrative collaborations, whereas MIT recently built a new 163,000-square-foot, 6-story facility for the Media Lab, partially funded by a $27 million philanthropic bequest (MIT Media Lab, "Building"). However, this obvious discrepancy should not create the impression that Media Lab is "better" than the Institute for Visual Studies. Researchers deliberately avoided such comparisons throughout this document specifically to refrain from creating such an unfair impression. Best practice does not lie in the amount of space devoted to arts integration, nor in budgets, numbers of participants, or other quantifiable factors. Rather, best practice becomes evident in a personal and institutional commitment to arts integration, leveraging available financial, physical, intellectual, and human resources advantageously, whether these are plentiful or scarce.

INSTITUTIONALIZATION

Best practice arises through moderation and sustainability, avoiding over-immersion in even the best of ideas lest they become fads, rapidly fading away. Arts integration should not merely be a buzzword without tangible substance. Institutions exhibiting best practice weave the arts into the fabric of academic life through programmatic structures and favorable policy allowing faculty to receive professional credit for arts-integrative, extra-disciplinary, or collaborative work. Institutionalization of arts integration creates a stable environment in which these philosophies and practices can take root and grow.

GENUINE PARTNERSHIPS

Collaborations should not treat the arts as a mere handmaiden to another discipline. Situations will certainly arise in which any given disciplinary area could serve to enhance inquiry in another. These can be genuinely valuable collaborations; nonetheless, the weight of these unequal partnerships should not consistently skew in a direction creating persistent inequities. Arts integration not only indicates how the arts can benefit teaching, learning, and research in other academic domains, but how the arts might derive value from these partnerships as well.

ENDURING VALUE

Although the Mellon Research Project's focus does not extend to the overall value of the arts within research universities, the arts possess enduring value of their own. Higher education continues to value monodisciplinarity, regardless of the academic domain under consideration, whether a beautiful solution in pure mathematics or an aria sung by a coloratura soprano. Of course, visualization of "big data," groundbreaking research projects leading to world-changing discoveries, and arts integration across the landscape of the university remain important, but the pure aesthetic experience afforded by the arts deserves attention, too. Interview participants notably maintain a baseline belief in the value and importance of the arts, not just in combination with other disciplines, but for their own sake.

The arts and artists benefit from arts-integrative engagement with other fields, just as others benefit from interaction and partnership with the arts, providing exposure to many types and tokens of creativity. Based on the most successful programs, partnerships, or courses discovered in the Mellon Research Project, we might identify three motivations for arts faculty members to engage in arts integration:[41]

- *Improved creative practice and personal enrichment: Collaborations expose scholars to new stimuli, provide productive frictions and creative challenges, and promote the development of professional relationships with partners from outside of the participants' primary areas of practice.*
- *Enhanced professional standing: Collaborations can allow participants to gain a deeper understanding of the creative process and its deep connections to research.*
- *Enriched student learning and career success: Educators hold students' academic and career success in high regard. Students who participate in the arts can gain demonstrable benefit from this experience, advantageous to arts educators and to the educational institution as a whole.*

Because these areas diverge somewhat from the original language in the first grant from The Andrew W. Mellon Foundation, further investigation of the benefits of arts integration to the arts and artists remains a potential subject of additional study. However, at the most basic level, arts integration requires the participation of artists, who may be reluctant to engage without knowledge of how this activity will be of benefit to their arts practice, professional activities, or teaching.

FINDINGS

- Co-teaching and cross-listing an arts-integrated course provides greater opportunities for faculty to establish such partnerships across diverse disciplines and to provide students with viable options to enroll in these courses. Beneficial administrative support for such courses includes consideration for faculty teaching loads, provision for faculty displacement, and support for course planning.

- Administrators' ability to impart a contagious vision and to exercise skillful leadership remains crucial to any academic endeavor's success, exemplified by many outstanding leaders participating in the Mellon Research Project. Among the areas of concern to faculty and administrators, liberal interpretation of existing policies for promotion and tenure allow faculty to receive due consideration for arts-integrative work outside of their primary discipline, thus mitigating a significant impediment to arts integration.

- Centers and institutes provide affiliated faculty with a professional community in which arts-integrative research and teaching can thrive. Collaboration with internal and external partners, including corporate and community organizations, provide students with genuine engagement in arts-integrative scholarship and research, fulfilling their desire for meaningful, impactful activities involving the arts. Funding models incorporating stable revenue sources, such as tuition or university-level funding, allow centers and institutes to succeed, and curricular connections add value by providing faculty with structures for promotion or tenure not always available in a research institute or center alone.

- Research in, through, with, or about the arts was present across the sites visited, from small individual projects to permanent, large-scale installations featuring high-level research partnerships. Inclusion of the arts as equal partners from the onset of a project ensures fairness, preventing perception of the arts as a mere handmaiden to another discipline. Similarly, research initiated by artists, in collaboration with scholars from other disciplines, can yield long-lasting, fruitful partnerships.

- Co-curricular arts programming represents a valued resource for students, providing a creative outlet and meeting needs not addressed through regular degree programs. Validation systems such as digital badges, e-portfolios, and co-curricular transcripts allow students to create an authoritative record of their co-curricular involvement.

- Other best practices encompass partnerships between stand-alone art schools and research universities, engagement between the arts and community organizations, and efforts to support and improve arts practice at study locations, moving beyond curricular, research, or co-curricular arts integration into efforts to improve the world outside of the university and to enhance the arts themselves within its borders.

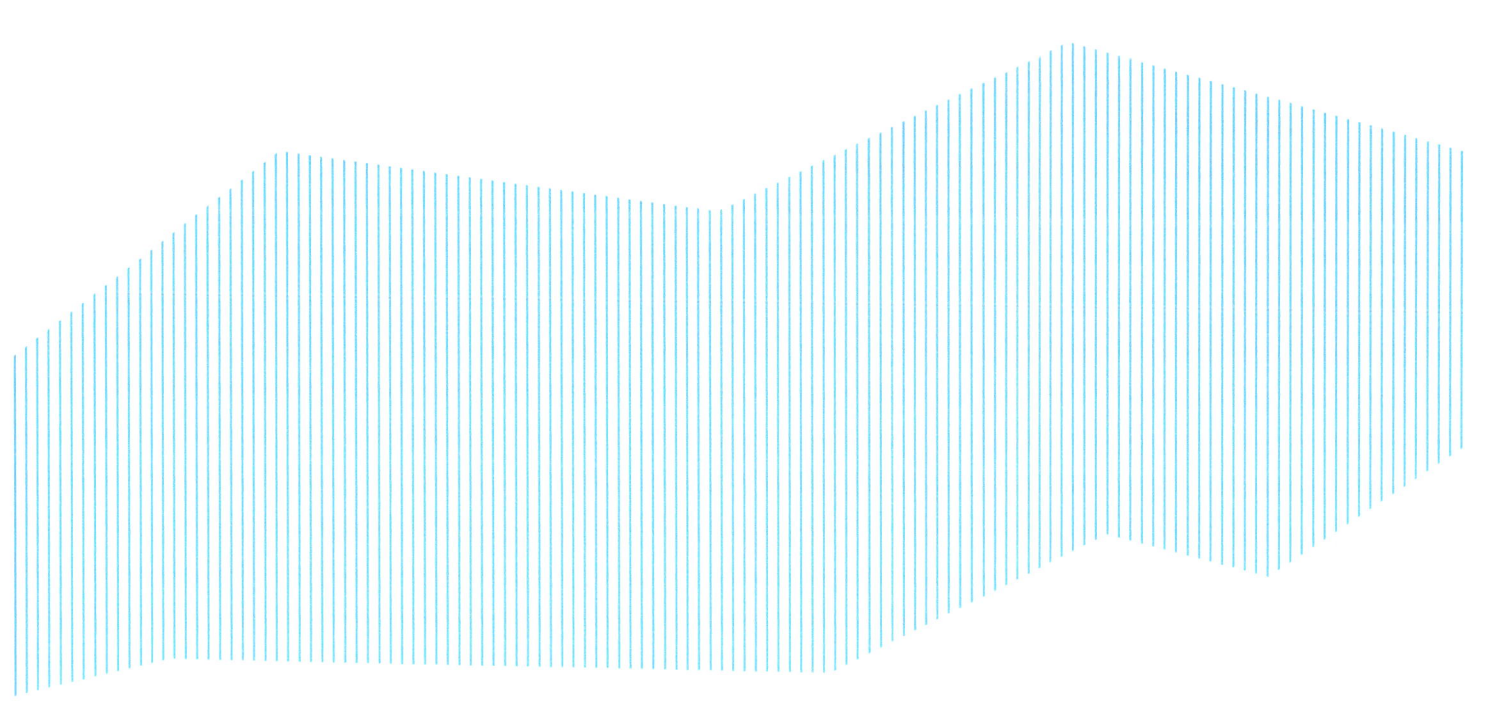

CHAPTER SIX

SUMMARY & RECOMMENDATIONS

The Mellon Research Project began as a mixed methodological study of arts integration at RU/VH universities, seeking to identify best practices in research, curricular, programmatic, and co-curricular areas in which arts integration takes place on the campuses of partner institutions. Researchers gathered the majority of data through site visits and interviews with individuals at all levels of the higher educational spectrum who engage in or are concerned with arts integration. The study's basic design yielded a vast storehouse of interview data, providing plentiful opportunities for further research. However, this proved too large a collection to examine in as much depth as would have been ideal, given the demands of protracted travel and tight scheduling. Interviews commenced in November 2012, less than two months after the Research Project Director joined the project, and concluded in February 2015, only four months before the deadline for completion of the final report. Truly, this could have been three large studies rather than one, and many more discoveries than this study is able to convey remain unexplored within the existing data set.

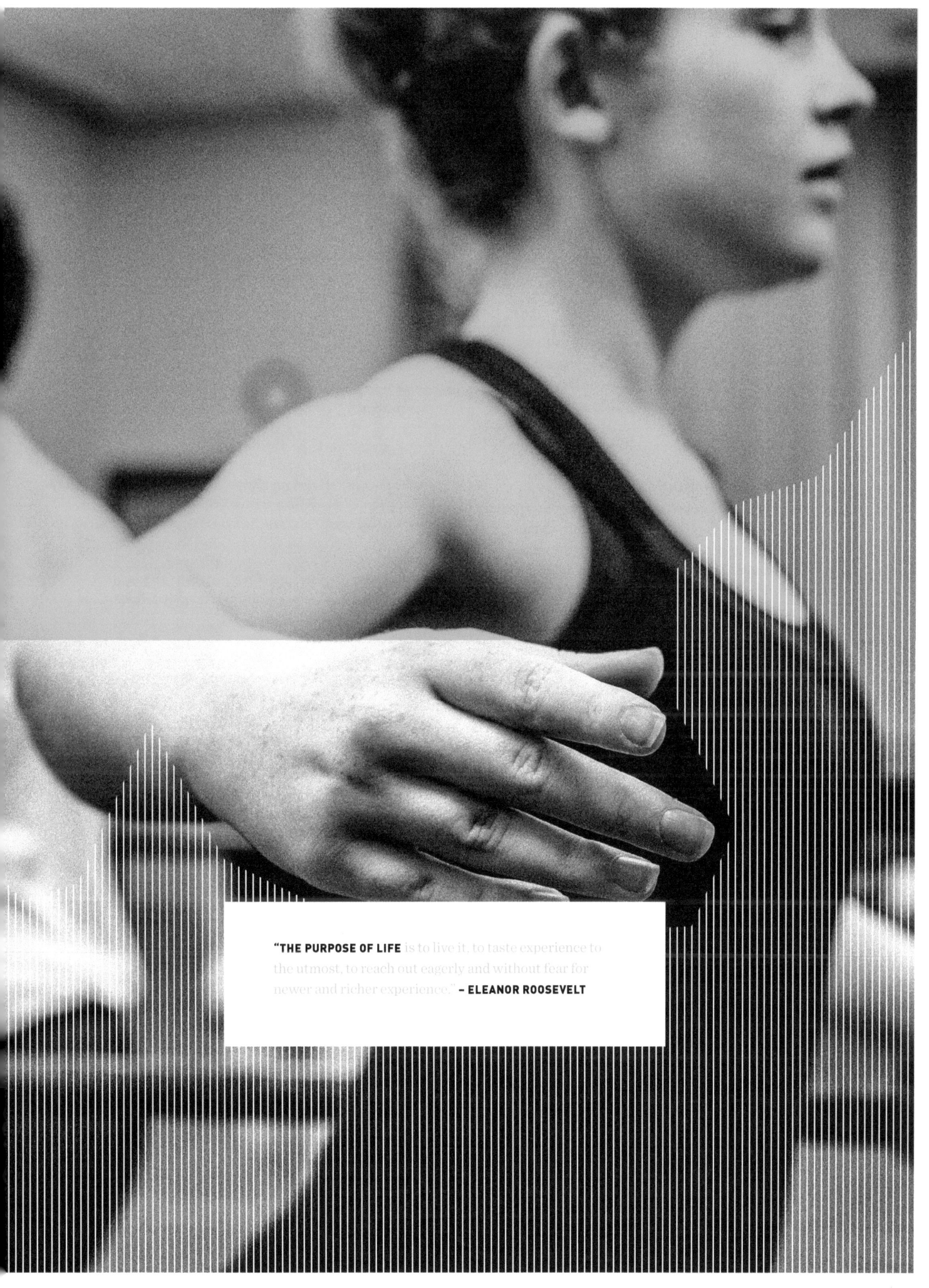

"**THE PURPOSE OF LIFE** is to live it, to taste experience to the utmost, to reach out eagerly and without fear for newer and richer experience." – **ELEANOR ROOSEVELT**

Although some participants provided limited numerical information regarding items such as budget or grant amounts, program costs and expenses, revenue generated, numbers of faculty or staff, or student enrollment figures, it did not lead to a sufficient compilation suitable for statistical analysis. Participant narratives generated thousands of pages of analysis and approximately 1,100 hours of video. The University of Michigan will archive this data for further study. Further research might collect more detailed program details in order to conduct comparative analyses. Since it was the first study of its kind, researchers came to understand some of the challenges of data collection, especially in cases where universities do not compile reports or annual accounts of arts-related activities across research, curricula, and co-curricular life.

SUMMARY OF FINDINGS

Project findings, as presented in the previous chapters, address the initial grant language specifying the project's purpose in identifying models, obstacles, implementation strategies, costs and impact on students and faculty as well as on research, practice, and teaching in other knowledge areas.

MODELS OF ARTS INTEGRATION

- *Curricular arts integration occurs through a range of practices, from collaborations in which the arts or design support instruction in a partnering discipline (infusion), students engage in the arts or design through an immersive creative experience (diffusion), or the arts or design partner equally with one or more other learning areas (fusion).*

- *Research collaborations involving the arts also occur across a continuum, spanning equal partnerships; situations in which a non-arts discipline supports research in, through, or about the arts; or circumstances in which the arts support research in a partnering discipline, mainly through data visualization, sonification, or other embodiment.*

- *Institutional or programmatic structures for arts integration exist in interdisciplinary degree programs and in centers or institutes fostering research and teaching that integrate the arts with diverse academic fields.*

- *Co-curricular programs integrate the arts with students' overall academic lives through direct participation in the arts or design. Such programs allow students to engage in the arts even when their programs of study might not accommodate coursework in the arts.*

- *Measurements of the success or impacts of arts-integrative activities resist generalization, manifesting differently in each specific instance. Further development of tools for assessment of arts-integrative activities represents an area for future study.*

STUDENT NEEDS AND PERCEPTIONS

- *Students described themselves as "native to interdisciplinarity," seeing a natural fit between their artistic and other academic pursuits and maintaining a fluid and flexible relationship to disciplinary identity.*

- *Students expressed a strong desire to be part of a community of like-minded people involved in arts integration.*

- *Students want to be part of something bigger than themselves and to make an impact on the world, using their artistic talents through involvement in local communities or shaping national or worldwide discussions as part of this generation's voice.*

- *Students reported becoming involved in arts integration by chance, discovering a new educational trajectory through happenstance rather than intention.*

- *Students desire authentic engagement and establishment of lasting arts-integrative, interdisciplinary learning communities.*

CHALLENGES AND ADMINISTRATIVE CONCERNS

- *Promotion and tenure emerged as primary concerns across faculty and administrative participants, who reported difficulties in obtaining or conferring consideration for aspects of teaching or research occurring outside of disciplinary norms.*

- *Considerations surrounding funding and associated perceptions of status pervade higher education. Participants reported beneficial partnerships between the arts and disciplines with greater access to financial resources, but they also spoke of difficulties encountered in perceived inequities with regard to resources or differentials in esteem between disciplinary areas.*

- *Disciplinary vernaculars or differing departmental cultures can complicate communication between individuals in diverse learning areas. However, such discrepancies can serve as productive frictions, enhancing participants' understanding of one another's perspectives and strengthening their partnerships.*

- *University structures may serve to complicate collaborations. Requirements regarding credit hours and contact hours, departmental policies or procedures, teaching loads, instructor displacement, or scheduling practices can impact efforts to co-teach across disciplinary areas or to engage in collaborative research.*

- *Like funding, facilities and space remain a problem at virtually every institution, not just those participating in the Mellon Research Project. Nevertheless, arts integration efforts may be particularly vulnerable to shortages in this regard, existing in addition to standard programing rather than replacing it, thus creating added burdens on available classroom, laboratory, or collaborative spaces. Furthermore, interdisciplinary collaborations may not fit comfortably within either of the partnering disciplines and may present needs for space or facilities unavailable in a given curricular area.*

- *Recognition of one's professional efforts and positive relationships with one's peers and supervisors provide motivation for individuals to engage in innovative, forward-thinking activities such as arts integration. However, absence of recognition, insufficient administrative support, or collegial difficulties can create obstacles to arts integration.*

- *Identifying problems common to arts integration allows for formulation of workable solutions, increasing the likelihood of success in collaborative curricular or research efforts involving the arts and design.*

BEST PRACTICES

- *Co-teaching and cross-listing an arts-integrated course provides greater opportunities for faculty to establish such partnerships across diverse disciplines and to provide students with viable options to enroll in these courses. Beneficial administrative support for such courses includes consideration for faculty teaching loads, provision for faculty displacement, and support for course planning.*

- *Administrators' ability to impart a contagious vision and to exercise skillful leadership remain crucial to any academic endeavor's success, exemplified by many outstanding leaders participating in the Mellon Research Project. Among the areas of concern to faculty and administrators, liberal interpretation of existing policies for promotion and tenure allow faculty to receive due consideration for arts-integrative work outside of their primary discipline, thus mitigating a significant impediment to arts integration.*

- *Centers and institutes provide affiliated faculty with a professional community in which arts-integrative research and teaching can thrive. Collaboration with internal and external partners, including corporate and community organizations, provides students with genuine engagement in arts-integrative scholarship and research, fulfilling their desire for meaningful, impactful activities involving the arts. Funding models incorporating stable revenue sources, such as tuition or university-level funding, allow centers and institutes to succeed, and curricular connections add value by providing faculty with structures for promotion or tenure not always available in a research center or institute alone.*

- *Research in, through, with, or about the arts was present across the sites visited, from small individual projects to permanent, large-scale installations featuring high-level research partnerships. Inclusion of the arts as equal partners from the onset of a project ensures fairness, preventing perception of the arts as a mere handmaiden to another discipline. Similarly, research initiated by artists, in collaboration with scholars from other disciplines, can yield long-lasting, fruitful partnerships.*

- *Co-curricular arts programming represents a valued resource for students, providing a creative outlet and meeting needs not addressed through regular degree programs. Validation systems such as digital badges, e-portfolios, or co-curricular transcripts allow students to create an authoritative record of their co-curricular involvement.*

- *Other best practices encompass partnerships between stand-alone art schools and research universities, engagement between the arts and community organizations, and efforts to support and improve arts practice at study locations, moving beyond curricular, research, or co-curricular arts integration into efforts to improve the world outside of the university and to enhance the arts themselves within its borders.*

OPPORTUNITIES FOR FURTHER RESEARCH

ArtsEngine and a2ru have received a second grant from **The Andrew W. Mellon Foundation**, which will help to create additional resources based on this rich database of participant information. Through this second grant, the following items will be completed:

- Complete transcription of interviews, to be archived and made available.
- Mining of the full transcriptions of participant narratives for additional quantitative data.
- Gathering additional documentation from partner institutions in order to update existing data and generate an archive and repository of supporting materials (see "Development of resources" bullet, below).
- Creation of Partner Profiles of each of the a2ru participating institutions to contain synthesized information gathered via interviews, peer comparisons and recommendations.
- Development of Shared Practice Modules, produced by a2ru partners, illuminating areas such as Arts and Health, Arts and Humanities, Arts and STEM, Creative Placemaking and other areas within emerging and evolving arts-integrative fields.
- Production of a "Keystone Guide" for facilitating arts-integrated teaching, learning, and research.
- Regional training workshops for arts-integrated interdisciplinary approaches to teaching, learning, practice, and research.
- Development of resources tailored to the informational needs of different groups featured in this report. Specifically:
  - **ADMINISTRATORS:** Create an archive of tenure and promotion policies supportive of arts-integrative efforts for use by administrators seeking to revise or reinterpret their existing policies.
  - **ARTISTS:** Compile a database of funding opportunities available to artists in order to build greater capacity to contribute to arts-integrative projects.
  - **STUDENTS:** Formulate a resource for students seeking to develop co-curricular groups, clubs, or organizations involving the arts, providing coaching on fundraising and group management.
  - **ALL PARTICIPANTS:** Generate guidelines for communicating between, across, and among disciplines, anticipating common obstacles and supporting skill development in conducting fluent discourse spanning diverse academic fields.

- Deeper examination of the complex relationship between institutional context or structure and the success of arts integration at a given institution. For example, considerations of organization of different colleges, schools, or departments in terms of governance structures, fundraising, affiliated learning areas, and the impact of these aspects on administrative and faculty actions when seeking to pursue arts integration. The overall strength of the arts at any given institution is the key to effective local arts integration.

CONCLUSION

With such a vast collection of ethnographic data, the best practices observed and recommended in this study represent only a fraction of the possible discoveries. Recognizable differences between institutions tend to prohibit broad recommendations since a viable strategy working at a stand-alone art school might not meet the needs of a large research university, and vice versa. Establishing centers and institutes can serve to promote and support arts integration, but not every institution possesses the ability to accomplish this, nor should it become a requirement. With such a diverse audience, a best practices guide covering a topic as complex as arts integration in the research university necessarily becomes a catalog rather than a manual, presenting a menu of examples and instances from which the reader can select the most appropriate means of addressing a given situation.

When the arts join with diverse academic fields, all manner of innovations, all kinds of collaborations, all brands of creativities become possible, discovered countless times during the site visits and interviews conducted for the Mellon Research Project. This study did not discern a single way to approach arts integration, nor did it produce an infallible formula for implementing arts integration at every higher educational institution. However, it was successful in identifying models of best practice in curricular arts integration, collaborative research, programmatic arts integration through centers and institutes, and co-curricular opportunities for students to engage with the arts. Undoubtedly, much learning remains, but institutions and individuals interested in adopting these identified best practices will, we hope, find this study to be a useful resource.

The reader should bear in mind that implementing a program of arts integration entails an iterative process regardless of scale or anticipated impact; in this way it mirrors arts practice itself. Perhaps the most important lesson of the Mellon Research Project is the recognition that there is a multiplicity of approaches to this task, just as works of art arise from limitless possibilities. At its heart, change occurs when a person with a contagious vision also possesses the will to bring it to reality, whether through a solitary course integrating the arts with another disciplinary area or through a university-wide initiative emphasizing the importance of the arts in all areas of human endeavor. Existing among such diverse possibilities, we must find similarly diverse methods.

Furthermore, arts integration is no easy task. The director of an international festival combining cinema and dance commented, "I've tried to change my focus to things within my reach because when I got here I thought, 'We can do this! It's not rocket science.' But then I realized that rocket science is easier than opening minds." Some see arts integration as a promise to restore wholeness to the university, moving beyond the disciplinary divisions so deeply ingrained in higher education. Others, however, prefer the status quo. Despite the testimony of the 965 participants who volunteered for this study, the vast majority of faculty and administrators working in higher education today – even at the 46 participating institutions – remain uninvolved in arts integration, creating ongoing challenges at all of the sites visited.

When asked for his definition of transdisciplinarity, the director of a research center said, "You know, I'm far more interested in tearing down the walls than in describing them. The better challenge is to reckon how we work when there are no walls. That's better than trying to figure out how to work with them." Arts integration, existing across so many different settings and implemented by so many different people, serves both purposes: it works without walls, but it also works with them, being endlessly flexible and constantly mutable. Arts integration can dissolve the boundaries between disciplines on a grand scale, as observed at research institutes, or it can support student experience in a single area of the arts, such as membership in a marching band. Arts integration encompasses fusion, infusion, and diffusion; it spans disciplinarity, interdisciplinarity, transdisciplinarity, and every type of hyphen-disciplinarity imaginable. No single definition, no one exemplar could suffice to describe it.

The lasting value of this study, then, is as a map of the landscape of arts integration in higher education. Rather than an itinerary to a specific destination, the array of programs and practices discovered through the Mellon Research Project offers a terrain rich in possibilities. Challenges or problems discussed in these pages allow others to find potential solutions when encountering similar obstacles, while discussions of best practice help others to begin or continue this journey at their own higher educational institutions. The journey of discovery merely began with the Mellon Research Project, creating a topographical survey allowing administrators, faculty, and staff to proceed with greater assurance and to find direction within an exciting and ever-changing academic field.

EPILOGUE

"The purpose of life is to live it, to taste experience to the utmost, to reach out eagerly and without fear for newer and richer experience."
– **ELEANOR ROOSEVELT**, *You Learn By Living*

The Mellon Research Project was an immense undertaking. Researchers collected an incredible amount of narrative and ethnographic data. The scope of data gathered cannot accurately be conveyed by this study in its entirety and still remain within the parameters of the original grant language.

Prior to publication, we sent the document out to select readers for their input. All of their ideas and reflections were incorporated into this study. Others who have consulted with us have noted an absence of quantitative data in support of qualitative analysis and reporting. I personally believe that more quantitative data would have helped those who are more familiar with this approach as a means of validation to accept the findings of this study. However, this was not possible. Due to unique circumstances experienced during the last three years, we could not fully mine the interviews for further quantitative data. As we have specified within this review, the next round of funding, generously provided by The Andrew W Mellon Foundation, includes resources for the full transcription of the recorded interviews. Thereafter, scholars will be able to mine the transcripts for additional quantitative and qualitative data, building upon the foundation established by this study.

Nonetheless, I hope those of you from academic fields more disciplinarily inclined toward an appreciation for quantitative data over qualitative analysis will view the information presented in this study as an opportunity to codify and instrumentally apply your efforts in arts integration. If you are able to consider this study for that purpose, then I consider it to be a success, in addition to an incredible learning opportunity.

"Experience is what you get when you didn't get what you wanted. And experience is often the most valuable thing you have to offer." – **RANDY PAUSCH**, *The Last Lecture*

With every good wish,
Bruce M. Mackh, PhD

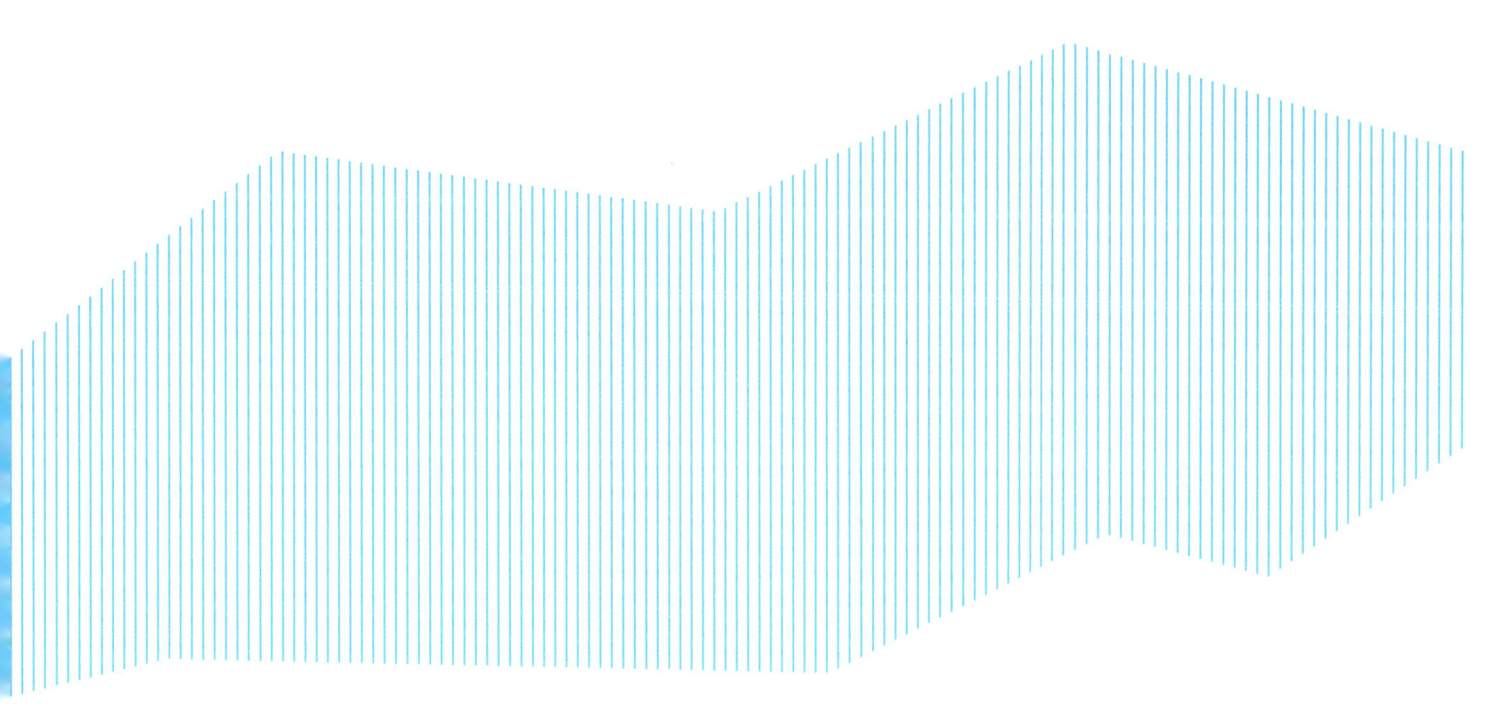

WORKS CITED

"10 Universities That Receive the Most Government Money." *Huff Post Business*. Huffington
        Post, 24/7 Wall St. 27 April 2013. Web. 23 June 2015. <http://www.huffingtonpost.
        com/2013/04/27/universities-government-money_n_3165186.html>.

a2ru: Alliance for the Arts in Research Universities. "Who We Are." Alliance for the Arts in Research
        Universities, n.d. Web. 7 June 2015. <http://a2ru.org/about/who-we-are>.

The AlloSphere Research Facility. U of California, Santa Barbara, 2010. Web.
        17 May 2015. <http://www.allosphere.ucsb.edu>.
---. "About the AlloSphere." U of California, Santa Barbara, 2010. Web. 17 May
        2015. <http://www.allosphere.ucsb.edu/about.php>.
---. "Research in the AlloSphere." U of California, Santa Barbara, 2010. Web. 17 May
        2015. <http://www.allosphere.ucsb.edu/research.php>.

American Academy of Arts & Sciences. "Humanities Report Card." American Academy of Arts & Sciences,
        2013. Web. 7 June 2015. <https://www.amacad.org/binaries/hum_report_card.pdf>.

Artble. "Vincent Van Gogh Biography." Artble, 2015. Web. 7 July 2015.
        <http://www.artble.com/artists/vincent_van_gogh/more_information/biography>.

Arts at Michigan. "About Us." U of Michigan, n.d. Web. 7 June 2015. <http://arts.umich.edu/about>.

Arts at MIT. "About Arts Scholars." MIT, n.d. Web. 5 July 2014. <http://arts.mit.edu/groups/arts-scholars/apply>.
---. "About CAST." MIT, n.d. Web. 16 May 2015. <http://arts.mit.edu/welcome/cast/about>.
---. "Members." MIT, n.d. Web. 5 July 2014. <http://arts.mit.edu/groups/arts-scholars/members>.
---. "Mission." MIT, n.d. Web. 16 May 2015. <http://arts.mit.edu/welcome/overview/mission>.

ArtsEngine National. "ArtsEngine National: Research Project Proposal." U of Michigan, n.d.
        Web. 5 August 2014. <http://artsengine.umich.edu/Mellon-Proposal.pdf>.

Arts Institute. "The Institute." U of Wisconsin-Madison, 2015. Web. 7 June 2015.
        <http://artsinstitute.wisc.edu/mission.htm>.
---. "Programs." U of Wisconsin, 2015. Web. 31 May 2014. <http://artsinstitute.wisc.edu/programs.htm>.
---. "Resources." U of Wisconsin, 2015. Web. 16 May 2015. <http://artsinstitute.wisc.edu/resources-facts-figures.htm>.

Arts Research Center. U of California, Berkeley, n.d. Web. 7 June 2015. <http://arts.berkeley.edu>.
---. "Research Focus: Art and Social Change." U of California, Berkeley, n.d. Web.
        7 June 2015. <http://arts.berkeley.edu/?page_id=955>.

Ash, Katie. "'Digital Badges' Would Represent Students' Skill Acquisition." *Education Week
        Digital Directions*. Education Week, 13 June 2012. Web. 7 June 2015.
        <http://www.edweek.org/dd/articles/2012/06/13/03badges.h05.html>.

The Association for Authentic, Experiential and Evidence-Based Learning. "About
        AAEEBL." The Association for Authentic, Experiential and Evidence-Based
        Learning, n.d. Web. 7 June 2015. <http://www.aaeebl.org/?page=about>.
---, "Academic Member Institutions." The Association for Authentic, Experiential, and Evidence-Based
        Learning, n.d. Web. 7 June 2015. <http://www.aaeebl.org/?page=academic_members>.

Bayles, David, and Ted Orland. *Art and Fear: Observations on the Perils (and Rewards) of Artmaking*. Eugene: Image Continuum P, 2001. Print.

Bowen, Stephen. "Engaged Learning: Are We All on the Same Page?" *Peer Review* 7.2 (2005): 4-7. Print.

Brain and Creativity Institute. U of Southern California, n.d. Web. 22 July 2015. <http://dornsife.usc.edu/bci>.

BU Arts Initiative. "About Us." Boston U, n.d. Web. 7 June 2015. <http://www.bu.edu/arts/about-us>.

Burnaford, Gail, Arnold Aprill, and Cynthia Weiss. *Renaissance in the Classroom: Arts Integration and Meaningful Learning*. Mahwah: Lawrence Erlbaum, 2001. Print.

Burton, Judith, Robert Horowitz, and Hal Abales. "Learning in and through the Arts." *Champions of Change: The Impact of the Arts on Learning*. Ed. Edward B. Fiske. Washington: President's Committee on the Arts and Humanities, 1999. 35-46. ERIC. Web. 21 July 2015. <http://eric.ed.gov/?id=ED435581>.

Buster, Kendall, and Paula Crawford. *The Critique Handbook: The Art Student's Sourcebook and Survival Guide*. 2nd ed. Upper Saddle River: Pearson, 2009. Print.

The Carnegie Classification of Institutions of Higher Education. "Classification Description." Indiana U, Bloomington, n.d. Web. 17 July 2015. <http://carnegieclassifications.iu.edu/descriptions/basic.php>.

Center for Arts in Medicine. "About the Center." U of Florida, n.d. Web. 16 May 2015. <http://arts.ufl.edu/academics/center-for-arts-in-medicine/about/mission>.
---. "AIM for Africa." U of Florida, 2015. Web. 16 May 2015. <http://arts.ufl.edu/academics/center-for-arts-in-medicine/programs/aim-for-africa>.

Creswell, John W. *Qualitative Inquiry and Research Design: Choosing among Five Approaches*. 3rd ed. Thousand Oaks: SAGE, 2013 Print.

The Curb Center for Art, Enterprise & Public Policy. "Program Overview." Vanderbilt U, n.d. Web. 7 June 2015. <http://www.vanderbilt.edu/curbcenter/?page_id=750>.

da Vinci Center. "About." Virginia Commonwealth U, 2012. Web. 7 June 2015. <http://www.davincicenter.vcu.edu/about>.

Davidson, Cathy N., and David Theo Goldberg. *The Future of Thinking: Learning Institutions in a Digital Age*. Cambridge: MIT P, 2010. Print.

Digication. N.d. Web. 7 June 2015. <https://www.digication.com>.

Diop, Corinne, and Elizabeth Brown. "ART 492/MATH 467: Math and Art: Beautiful Rigor." James Madison U, n.d. Web. 15 May 2015. <http://www.jmu.edu/ivs/Math.Art.09.pdf>.

Edwards, Chris. "Seeing Differently." *Madison Magazine* Winter 2011: 24-27. Web. 7 June 2015. <http://www.myvirtualpaper.com/doc/JMU/madison-arts-winter2011-final/2010112401/#0>.

El Museo del Norte. "The Boulevard House." El Museo del Norte, n.d. Web. 24 May 2015. <http://www.elmuseodelnorte.org/boulevard-house.html>.

Elkins, James. *Art Critiques: A Guide.* 3rd ed. Washington: New Academia Publishing, 2014. Print.

Foliotek. N.d. Web. 7 June 2015. <http://www.foliotek.com>.

Gant, Larry M. "'The Boulevard House': A Settlement House Approach to Project Based Learning in Urban Communities." *Deep Blue.* U of Michigan, 17 February 2014. Web. 24 May 2015. <http://deepblue.lib. umich.edu/bitstream/handle/2027.42/102739/concept%20paper%20about%20the%20boulevard%20 house%20and%20community%20practice%20winter%202014%20feb%2017.pdf?sequence=1>.

Gifts of Art. "Programs." U of Michigan Health System, n.d. Web. 17 May 2015. <http://www.med.umich.edu/goa/programs.htm>.

Gifts of Art, Life Sciences Orchestra. "About." U of Michigan Health System, 2013. Web. 25 May 2015. <http://lso.med.umich.edu/about>.

Gladwell, Malcolm. *Outliers: The Story of Success.* New York: Little, Brown, 2008.

Hardiman, Mariale. *The Brain-Targeted Teaching Model for 21st-Century Schools.* Thousand Oaks: Corwin/SAGE, 2012. Print.

Hart Research Associates. "Falling Short? College Learning and Career Success." Washington: Association of American Colleges & Universities, 20 January 2015. Web. 25 May 2015. <http://www.aacu.org/leap/public-opinion-research/2015-survey-results>.

Hasan, Ali, and Richard Fumerton. "Knowledge by Acquaintance vs. Description." *The Stanford Encyclopedia of Philosophy.* Ed. Edward N. Zalta. Stanford: Stanford U, Spring 2014. Web. 7 June 2015. <http://plato.stanford.edu/archives/spr2014/entries/knowledge-acquaindescrip>.

Healy, Patrick. "'Angels in America' Earns Place in Pantheon." *New York Times* 24 October 2010. Web. 7 July 2015. <http://www.nytimes.com/2010/10/25/theater/25angels.html?_r=2>.

Heidegger, Martin. "The Origin of the Work of Art." *Poetry, Language, Thought.* Trans. Albert Hofstadter. New York: Harper and Row, 1971. Print.

Herpin, Sharon A., Adrienne Quinn Washington, and Jian Li. *Improving the Assessment of Student Learning in the Arts – State of the Field and Recommendations.* Washington: National Endowment for the Arts, 2012. Web. 17 June 2015. <http://arts.gov/sites/default/files/WestEd.pdf>.

Hesterman, Donna. "Experimental Palette." *Explore Research Magazine* Spring 2013. Web. 1 July 2015. <https://research.ufl.edu/publications/exploremagazine/spring-2013/experimental-palette.html>.

Hoey, Brian A. "What Is Ethnography?" Brian A. Hoey, n.d. Web. 7 June 2015. <http://brianhoey.com/research/ethnography>.

Husserl, Edmund. *The Crisis of European Sciences and Transcendental Phenomenology.* Trans. David Carr. Evanston: Northwestern UP, 1970. Print.

IBM. "Capitalizing on Complexity: Insights from the 2010 IBM Global CEO Study." IBM, 2010. Web. 7 June 2015. <http://www-935.ibm.com/services/us/ceo/ceostudy2010>.
---. "Leading Through Connections: Insights from the IBM Global CEO Study." IBM, 2012. Web. 7 June 2015. <http://www-935.ibm.com/services/us/en/c-suite/ceostudy2012>.

Illinois Program for Research in the Humanities. "IPRH Research Clusters." U of Illinois at Urbana-Champaign, n.d. Web. 30 June 2015. <http://www.iprh.illinois.edu/programs/clusters.html>.

Institute for Creativity, Arts, and Technology. "The Cube." Virginia Tech, n.d. Web. 24 May 2015. <http://www.icat.vt.edu/content/cube-0>.
---. "General Handout." Virginia Tech, n.d. Web. 24 May 2015. <http://www.icat.vt.edu/sites/default/files/ICAT_General_Handout.pdf>.
---. "ICAT Overview." Virginia Tech, n.d. Web. 24 May 2015. <https://www.icat.vt.edu/content/icat-overview>.
---. "K-to-12 Projects." Virginia Tech, n.d. Web. 24 May 2015. <http://www.icat.vt.edu/education/k-12>.

Institute for the Arts & Humanities. "Programs and Partnerships." Pennsylvania State U, 2015. Web. 15 June 2015. <http://iah.psu.edu/programs-and-partnerships/programs-and-partnerships>.

Institute for Visual Studies. James Madison U, n.d. Web. 7 June 2015. <http://www.jmu.edu/ivs>.
---. "Courses." James Madison U, n.d. 10 May 2015. <www.jmu.edu/ivs/courses.html>.
---. "Math and Art: Beautiful Rigor." James Madison U, n.d. Web. 10 May 2015. <http://www.jmu.edu/ivs/Math.Art.09.pdf>.

Johns Hopkins Medicine. "The Musical Brain: Novel Study of Jazz Players Shows Common Brain Circuitry Processes Both Music and Language." Johns Hopkins U, 19 February 2014. Web. 14 June 2015. <http://www.hopkinsmedicine.org/news/media/releases/the_musical_brain_novel_study_of_jazz_players_shows_common_brain_circuitry_processes_both_music_and_language>.

Johns Hopkins University. "Parents Advising Handbook: Co-Curricular Activities, Student Employment, and Community Service." Johns Hopkins U, n.d. Web. 10 May 2015. <http://web.jhu.edu/parentsadvisinghandbook/experience/other>.

Kelly, Thomas. "Igor Stravinsky's 'The Rite of Spring.'" *NPR*. NPR, 1999. Web. 7 Aug. 2015. <http://www.npr.org/programs/specials/milestones/991110.motm.riteofspring.html>.

Kolenic, Anthony J., and Bruce M. Mackh. *ArtsEngine Mellon Research Project: Round 1 Interim Report, Curricular Integration*. Alliance for the Arts in Research Universities, 2 October 2013. Web. 20 June 2015. <http://a2ru.org/wp-content/uploads/2013/10/Mellon-Round-I-Curricular-Report-1-Kolenic.pdf>.

Kuh, George D. "High-Impact Educational Practices: A Brief Overview." Association of American Colleges & Universities, 2008. Web. 14 June 2015. <https://www.aacu.org/leap/hips>.

Lacey, Sharon. "MIT Center for Art, Science, & Technology (CAST) Receives $1.5 Million Grant from The Andrew W. Mellon Foundation." 22 April 2015. Web. 16 May 2015. <http://arts.mit.edu/mit-center-for-art-science-technology-cast-receives-1-5-million-grant-from-the-andrew-w-mellon-foundation>.

Latour, Bruno. *Pandora's Hope: Essays on the Reality of Science Studies*. Cambridge: Harvard UP, 1999. Print.

Light, Richard J. *Making the Most of College: Students Speak Their Minds*. Cambridge: Harvard UP, 2004. Print.

Living Arts. U of Michigan, 2015. Web. 31 May 2015. <http://www.livingarts.umich.edu>.

Mackh, Bruce M. *Achieving Successful Collaboration in Higher Education.* Bruce M. Mackh, 6 December 2014. Web. 20 July 2015. <http://brucemackh.weebly.com/achieving-successful-collaboration-in-higher-education.html>.

---. *From the Outside In: The Benefits of Arts-Integration to Arts Practice.* Alliance for the Arts in Research Universities, 17 June 2014. Web. 20 July 2015. <http://a2ru.org/wp-content/uploads/2015/04/a2ru-Mackh-OutsideIn-O16.17.14.pdf>.

Mackh, Bruce M., and Laurie Baefsky. *ArtsEngine Mellon Research Project: Round II Interim Report, Co-Curricular Programs.* Alliance for the Arts in Research Universities, 3 December 2014. Web. 20 June 2015. <http://a2ru.org/wp-content/uploads/2013/05/Mellon-Co-Curricular-FINAL.12-3-1.pdf>.

Mackh, Bruce M., and Anthony J. Kolenic. *ArtsEngine Mellon Research Project: Round I Interim Report, Collaborative Research.* Alliance for the Arts in Research Universities, 2 October 2013. Web. 20 June 2015. <http://a2ru.org/wp-content/uploads/2013/10/Mellon-Round-I-Research-Report-Mackh.pdf>.

Manderscheid, David. "Team Teaching Proposals." Memo to ASC Executive Deans Office, All Department Chairs & Directors, All ASC Faculty, College of Arts and Sciences, Ohio State University, Columbus. 29 September 2014. Web. 17 May 2015. <http://artsandsciences.osu.edu/sites/artsandsciences.osu.edu/files/ASC%20Strategic%20Plan%20-Team%20Teaching%20Plan%20092914.pdf>.

McKeon, Matthew. "Argument." *The Internet Encyclopedia of Philosophy,* n.d. Web. 7 June 2015. <http://www.iep.utm.edu/argument>.

Mervis, Jeffrey. "NSF's 2015 Budget: A Small Increase and a Big Pat on the Back." *Science* 10 December 2014. Web. 10 May 2015. <http://news.sciencemag.org/funding/2014/12/nsf-s-2015-budget-small-increase-and-big-pat-back>.

MIT Media Lab. "Building." MIT, n.d. Web. 22 July 2015. <https://www.media.mit.edu/about/building>.

---. "The MIT Media Lab at a Glance." MIT, March 2015. Web. 16 May 2015. <http://www.media.mit.edu/files/overview.pdf>.

MIT Program in Art, Culture, and Technology. "About ACT." MIT, n.d. Web. 16 May 2015. <http://act.mit.edu/about-act>.

National Academy of Sciences, National Academy of Engineering, and Institute of Medicine. *Facilitating Interdisciplinary Research.* Washington: National Academies P, 2004. Print.

National Endowment for the Arts. "President Obama Releases FY 2015 Budget Number for the National Endowment for the Arts." National Endowment for the Arts, 4 March 2014. Web. 12 May 2015. <http://arts.gov/news/2014/president-obama-releases-fy-2015-budget-number-national-endowment-arts>.

New College. "History." University of Alabama, n.d. Web. 13 June 2015. <http://nc.as.ua.edu/about/history>.

---. "New College Seminars." University of Alabama, n.d. Web. 15 May 2015. <http://nc.as.ua.edu/degree-program/new-college-seminars>.

Oakes, John Warren. "How the Servicemen's Readjustment Act of 1944 (GI Bill) Impacted Women Artists' Career Opportunities." *Visual Culture & Gender* 1 (2006): 21-30. Print.

Office of Research. "Battelle Engineering, Technology, and Human Affairs (BETHA) Endowment." Ohio State U, n.d. Web. 17 May 2015. <http://research.osu.edu/researchers/funding/betha>.

OpenGrounds. "Mission." U of Virginia, 2015. Web. 24 May 2015. <http://opengrounds.virginia.edu/about/mission>.

Otis College of Art and Design. "Creative Action." Otis College of Art and Design, n.d. Web. 23 May 2015.
      <http://www.otis.edu/creative-action>.

Parker, Kristen, Eileen Roraback, and Rex LaMore. "A Young Picasso or Beethoven Could Be the
      Next Edison." *MSU Today.* Michigan State U, 23 October 2013. Web. 24 May 2014.
      <http://msutoday.msu.edu/news/2013/a-young-picasso-or-beethoven-could-be-the-next-edison>.

Pass-Port. "What Is PASS-PORT?" Pass-Port, n.d. Web. 7 June 2015. <http://www.pass-port.org/?q=node/20>.

Patterson, Jim. "Chancellor: Four Ideas Will Define Vanderbilt's Destiny." *My VU.* Vanderbilt U, 3 April
      2013. Web. 7 June 2015. <http://news.vanderbilt.edu/2013/04/faculty-assembly-chancellor>.

Pausch, Randy. *The Last Lecture.* New York: Hyperion, 2008. Print.

Penn State Undergraduate Admissions. "Admission and University Statistics." Pennsylvania
      State U, 2013. Web. 14 June 2015. <http://admissions.psu.edu/apply/statistics>.

Pennsylvania State University. "Interdisciplinary Research." Pennsylvania State U, 2015. Web.
      17 May 2015. <http://www.psu.edu/research/interdisciplinary-research>.

Pippen, Carolyn. "Interdisciplinary Majors at Vanderbilt." Vanderbilt U, 30 September 2013. Web. 7 June 2015.
      <http://admissions.vanderbilt.edu/vandybloggers/2013/09/interdisciplinary-majors-at-vanderbilt>.

Porter, Eduardo. "Government R&D, Private Profits and the American Taxpayer." *New York Times*
      26 May 2015. Web. 15 May 2015. <http://www.nytimes.com/2015/05/27/business/
      giving-taxpayers-a-cut-when-government-rd-pays-off-for-industry.html?_r=1>.

Preminger, Son. "Transformative Art: Art as Means for Long-Term Neurocognitive
      Change." *Frontiers in Human Neuroscience* 6 (2012): n. pag. Web. 20 July 2015.
      <http://www.ncbi.nlm.nih.gov/pmc/articles/PMC3334843>.

Purdue University Calumet. "What Is a Co-Curricular Transcript?" Purdue U Calumet,
      n.d. Web. 7 June 2015. <http://webs.purduecal.edu/cct>.

Reid, Theresa. *Art-Making and the Arts in Research Universities: Strategic Task Forces, March 2012 Interim Report.*
      Alliance for the Arts in Research Universities, March 2012. Web. 28 June 2015. <http://a2ru.org//wp-
      content/uploads/2013/06/ArtsEngine-National-Strategic-Task-Forces-Interim-Report-March-2012.pdf>.

Rinne, Luke, Emma Gregory, Julia Yarmolinskaya, and Mariale Hardiman. "Why Arts Integration Improves
      Long-Term Retention of Content." *Mind, Brain, and Education* 5.2 (2011): 89-96. Print.

Robinson, Ken, and Lou Aronica. *Creative Schools: The Grassroots Revolution That's
      Transforming Education.* New York: Viking, 2015. Print.

Roosevelt, Eleanor. *You Learn By Living.* New York: Harper & Brothers, 1960. xii. Print.

Rorty, Richard. *Philosophy and the Mirror of Nature.* Princeton: Princeton UP, 1979. Print.

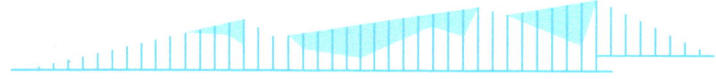

Sam Fox School. "Alberti Program." Washington University in St. Louis, n.d. Web. 24
        May 2015. <http://samfoxschool.wustl.edu/alberti_program>.
---. "CityStudioSTL." Washington University in St. Louis, n.d. Web. 24 May
        2015. <http://samfoxschool.wustl.edu/citystudiostl>.
---. "University City Gallery Series." Washington University in St. Louis, n.d. Web.
        24 May 2015. <http://samfoxschool.wustl.edu/node/10652>.
---. "University City Sculpture Series." Washington University in St. Louis, n.d. Web.
        24 May 2015. <http://samfoxschool.wustl.edu/ucity-sculpture>.
---. "WashUCity Design Program." Washington University in St. Louis, n.d. Web. 24 May
        2015. <http://samfoxschool.wustl.edu/artarch/research/washucity>.

Sawyer, R. Keith. *Explaining Creativity: The Science of Human Innovation.* 2nd ed. Oxford: Oxford UP, 2012.

School of the Art Institute of Chicago. "Art and Science: Archive." School of the Art Institute
        of Chicago, 2015. Web. 23 May 2015. <http://www.saic.edu/academics/areasofstudy/
        artandscience/conversationsonartandscienceseries/archive>.
---. "Big Beautiful Data: Collaboration with Northwestern U. Inspires New Exhibition." School of the
        Art Institute of Chicago, 30 July 2013. Web. 23 May 2015. <http://www.saic.edu/press/2013/
        bigbeautifuldatacollaborationwithnorthwesternuinspiresnewexhibition>.
---. "SAIC Welcomes Its First-Ever Scientist-in-Residence." School of the Art
        Institute of Chicago, 23 January 2014. Web. 23 May 2015.
        <http://www.saic.edu/news/saic-welcomes-its-first-ever-scientist-in-residence-.html>.
---. "Shapiro Center for Research and Collaboration: Research Partnerships." School of the Art Institute of Chicago,
        2015. Web. 23 May 2015. <http://www.saic.edu/academics/shapirocenter/researchpartnerships>.
---. "Shapiro Center for Research and Collaboration: Sponsored Classes." School of the Art Institute of Chicago,
        2015. Web. 23 May 2015. <http://www.saic.edu/academics/shapirocenter/sponsoredclasses>.

Segal Design Institute at Northwestern University. "Engineers and Artists Team up for Data
        as Art Class." Northwestern U, 20 January 2015. Web. 23 May 2015.
        <http://segal.northwestern.edu/news-events/articles/Data-as-art-2014.html#.VWC8YVLJYrg>.

Selingo, Jeffrey J. "Why Are So Many College Students Failing to Gain Job Skills Before Graduation?" *Washington
        Post,* 26 January 2015. Web. 25 May 2015. <http://www.washingtonpost.com/news/grade-point/
        wp/2015/01/26/why-are-so-many-college-students-failing-to-gain-job-skills-before-graduation>.

Silverstein, Lynne B., and Sean Layne. "Defining Arts Integration." ArtsEdge. The John F. Kennedy
        Center for the Performing Arts, 2010. Web. 30 May 2015. <http://www.kennedy-center.
        org/education/partners/defining_arts_integration.pdf>. Singerman, Howard. *Art Subjects:
        Making Artists in the American University.* Berkeley: U of California P, 1999. Print.

Sonke, Jill. "TEDxUF Talk about Arts in Medicine." U of Florida Health, 28 April 2015. Web. 16 May 2015.
        <http://artsinmedicine.ufhealth.org/2015/04/28/program-spotlight-tedxuf-talk-about-arts-in-medicine>.

Student Development. "Co-Curricular Transcript." U of Dayton, n.d. Web. 7 June 2015. <https://
        udayton.edu/studev/leadership/studentleadershipprograms/CCT/index.php>.

Studio|Lab. Pennsylvania State U, n.d. Web. 17 May 2015. <https://studiolab.psu.edu>.
---. "Studio|Lab Partners." Pennsylvania State U, n.d. Web. 17 May 2015. <https://studiolab.psu.edu/partners>.
---. "Studio|Lab People." Pennsylvania State U, n.d. Web. 17 May 2015. <https://studiolab.psu.edu/people>.
---. "What Is Studio|Lab?" Pennsylvania State U, n.d. Web. 17 May 2015. <https://studiolab.psu.edu/more-info>.

Thompson, Lauren Fretz, and Anthony J. Kolenic. "Perspectives on Arts-Integrative Interdisciplinary
         Training: Student Views and Experiences on a2ru University Campuses." Alliance
         for the Arts in Research Universities, 2014. Web. 20 July 2015. <http://a2ru.org/wp-
         content/uploads/2015/03/a2ru-White-Paper-Student-Perspectives.pdf>.

Today in Science History. "Albert Szent-Gyorgyi." Today in Science History, n.d. Web. 19 July 2015.
         <http://todayinsci.com/S/SzentGyorgyi_Albert/SzentGyorgyiAlbert-Quotations.htm>.

Transart Institute. "About." Transart Institute, 2015. Web. 14 July 2015. <http://www.transart.org/about>.

USC Cinematic Arts. "DADA Students Featured in 'USC Arts After Dark' Short Film." U of Southern California,
         2014. Web. 22 July 2015. <http://anim.usc.edu/student-related/dada-students-featured-usc-arts-dark>.
---. "Institute for Multimedia Literacy." U of Southern California, n.d. Web. 22 July 2015.
         <https://cinema.usc.edu/faculty/iml.cfm>.

USC International Artist Fellowship. U of Southern California, n.d. Web. 22 July 2015. <http://globalartists.usc.edu>.

USC Jimmy Iovine and Andre Young Academy. U of Southern California, n.d. Web. 22 July 2015.
         <http://iovine-young.usc.edu>.
---. "The Academy Experiernce." U of Southern California, 2015. Web. 22 July 2015.
         <http://iovine-young.usc.edu/program/index.html>.

Visions and Voices. "About the Initiative." U of Southern California, n.d. Web. 7 June 2015.
         <http://www.usc.edu/dept/pubrel/visionsandvoices/about.php>.

Winter, Abigail J., Marisha B. McAuliffe, Douglas J. Hargreaves, and Gary Chadwick. "The
         Transition to Academagogy." *Proceedings of Philosophy of Education Society of
         Australasia (PESA) Conference 2008.* Brisbane: Queensland U of Technology, 2009.
         1-6. Web. 24 May 2015. <http://eprints.qut.edu.au/17367/5/17367b.pdf>.

Zehner, Andy. "Nothing to Do and No Time to Do It: A Study of Students Who Fail to Get Involved in Co-
         Curricular Activities." *Student Affairs Assessment.* Purdue U, September 2012. Web. 4 June 2015.
         <https://www.purdue.edu/vpsa/assessment/archives/Nothing to do and no time to do it.pdf>.

APPENDIX 1: RECOMMENDED READING

Barkley, Elizabeth F., K. Patricia Cross, and Claire Howell Major. *Collaborative Learning Techniques: A Handbook for College Faculty*. San Francisco: Jossey-Bass, 2004. Print.

Barone, Tom, and Elliot W. Eisner. *Arts Based Research*. Thousand Oaks: SAGE, 2011. Print.

Bean, John C., and Maryellen Weimer. *Engaging Ideas: The Professor's Guide to Integrating Writing, Critical Thinking, and Active Learning in the Classroom*. 2nd ed. San Francisco: Jossey-Bass, 2011. Print.

Biggs, Michael, and Daniela Buchler. "Eight Criteria for Practice-Based Research in the Creative and Cultural Industries." *Art, Design & Communication in Higher Education* 7.1 (2008): 5-18. Print.

Boix Mansilla, Veronica. "Learning to Synthesize: The Development of Interdisciplinary Understanding." *The Oxford Handbook of Interdisciplinarity*. Eds. Robert Frodeman, Julie Thompson Klein, and Carl Mitcham. Oxford: Oxford UP, 2010. 288-306. Print.

Boix Mansilla, Veronica, Elizabeth Dawes Duraisingh, Christopher R. Wolfe, and Carolyn Haynes. "Targeted Assessment Rubric: An Empirically Grounded Rubric for Interdisciplinary Writing." *The Journal of Higher Education* 80.3 (2009): 334-353. Print.

Boix Mansilla, Veronica, and Howard Gardner. "Assessing Interdisciplinary Work at the Frontier: An Empirical Exploration of 'Symptoms of Quality.'" GoodWork Project Report Series, Number 26. 1 December 2003. Web. 10 May 2015. <http://evergreen.edu/washingtoncenter/docs/resources/boixgardner.pdf>.

Brookhart, Susan M. *How to Assess Higher-Order Thinking Skills in Your Classroom*. Alexandria: ASCD, 2010. Print. See especially chapter 6, "Assessing Creativity and Creative Thinking."

Candy, Linda. *Practice Based Research: A Guide*. CCS Report: 2006-V1.0. Creativity & Cognition Studios, U of Technology, Sydney, November 2006. Web. 20 June 2015. <http://www.creativityandcognition.com/wp-content/uploads/2011/04/PBR-Guide-1.1-2006.pdf>.

Carey, John. *What Good Are the Arts?* Oxford: Oxford UP, 2006. Print.

Cowdroy, Rob, and Anthony Williams. "Assessing Creativity in the Creative Arts." *Art, Design & Communication in Higher Education* 5.2 (2006): 97-117. Print.

Cropley, Arthur, and David Cropley. *Fostering Creativity: A Diagnostic Approach for Higher Education and Organizations*. New York: Hampton Press, 2009. Perspectives on Creativity Research. Print.

Crossick, Geoffrey, ed. *Creating Prosperity: The Role of Higher Education in Driving the UK's Creative Economy*. London: Universities UK, 2010. Web. 20 July 2015. <http://www.universitiesuk.ac.uk/highereducation/Documents/2010/CreatingProsperityTheRoleOfHigherEducation.pdf>.

Darso, Lotte. *Artful Creation: Learning-Tales of Arts-in-Business*. Frederiksberg: Samfundslitteratur, 2004. Print.

Daston, Lorraine, and Peter Galison. "The Image of Objectivity." *Representations* 40 (Autumn 1992): 81-128. Print.

Dubberly Design Office. *A Model of the Creative Process*. 20 March 2009. Web. 28 April 2015. < http://www.dubberly.com/concept-maps/creative-process.html>.

Eisner, Elliot W. *The Arts and the Creation of Mind.* New Haven: Yale UP, 2004. Print.

---. *The Enlightened Eye: Qualitative Inquiry and the Enhancement of Educational Practice.* 2nd ed. Upper Saddle River: Pearson, 1997. Print.

---, ed. *Learning and Teaching the Ways of Knowing: Eighty-Fourth Yearbook of the National Society for the Study of Education.* 2 vols. Chicago: U of Chicago P, 1985. Print.

Elton, Lewis. "Assessing Creativity in an Unhelpful Climate." *Art, Design & Communication in Higher Education* 5.2 (2007): 119-130. Print.

Foshay, Raphael, ed. *Valences of Interdisciplinarity: Theory, Practice, Pedagogy.* Edmonton: Athabasca UP, 2012. Print.

Frayling, Christopher. "Research in Art and Design." *Royal College of Art Research Papers* 1.1 (1993/1994): 1-5. Print.

Fry, Blake Edward. "The Interrelationship Between Co-Curricular Student Leadership Experiences and Moral Development." Diss. Oklahoma State U, 2008. *Google Books.* Web. 13 June 2014. <http://books.google.com/books?id=3kU3ZVDt7c4C&dq=benefits+of+co-curricular+engagement&source=gbs_navlinks_s>.

Gherardi, Silvia. "Practice-Based Theorizing on Learning and Knowing in Organizations." *Organization* 7.2 (2000): 211-223. Print.

Gray, Carole, and Julian Malins. *Visualizing Research: A Guide to the Research Process in Art and Design.* Burlington: Ashgate, 2004. Print.

Halsall, Francis, Julia Jansen, and Tony O'Connor, eds. *Rediscovering Aesthetics: Transdisciplinary Voices from Art History, Philosophy, and Art Practice.* Stanford: Stanford UP, 2009. Print.

Harrell, D. Fox, and Sneha Veeragoudar Harrell. "Strategies for Arts + Science + Technology Research: Executive Report on a Joint Meeting of the National Science Foundation and National Endowment for the Arts." N.p. N.d. Web. 5 June 2015. <http://groups.csail.mit.edu/icelab/sites/default/files/pictures/Harrell-NSF-NEA-Workshop-ExecutiveReportFinalDraft_0.pdf>.

Hetland, Lois, Ellen Winner, Shirley Veenema, and Kimberly M. Sheridan. *Studio Thinking 2: The Real Benefits of Visual Arts Education.* 2nd ed. New York: Teachers College P, 2013. Print.

Hoffert, Bernard. "Taking Art Seriously: Understanding Studio Research." *Art & Education, n.d. Web.* 9 October 2012. <http://www.artandeducation.net/paper/taking-art-seriously-understanding-studio-research>.

IBM. "Capitalizing on Complexity: Insights from the 2010 IBM Global CEO Study." IBM, 2010. Web. 9 September 2012. <http://www-935.ibm.com/services/us/ceo/ceostudy2010>.

Jackson, Norman, Martin Oliver, Malcolm Shaw, and James Wisdom, eds. *Developing Creativity in Higher Education: An Imaginative Curriculum.* New York: Routledge, 2006. Print.

Kirshner, Andy. *The Musical Image.* University of Michigan. *YouTube,* 18 October 2007. Web. 14 April 2015. <https://www.youtube.com/watch?v=EY9xa4pLP74&list=PLisZMo1SW-RhIfFfQf3uekiDGidcDqACe&index=1>.

Kockelmans, Joseph J., ed. *Interdisciplinarity and Higher Education.* University Park: Penn State UP, 1979. Print.

Kuh, George D. "High-Impact Educational Practices: A Brief Overview." Association of American Colleges & Universities, 2008. Web. 14 June 2015. <https://www.aacu.org/leap/hips>.

Kuh, George D., Jillian Kinzie, John H. Schuh, and Elizabeth J. Whitt. *Student Success in College: Creating Conditions That Matter.* San Francisco: Jossey-Bass, 2010. Print.

Lackney, Jeffery A. "A History of the Studio-Based Learning Model." Mississippi State U, 2 August 1999. Web. 5 Jul 2015. <http://edi.msstate.edu/work/pdf/history_studio_based_learning.pdf>.

LaJevic, Lisa. *"Arts Integration: An Exploration of the Dis/Connect between Policy and Live(d) Practice."* Diss. Pennsylvania State U, 2009. Web. 14 July 2015. <https://etda.libraries.psu.edu/paper/9913>.

Light, Richard J. *Making the Most of College: Students Speak Their Minds.* Cambridge: Harvard UP, 2004. Print.

Madoff, Steven Henry, ed. *Art School: (Propositions for the 21st Century).* Cambridge: The MIT P, 2009. Print.

Marshall, Cora. "A Research Design for Studio-Based Research in Art." *Teaching Artist Journal* 8.2 (2010): 77-87. Print.

McGregor, Sue L. T., and Russ Volckmann. *Transversity: Transdisciplinary Approaches in Higher Education.* N.p.: Integral Publishers, 2011. Print.

Michaelsen, Larry K., Arletta Bauman Knight, and L. Dee Fink, eds. *Team-Based Learning: A Transformative Use of Small Groups in College Teaching.* Sterling: Stylus Publishing, 2004. Print.

Millis, Barbara J., ed. *Cooperative Learning in Higher Education: Across the Disciplines, Across the Academy.* Sterling: Stylus Publishing, 2010. Print. New Pedagogies and Practices for Teaching in Higher Education.

National Endowment for the Arts. *How Art Works: The National Endowment for the Arts' Five-Year Research Agenda, with a System Map and Measurement Model.* National Endowment for the Arts, September 2012. Web. 20 July 2015. <http://arts.gov/sites/default/files/How-Art-Works_0.pdf>.

Nicolescu, Basarab, ed. *Transdisciplinarity: Theory and Practice.* New York: Hampton Press, 2008. Print.

Niedderer, Kristina, and Seymour Roworth-Stokes. "The Role and Use of Creative Practice in Research and Its Contribution to Knowledge." *Proceedings of the IASDR International Conference 2007.* Ed. Sharon Poggenpohl. Hong Kong: International Association of Societies of Design Research and Hong Kong Polytechnic U, 2007. CD.

Oakley, Kate, Brooke Sperry, and Andy Pratt. *The Art of Innovation: How Fine Arts Graduates Contribute to Innovation.* National Endowment for Science, Technology, and the Arts (UK), 1 September 2008. Web. 3 March 2013. <http://www.nesta.org.uk/sites/default/files/art_of_innovation.pdf>.

Pascarella, Ernest T., and Patrick T. Terenzini. *How College Affects Students: A Third Decade of Research.* San Francisco: Jossey-Bass, 2005. Print.

Preminger, Son. "Transformative Art: Art as Means for Long-Term Neurocognitive Change." *Frontiers in Human Neuroscience* 6 (2012): n. pag. Web. 20 July 2015. <http://www.ncbi.nlm.nih.gov/pmc/articles/PMC3334843>.

Quaye, Stephen John, and Shaun R. Harper, eds. *Student Engagement in Higher Education: Theoretical Perspectives and Practical Approaches for Diverse Populations.* 2nd ed. New York: Routledge, 2014. Print.

Reid, Anna, and Solmonides, Ian. "Design Students' Experience of Engagement and Creativity." *Art, Design & Communication in Higher Education* 6.1 (2007): 27-39. Print.

Report of the Task Force on the Arts. Harvard University, September 2008. Web. 8 July 2015. <http://media.www.harvard.edu/content/arts_report.pdf>.

Ritchhart, Ron, Mark Church, and Karin Morrison. *Making Thinking Visible: How to Promote Engagement, Understanding, and Independence for All Learners*. San Francisco: Jossey-Bass, 2011. Print.

Root-Bernstein, Robert S., and Michele M. Root-Bernstein. *Sparks of Genius: The Thirteen Thinking Tools of the World's Most Creative People*. New York: Mariner Books, 2001. Print.

Sawyer, Keith. *Zig Zag: The Surprising Path to Greater Creativity*. San Francisco: Jossey-Bass, 2013. Print.

Sawyer, R. Keith. "Learning How to Create: Toward a Learning Sciences of Art and Design." *The Future of Learning: Proceedings of the 10th International Conference of the Learning Sciences (ICLS 2012) – Volume 1, Full Papers*. Eds. Jan van Aalst, Kate Thompson, Michael J. Jacobson, and Peter Reimann. Sydney: International Society of the Learning Sciences, 2012. 33-39. Print.

---. "The Western Cultural Model of Creativity: Its Influence on Intellectual Property Law." *Notre Dame Law Review* 86.5 (2011): 2027-2056. Web. 5 June 2015. <http://scholarship.law.nd.edu/cgi/viewcontent.cgi?article=1099&context=ndlr>.

Skorton, David J. "The Arts Are Essential." *Edutopia*. George Lucas Educational Foundation, 28 January 2009. Web. 30 April 2013. <http://www.edutopia.org/arts-education-humanities-creativity>.

Smith, Fran. "Why Arts Education Is Crucial, and Who's Doing It Best." *Edutopia*. George Lucas Educational Foundation, 28 January 2009. Web. 30 April 2013. <http://www.edutopia.org/arts-music-curriculum-child-development>.

Sullivan, Graeme. *Art Practice as Research: Inquiry in Visual Arts*. 2nd ed. Thousand Oaks: SAGE, 2010. Print.

Treffinger, Donald J., Grover C. Young, Edwin C. Selby, and Cindy Shepardson. *Assessing Creativity: A Guide for Educators*. Storrs: U of Connecticut, The National Research Center on the Gifted and Talented, 2002. Web. 25 April 2013. <http://files.eric.ed.gov/fulltext/ED505548.pdf>.

Tyler, Christopher W., and Lora T. Likova. "The Role of Visual Arts in Enhancing the Learning Process." *Frontiers in Human Neuroscience* 6 (2012): n. pag. Web. 8 October 2013. <http://www.ncbi.nlm.nih.gov/pmc/articles/PMC3274761>.

Upcraft, M. Lee, and John H. Schuh. *Assessment in Student Affairs: A Guide for Practitioners*. San Francisco: Jossey-Bass, 1996. Print.

Van Hartesveldt, Carol, and Judith Giordan. *Impact of Transformative Interdisciplinary Research and Graduate Education on Academic Institutions: Workshop Report*. National Science Foundation, May 2008. Web. 21 June 2015. <http://www.nsf.gov/pubs/2009/nsf0933/igert_workshop08.pdf>.

Zehner, Andy. "Nothing to Do and No Time to Do It: A Study of Students Who Fail to Get Involved in Co-Curricular Activities." *Student Affairs Assessment*. Purdue U, September 2012. Web. 4 June 2015. <https://www.purdue.edu/vpsa/assessment/archives/Nothing to do and no time to do it.pdf>.

Zull, James E. "The Art of the Changing Brain." New Horizons for Learning. Johns Hopkins U, 2012. Web. 21 July 2015. <http://education.jhu.edu/PD/newhorizons/ Neurosciences/articles/The%20Art%20of%20the%20Changing%20Brain>.

---. *"Arts, Neurosciences, and Learning." New Horizons for Learning. Johns Hopkins U, 2005. Web. 21 July 2015.* <http://education.jhu.edu/PD/newhorizons/Neurosciences/articles/Arts-neurosciences-and-learning>.

APPENDIX 2: CARNEGIE BASIC CLASSIFICATIONS
OF PARTICIPATING INSTITUTIONS (2010)

Name	Carnegie Basic Classification	Control	Student Population
Arizona State University	RU/VH	Public	68,064
Boston University	RU/VH	Private not-for-profit	31,960
Carnegie Mellon University	RU/VH	Private not-for-profit	11,197
Dartmouth College	RU/VH	Private not-for-profit	5,987
Goldsmiths College, University of London, UK	---	Public	8,884[42]
Harvard University	RU/VH	Private not-for-profit	27.651
Indiana University	RU/VH	Public	42,346
Iowa State University	RU/VH	Public	27,945
James Madison University	Master's L	Public	18,971
Johns Hopkins University	RU/VH	Private not-for-profit	20,383
King's College, London, UK	---	Public	25,187[43]
Lancaster University, UK	---	Public	12,000[44]
Louisiana State University	RU/VH	Public	28,643
Massachusetts Institute of Technology	RU/VH	Private not-for-profit	10,384
New York University	RU/VH	Private not-for-profit	43,404
The Ohio State University	RU/VH	Public	55,014
Otis College of Art and Design	Spec/Arts	Private not-for-profit	1,221
Pennsylvania State University	RU/VH	Public	45,185
School of the Art Institute of Chicago	Spec/arts	Private not-for-profit	3,164
Stanford University	RU/VH	Private not-for-profit	18,498
Syracuse University	RU/H	Private not-for-profit	19,638
Texas Tech University	RU/H	Public	30,049
Transart Institute	---	Private not-for-profit	100
Tufts University	RU/VH	Public	10,252
The University of Alabama (Tuscaloosa)	RU/H	Public	36,155
The University of Alabama, Birmingham	RU/VH	Public	16,874
University of California, Berkeley	RU/VH	Public	35,830
University of California, Santa Barbara	RU/VH	Public	22,850
University of Chicago	RU/VH	Private not-for-profit	15,094
University of Colorado Boulder	RU/VH	Public	33,010
University of Florida	RU/VH	Public	50,691
University of Illinois	RU/VH	Public	43,881
University of Iowa	RU/VH	Public	28,987
University of Kansas	RU/VH	Public	29,242
University of Manchester, UK	---	Public	38,430[45]
University of Maryland	RU/VH	Public	37,195
University of Michigan	RU/VH	Public	41,674
University of Nebraska	RU/VH	Public	24,100
University of Southern California	RU/VH	Private not-for-profit	34,824
University of Utah	RU/VH	Public	29,284
University of Virginia	RU/VH	Public	24,355
University of Wisconsin, Madison	RU/VH	Public	41,654
Vanderbilt University	RU/VH	Private not-for-profit	12,506
Virginia Commonwealth University	RU/VH	Public	32,172
Virginia Tech	RU/VH	Public	30,870
Washington University, St. Louis	RU/VH	Public	13,575

42 http://www.gold.ac.uk/statistics/#d.en.8548
43 http://www.kcl.ac.uk/aboutkings/facts/profile.aspx
44 http://www.lancaster.ac.uk/about-us/rankings-and-reputation/quick-facts/
45 http://documents.manchester.ac.uk/display.aspx?DocID=19310

APPENDIX 3: INTERVIEW SCRIPTS

FACULTY SCRIPT

Professor / Doctor _____,

• May I ask you to briefly tell me about yourself?

  - How long have you been employed at the university?

  - In what capacities have you been employed?

  - What is your current position?

  - What is your educational background?

  - What is your primary discipline?

• How do you define "research"?

• What do you understand "arts research" to be?

• Are you aware of "arts research," as you define it, going on here at the university? If so, where?

• What does the phrase "arts integration" mean to you?

• Do you differentiate between interdisciplinarity and transdisciplinarity? If so, how?

• What arts integration programs are you aware of here at the university?

• Is your course/program curricular, co-curricular, or both?

• With what other disciplines do you partner?

• Who initiated the contact?

• What, if any, disciplinary assumptions caused difficulties between you and your partners or collaborators?

• How did you and your colleagues address those obstacles in developing the course/grant/ proposal? Were you explicit about any theoretical bases for negotiating clashing disciplinary assumptions or expectations?

• Please tell me more about the process of putting this course/program/grant proposal together. What were you hoping to accomplish?

• What kind of support have you received from your college to pursue this?

• What difficulties did you encounter in terms of operations, university structures, and others in the process of development? How did the obstacles affect your implementation, planning, and strategies?

• Did your course/grant require extraordinary resources (faculty time, materials, facilities, etc.)? If so, what were they, and how willing was the university to provide them?

• Is your course economically sustainable? If so, how? If not, why?

• Of course, we're interested in impact – both short and long term, on both faculty and students. What impact did you hope to see, what impact are you actually seeing, and how are you measuring it?

• How has teaching this course affected your research?

• Has this course/grant affected the research and/or teaching of your colleagues? If so, how?

• How have your university's leaders responded to the course/grant? Are they knowledgeable about it? Interested? Supportive? If so, how are they showing it?

ADMINISTRATIVE SCRIPT

• What is your primary discipline?

• *The role and application of the arts in society has been expanding from high art to entrepreneurship to arts in medicine.* Taking into account the statement I've just read, in your view, what disciplines and practices constitute "the arts"?

• What do you understand "arts research" to be?

• What does the phrase "arts integration" mean to you?

• Are you aware of any instances of arts integration at the university?

• Are you a funder of these programs? If so, what are your criteria? What is the value of these programs?

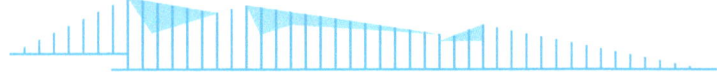

- How does research in, through, or about the arts fit into your university's research agenda? How would you like it to fit?
- How does your university include the arts in its research discussions or committees at the college and university level?
- Does your university have incentives or awards in place to foster interdisciplinary research with the arts?
- At what stage do you hear of collaboration/curricular proposals involving the arts? How formalized are they when you first see them (nascent, complete)? When these are proposed, are they usually accompanied by attempts to secure competitive funding?
- How do you imagine future support for the arts and research and creative practice?
- As an administrator, what do you feel the role of a provost/dean/director/chair should be in shaping, maintaining, or permeating disciplinary boundaries? Who else has a role in shaping this?

HIGH-LEVEL RESEARCH PARTNERSHIPS SCRIPT

- How do you define "research"?
- What do you understand "arts research" to be?
- What does the phrase "arts integration" mean to you?
- Do you differentiate between interdisciplinarity and transdisciplinarity? If so, how?
- What is your primary discipline, and with what other disciplines do you partner?
- Who initiated the contact?
- With whom are arts colleges partnering? Where are the partnerships? Who's doing it? Junior or senior faculty?
- What is the depth of the partnerships?
    - Where are you in the partnership?
    - Exploratory? Funded? If so, how? For what duration?
- How did the project form?
- How did you find your partners?
- Why consider a transdisciplinary partnership? In those early days, what did you believe the value to be?
- To what extent did you have to modify your usual language or methodological approach to meet partner requirements?
- How did you conceive of the model for your collaboration? Were there others that you consulted or examined?
- How has the university supported it? Or impeded it?
- Is there a particular cultural perception within your department of this kind of work? Does your collaboration count toward tenure and promotion?
- How well do these show up in communications with important constituencies?

APPENDIX 4: NARRATIVE EXAMPLES

A full monologue provided by a professor in the visual arts points out the successes and complications occurring while creating arts-integrated courses.

A few years ago, I wanted to use a more interdisciplinary approach and to look at student retention. I noticed they weren't completing their degrees: they were having a hard time getting their science credits. So my idea was to take advantage of the [off-campus science] research center, creating a class incorporating science and art to help get the students their science requirements and help scientists get their art requirements. I brought this idea to then-director of [the research center]. I wanted to do it during the two-week interim in the summer.

It didn't turn out as interdisciplinary as I wanted. The major issue is the student credit hours model (SCH). For every student enrolled in a class, that department gets money. The problem is if you're doing these classes, who gets the money? So if we create a truly interdisciplinary class between art and science, who gets the money? . . . [We] were working with two different colleges, landscape ecology and painting. Two-week long residency 300 miles away in [the science center]. The facility didn't totally work; it never had that many students there before. But it's been improved since then.

We wanted to teach this every other year, but it only happened once. My co-teacher from biology got promoted and decided not to do it anymore. No other faculty from biology will teach – it takes too much time; it's a lot of work. All of the interdisciplinary classes are three to four times more work.

I had to write grants twice for this because biology was first in, then out, then back in again for this course. I got a teaching grant for the art part. Got supplies, built special pallet kits. Renting vans, food, menu, getting students there. It was a huge undertaking.

I wanted to offer the biologists the opportunity to take this class with a non-major credit. We already had the painting [component] accepted as credit in our department so also had to write to undergraduate studies to get the painting reclassified as fulfilling FF [fine arts and fine arts explorations] requirements for biologists. What happened was that both sides wouldn't let us do it – they couldn't get the vision that an integrated class would be different but just as valid.

They both said this, but biology much more so. "It's not going to have the rigor, won't have the same things we require from this class." It's true. To a certain extent, for true integration you're looking for a different set of skills coming out – you're trying to create something new. So what happened for us was we had to keep them fairly separate. We did painting in the mornings; afternoons were biology. We had to create two separate syllabi.

It took a while to have the undergraduate school change the designation of the painting class. But it doesn't count both ways – not for biology. Never got it to work. A lot of it has to do with the SCH model. Both sides got credit, just under two separate headings. Biology class for an art minor – or a biology class for an art major.

[We both] taught in the same place, which was one thing neat for the students, even though they were still working on their own majors and credits. But the students understood what was happening. There was mixing of dialogues and perspectives; they were able to see crossover.

[Based on submitted student reflections], we saw that the artists on the team caused the research output to be different. The artists weren't just doing what the scientists were doing: they were interacting. The scientists also walked away with a new respect for artists. Frankly the arts are looked at as we are children and we play. But scientists found out that there are rules we follow, and we think conceptually. So that was exciting. Also because the science courses are usually so big, they had never had such close interaction with the other students and the faculty! It helped them in their communication skills.

At the end of this, we had an exhibition. The scientific research and paintings of the scientists were displayed. I hope I can find another partner to do this with because it was very beneficial, however very laborious.

Another example of course development, this time between physics and theater, illustrates navigation of significant challenges.

I have developed a course with two colleagues . . . through the lens of live performance looking at how science and scientists are represented and ethical issues. Tend to focus on real science rather than science fiction. Opens up lots of interesting dialogue [between] physics, theater, and medicine.

Physics professor contacted us first. He was interested in doing outreach to younger people maybe using theater. I was contacted by my department chair. We started our collaboration with a playwright, which ended up falling apart. A play came out of it, tangentially. But there was a call from our university for proposals for research or courses, so I contacted faculty in physics and decided to write a proposal for the course. In the midst of this, I was introduced to [another professor] in medicine [with a background in theater]. Seemed like the perfect group to develop this course.

The physics faculty gave me lot of latitude in selecting plays. Then we together (all three) looked at plays and selected from those. A lot of science plays out there that are not good, so it took work to find quality material.

[The professor in medicine] has a theater background even though she's teaching in medicine. So she and I tend to be more on the same page in terms of how we think about theater and performance. Our physics collaborator, on the other hand, approaches things differently. Doesn't have tools to analyze a play but reacts to it and focuses on how scientists are represented in the plays. He's also focused on the accuracy of the science. So we focus on different things, but they complement each other.

We wanted to model and create a space for students from different disciplines to come together. This comes back to [having a] large research university where faculty and students are siloed – encouraged to declare majors as soon as possible. So the students are not developing relationships with other students as much. So we wanted to develop a place for this exchange to happen.

We have general education requirements for the arts here. The thing is that the college is saturated with courses to fulfill that. So even if we [get our course] to meet this, that's no guarantee you'll get people to take it. More students are taking sexy large courses such as "History of Rock and Roll." Might be able to get humanities or upper-division writing. But that adds another layer to what we have to do in the course.

[As to whether our course is economically sustainable,] I don't know. It's tough. For theater, it is because we have smaller seminar classes – between 6 and 18 students. For physics, it's trickier. For physics faculty to get release, we had to fight for it; they are much more suspicious, [even though] it was reviewed by the physics department (physics faculty sat in on the class) and got great reviews. But we still had to fight for it.

APPENDIX 5: PLANNING FOR COLLABORATIVE RESEARCH OR TEACHING

PRE-COLLABORATION INTERVIEW QUESTIONNAIRE[46]

1. What is my vision for this project? (*Be as specific as possible.*)
2. As I understand it, what is the scope and purpose of this project?
3. How will the project be funded? (*If this has not yet been determined, what possible funding sources do you recommend?*)
4. What do I hope to gain from this collaboration? (*Rank the following statements in order, with 1 being your most important motivation for participating in this collaboration. Select only those that are relevant to you.*)

   _____ improved student learning

   _____ improved pedagogical practice

   _____ advancement of personal/professional research

   _____ enhanced creative practice

   _____ discovery of new knowledge that can subsequently enhance student learning

   _____ discovery of new knowledge that can improve the quality of human life

   _____ enhanced professional standing via publication

   _____ enhanced professional standing via an exhibition or performance

   _____ documenting achievement that can be applied towards promotion or tenure

   _____ meeting an external requirement (department, institution, or third-party)

   _____ enhanced status or recognition from/in/among: (check all that apply)

        _____ my department

        _____ the institution

        _____ other scholars in my discipline

   _____ enhanced institutional status

   _____ competition with/emulation of peer institution(s), organization(s), or individual(s)

   _____ direct financial reward

   _____ other (please specify): _____

5. What is my availability? (*Input your weekly schedule below.*)

	MONDAY	TUESDAY	WEDNESDAY	THURSDAY	FRIDAY
8AM					
9					
10					
11					
12NOON					
1PM					
2					
3					
4					
5					
EVENING HOURS					
WEEKEND AVAILABAILITY (IF ANY)					

6. What other commitments do I have that might impact or conflict with this collaboration? (*Ex: speaking engagements, upcoming professional conferences, upcoming performances or exhibitions, personal factors*)
7. What are my expectations regarding our meetings and/or shared work sessions:
   a. Where will we meet?
   b. When will we meet?
   c. How often will we meet?
   d. How long will our meetings be?
   e. Who else should be present at our meetings?
8. Deliverables:
   a. What deliverables do you expect from me, and when?
   b. What deliverables do I expect from you, and when?
9. Though redundant, what is the written timetable and schedule for accomplishment of these deliverables?
10. What challenges or impediments do I anticipate?
11. How do I suggest we prepare for these challenges or impediments?
12. How will this collaboration enhance learning?
    a. How will my students benefit?
    b. How will your students benefit?
    c. What do you and I expect to learn from one another?
    d. How will our learning in the project impact our teaching and/or service?
13. How will this collaboration enhance the reputation or status of the college or university?
14. How will we ensure that this is an equitable partnership?
15. What are my preferences for contact and communication? (*College/university email, personal email, text message, office phone, home phone*).
16. Do I want to set restrictions on contact methods or timeframes?
17. What other information do I feel you should know prior to entering into a partnership with me?

PROJECT ESTIMATE
1. A preliminary estimate of the project's scope and purpose
2. A schedule of meeting times, places, and work to be accomplished
3. An outline of each participant's responsibilities and duties
4. A list of other participants and their roles, including full contact information and professional profiles
5. A list of required materials and equipment needed, itemizing supplies already on hand and those that must be acquired, including estimated costs
6. A project budget, including specific funding sources or proposals for securing funding
7. Other considerations unique to the project. For instance, a theatrical production portraying a concept in quantum physics will have different requirements than a project involving the creation of computer graphics to conceptualize a mathematical theorem.
8. A clearly defined schedule outlining expected execution of deliverables

ENVIRONMENTAL ANALYSIS

1. Have similar collaborations previously occurred at this institution?
    a. Who were the participants?
    b. Can we contact them in order to find additional information?
    c. Was the collaboration successful?
        i. If so, why?
        ii. If not, why not?
    d. What obstacles did the participants face?
    e. How did they overcome these obstacles?
2. Have similar collaborations occurred elsewhere?
    a. What can we learn from these?
    b. Who was involved?
    c. Can we contact these individuals to learn more about their experiences?
3. What institutional supports are available to us?
    a. In my department?
    b. In your department?
    c. From other sources within the institution?
4. Which of our departments will be the home of our project?
5. To whom do we report our progress and/or findings?
6. What resources do we have available to us at present?
    a. Facilities and equipment, including specific locations and restrictions to access
    b. Departmental funding
    c. External funding
        i. What are the stipulations or requirements set out by the funding organization?
7. What can we expect from our departmental colleagues in the way of support, encouragement, or opposition?
    a. How will my work be evaluated by my peers?
    b. How does this differ from the way your work will be evaluated?

APPENDIX 6: INSTITUTIONAL AND ORGANIZATIONAL REFERENCES

Lists of the institutions and organizations involved in this study are provided on pages 22 and 152. Specific centers, institutes and programs affiliated with these institutions are not listed. These can be found by searching the web pages of their parent institutions.

www.ingramcontent.com/pod-product-compliance
Lightning Source LLC
Chambersburg PA
CBHW041923180526

45172CB00014B/1366